Business Process Excellence

Springer-Verlag Berlin Heidelberg GmbH

August-Wilhelm Scheer
Ferri Abolhassan · Wolfram Jost
Mathias Kirchmer
Editors

Business Process Excellence

ARIS in Practice

With 124 Figures
and 2 Tables

Springer

Professor Dr. Dr. h.c. mult. August-Wilhelm Scheer
Dr. Ferri Abolhassan
Dr. Wolfram Jost
IDS Scheer AG
Postfach 101534
66015 Saarbrücken
Germany

Dr. Mathias Kirchmer
IDS Scheer AG
1205 Westlakes Drive, Suite 270
Berwyn, PA 19312
USA

ISBN 978-3-642-53419-5 ISBN 978-3-540-24705-0 (eBook)
DOI 10.1007/978-3-540-24705-0

Library of Congress Cataloging-in-Publication Data applied for
Die Deutsche Bibliothek – CIP-Einheitsaufnahme

Business Process Excellence: ARIS in Practice; with 2 Tables /
August-Wilhelm Scheer ... Ed. –Berlin; Heidelberg; New York; Barcelona;
Hong Kong; London; Milan; Paris; Tokyo: Springer, 2002

http://www.springer.de

Originally published by Springer-Verlag Berlin Heidelberg New York in 2002
Softcover reprint of the hardcover 1st edition 2002

Hard cover design: Erich Kirchner, Heidelberg

42/3111-5 4 3 – Printed on acid-free paper

Foreword

Business has never changed as fast and as radically as at the moment. Business process management is the basis for all major business initiatives like Supply Chain Management (SCM), Customer Relationship Management (CRM), Enterprise Resource Planning (ERP), or Business Intelligence. New component and internet-based software architectures and web services require a solid process management to deliver the expected business success. An effective business process design is the only way to combine software components in a business driven way using new technologies like Enterprise Application Integration (EAI).

However, many organizations still struggle to find the right approach to business process management. After having decided to move forward in a business process oriented way, the question is in many cases HOW to do that. IDS Scheer delivers with ARIS the framework and procedures to meet this challenge successfully and answer the resulting questions.

IDS Scheer has successfully applied its ARIS business process management approach at thousands of organizations worldwide like Intel, Siemens, Air France, or the US Navy. Numerous highly appreciated universities and educational institutions like the University of Pennsylvania, Philadelphia, Widener University, Philadelphia, George Mason University, Washington, or the University of Southern California (USC), Los Angeles, use ARIS as basis for their information systems and business process classes.

This book presents international case studies in various manufacturing and service industries as well as the public sector. Leading organizations explain how they manage their business processes using ARIS. The book shows how to achieve business process excellence in practice.

In addition to this book which has an international focus, especially on North America, we also publish another collection of case studies under the title "ARIS in Praxis" for German speaking countries. Both books have only a minimal overlap.

We would like to thank all authors who contributed to this book. Their willingness to share their lessons learned will help many other organizations. Special thanks also to Carmen Doell who supported this book project in an excellent way from an administrative point of view.

Saarbrücken / Philadelphia, April 2002

Prof. Dr. Dr. h.c. mult. A.-W. Scheer | Dr. Ferri Abolhassan

Dr. Wolfram Jost | Dr. Mathias Kirchmer

Table of Content

ARIS - From the Vision to Practical Process Control

August-Wilhelm Scheer
IDS Scheer AG

Summary

The concept of a unified view of information systems that was aligned to the business processes within a company was born at the Institute for Information Systems (IWi) as a natural development of the fundamental notion of a company-wide data model – construction began on ARIS House. At the heart of this view concept, tool-supported modeling of business processes was explored initially in the context of research projects, and later as part of the product development effort in the spin-off company IDS Scheer. The ARIS Toolset by IDS Scheer was developed further so that now it has become the most successful business process modeling tool in the world.

Key Words

Architecture of integrated information systems (ARIS), ARIS House, ARIS House of Business Engineering (HOBE), event-driven process chain (EPC), research projects, IDS Scheer, Institute for Information Systems (IWi), modeling, prototype development, SAP, formation of company, business information systems

1. The Vision - A Common Language for IT and Management

In 1975, when I took the newly established chair for business information systems at the University of the Saarland, I had to completely rewrite my lecture notes. I myself had never heard a lecture on business information systems, since at the University of Hamburg, where I had lectured as a privatdozent until that time, the subject did not yet exist. As I revised my notes, I tried to disengage myself to the extent possible from the breakneck pace of development in information technology, and to strive in my description of commercial information systems for a level of abstraction that that would not be too heavily influenced by those developments. Otherwise, I would have spent much of my time changing my lectures to reflect technological innovations, and my students would have received information with a very short half-life.

The level of abstraction I chose at the time was a decription of information systems with the aid of data models. Peter Chen had just published his highly acclaimed article, "Towards a Unified View of Data" (1976), and the relational data model was making the journey from theory to practice. My interest was in analyzing the influence of information technology on new commercial organizational and decision-making processes. I found that the description yielded by data models was correct in its approach, but unsatisfactory in its range. Most importantly, data models could be used to represent the effect of integrated information systems. Integrate information systems, which reached full maturity with the addition of ERP systems, are identified by a company-wide database. Consequently, their logical design and their description on the basis of a company-wide data model also became central themes in my research and teaching. All the while, I wanted to use data models, particularly the language of the entity-relationship model, to create a common language for information technology specialists (programmers, systems analysts, users) and management (managers of Logistics, Sales, Accounting, and Product Development divisions). Only when these two groups understand the substance of each other's dialog would it be possible to use the capabilities of information technology in new business models, that is to say new digital products and new business processes.

However, I soon realized that method of the Entity-Relationship model was too abstract for the practically minded managers. A logistics manager who is working on a new idea for production scheduling does not want to interrupt his activities to attend a course on data modeling. The notion of integration applied not only to the integration of data, but also to the reconfiguration of the business processes that are possible on an integrated database. It was here that I had approach the problem according to a different logic: The modern organizational configuration would no longer be characterized by the established arrangement of division of labor, with its compartmentalized partial processing sequences, but by the dismantling of departmental boundaries with the aid of integrated business processes, which would encompass all corporate functional units, such as Sales, Marketing, Production,

Accounting, Purchasing and Human Resources. In order to achieve this, I had to expand the descriptive language of data modeling to arrive at a comprehensive descriptive approach for business processes.

When I researched the enormous volume of writings on software engineering, it became clear to me that, though scores, if not hundreds of methods and languages were presented for "Requirement Engineering", they were all designed with the single purpose of providing an interface for subsequent software development. Because of their technological orientation, they were not suited for use as a powerful language that would support the user in developing unprecedented new ideas in business processes. Just as before, the fact remained that a manager would not want to take a course in Petri nets or SADT techniques before formulating his business ideas. So, I continued my search for a language that was easy to understand, but could be used to encompass business processes in all their complexity.

To ensure that I was working from a solid position, I withdrew, therefore, and worked with the ARIS concept to produce an architecture that would allow of such an all-embracing description. It must not be biased for subsequent implementation of business processes in information systems, because otherwise this aspect would predominate too heavily, as was the case with the software engineering methods. It must also allow the inclusion of descriptive aspect that, though they have next to nothing to do with a technical information system, do have benefits in organizational terms.

With the ARIS House (see figure 1), I set out to describe a business process, assigning equal importance to the questions of organization, functionality and the required documentation. It had to be possible in the first instance to isolate these questions for separate treatment, in order to reduce the complexity of the description field, but then all the relationships must be restored using the Control view introduced for that purpose.

A three-tiered Life-Cycle design, consisting of the Requirements Definition, the Design Specification and the Implementation Description levels, was used so that it would be possible to track implementation from the technical organizational descriptions down to the implementation level of the systems. A performance level was later added to the ARIS views to allow explicit recording of the results (products, deliverables) of a business process and all its functions.

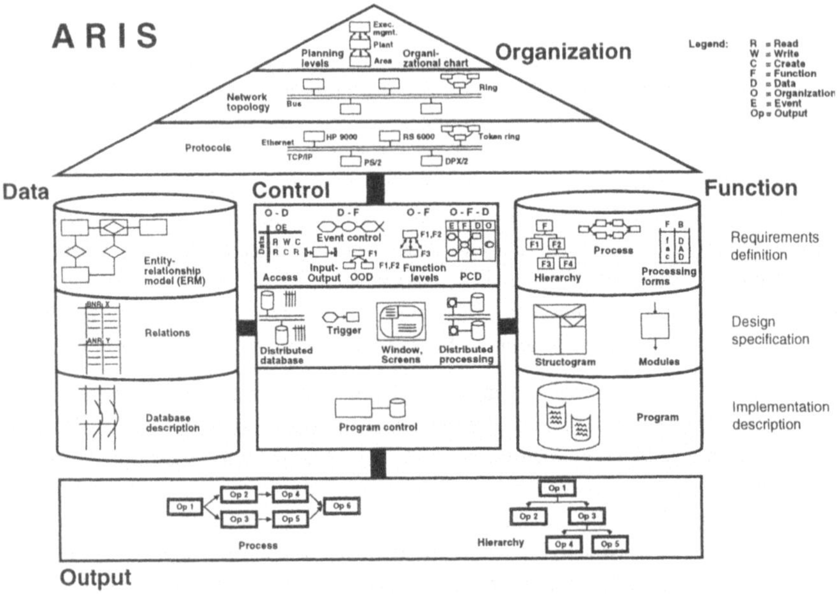

Figure 1: ARIS House

Although I had finally obtained my simple concept, which can be described in a few words, and which had even been given a graphical identity, the ARIS House, the development of this basic idea would still require considerable intellectual effort. Indeed, it is much more difficult to represent a complex system of relationships simply than it is to describe it using a complicated methodology. I still remember how I wrestled with formulations in order to achieve an even simpler, clearer system of expression. I had withdrawn to my apartment in Munich, so that I could concentrate as fully as possible on writing the ARIS book. The first edition was published in 1991, the fourth edition is now available, and the book has been translated into five languages. As I was working on the development of ARIS, my colleagues at the institute were working on subsidiary aspects in the context of various research projects, and as a result, when my approach was complete, I was able to present it to a discussion group that was able to provide informed criticism of my work.

ARIS House constitutes a framework concept in which the descriptive procedures for all views and levels of the Life Cycle are organized. Since the individual aspects and also the relationship systems of the individual views are highly dissimilar, it is not possible to apply a unified descriptive language, but different, problem-specific methods such as data modeling, organizational chart representations, functional descriptions and product structures must be used. As far as possible, I tried to cover the necessary aspects using descriptive procedures that were known from published works. However, we were unable to find a method for the overall representation of business processes that satisfied our requirements. So, in collaboration with SAP, the Institute developed the method of Event-driven Process Chains (EPCs). In essence, this is not a new method, containing as it does elements of the Petri net method and stochastic networks propounded by Elmaghraby, particularly the GERT procedure (Graphical Evaluation and Review Technique), with which I had worked previously as part of my doctoral thesis.

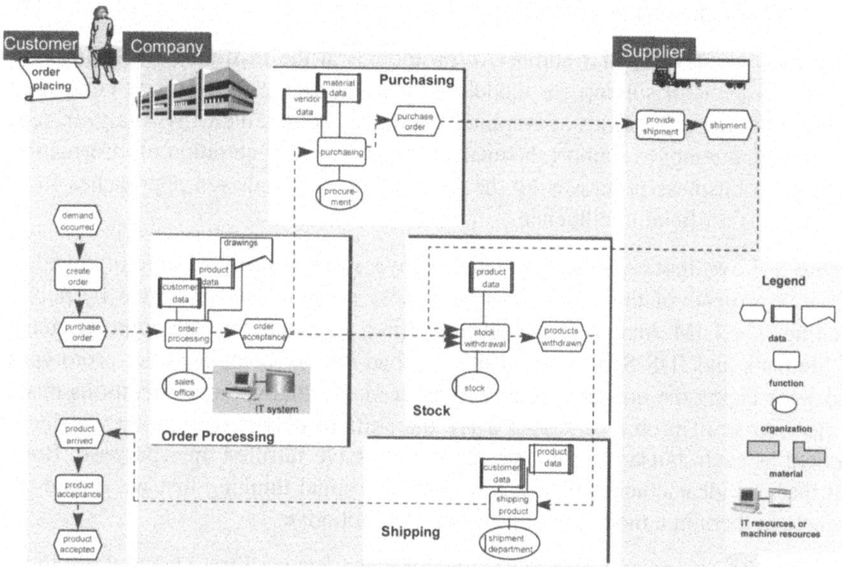

Figure 2: Event-driven Process Chain (EPC)

Figure 2 shows a simple example including the basic elements of the Event-driven Process Chain. The business process for processing an order illustrated here is self-explanatory and thus also demonstrates the simplicity of the descriptive language I was striving to achieve.

In an earlier book, "Principles of Efficient Information Management", published in 1984, I had already presented a table-oriented procedure with process chain diagrams (PCDs) that we had also used at the Institute to describe business processes. Since this was based on table structures, the models were relatively simple and clear. In the EPC method, on the other hand, we follow an unformatted presentation mode, so that we can better map complicated logical nesting arrangements of functions within process courses.

2. From the Research Prototype to the Product

It was clear to us that in the practical description of large information systems according to the ARIS concept, it would be necessary to use computer-supported tools to create the models in the first instance, but also particularly to support the stored model inventory with a wide range of evaluation capabilities. The most applicable for this purpose were existing CASE tools that also enabled the creation of data models or SADT descriptions for the requirement engineering stage. However, their emphasis lay less in support for organizational questions than in the subsequent generation of program code. As a result, they were not sufficiently user-friendly for our needs, which were chiefly centered on creating organizational and commercial process descriptions.

Therefore, we developed a number of prototypes at the Institute, which included different aspects of support for modeling methods. One prototype was concerned mainly with the capabilities of graphical displays, another, the CIM-Analyzer, represented an attempt to support the analysis of degree of penetration of information systems in business processes by the application of rule-driven approaches from the realm of artificial intelligence.

Figure 3 shows that no more than ten employees of my Institute were involved in research projects of this nature. None of these projects was supported by public funding. The CIM-Analyzer was developed in a joint venture with corporate units of Siemens and IDS Scheer. By 1992, we had largely completed the prototypes and were facing the question of how to proceed. Normally, the observations made in the course of prototype research are the stuff of dissertations, they are documented as such, but not further pursued. They have fulfilled their purpose. But I felt that our ideas contained such a wealth of original thinking that we should try to include them in a modeling tool on our own initiative.

In many discussions with IDS Scheer senior management, I tried to convince them of the opportunities offered by a product of this kind. Of course, the risks were also all too evident. Ultimately, the young company would be required to make a considerable investment in development. But in the end, a positive decision was reached in spite of the dangers. The decision was made easier when Dr. Wolfram Jost and Dr. Helge Hess, two leading technology experts at the Institute, declared their willingness to direct development at IDS Scheer. Dr. Wolfram Jost in particular was able to contribute a wealth of experience and ideas, gained through his previous management of the CIM-Analyzer research project. In the space of a few months, a development team had to be put together at IDS Scheer, and corresponding employees had to be hired to carry out product marketing and ARIS consulting, so that within a short time, the number of employees engaged in the ARIS project at IDS Scheer grew to about 120 by 1996.

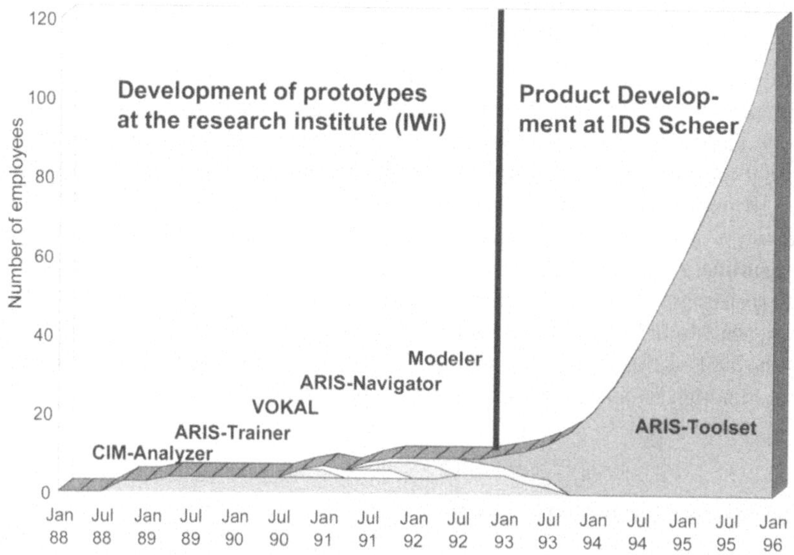

Figure 3: Development of research prototypes and the ARIS Toolset

The graph in figure 3 shows prototype development in a research institute compared with examples of product development in an industrial setting. Whereas the purpose of a research prototype is merely to demonstrate in principle how the task might be solved, a commercial product must be capable of providing reliable service in daily use by hundreds or thousands of users. A prototype does not need to be stable, whereas this is of course a prerequisite for a product. There is normally no development strategy for a prototype, no duty to guarantee its operation, no continuity in the development team – a commercial product must satisfy all of these requirements.

The transition from research ideas to products and marketing success that we were able to achieve with the ARIS Toolset was later applauded as an example of the greater efficiency of research expenditure in Germany. In our universities and public research facilities we Germans are "world beaters" when it comes to building prototypes, but too few of our ideas are built into new products, marketing successes, and consequently jobs. In Germany generally, the plot in Fig. 3 becomes bogged down at the bold vertical line just in front of the practical implementation. Efforts are in hand to reverse this situation, with the encouraging support for research institute spin-offs in recent years. But when we were developing the ARIS product, this notion was all but unprecedented. Fig. 3 also shows that after the employees, with their expertise, were transferred from the research institute to the IDS Scheer research projects, no more projects were undertaken in this field. The difference in the resource capabilities of IDS Scheer and IWi was simply too great, and they would have had to concentrate on new areas of research dealing with highly specialized problems with limited application. Mainstream development was taken over by IDS Scheer. Even so, IDS Scheer and IWi continued to nurture close ties during the following years.

The high degree of innovation in our ARIS product, the result of many years' work in research projects, was also decisive in eliciting a positive evaluation of the product by Gartner Group. Based on years of experience, I have come to the conclusion that an innovative creation is not hatched overnight, but is rather the culmination of long periods of brooding. The preparatory research in my books and my research projects with the Institute could not be reproduced without first negotiating significant hurdles. This is also one reason for the failure of so many dot-com enterprises in recent years; their product development was not founded on their own, well-founded ideas, but was instead copied from ideas that already existed in the United States, or consisted in very minor original ideas that were not substantial enough to bear longer term product development.

3. Collaboration with SAP

An critical factor in the development of the basic ideas for the ARIS concept was the connection between the organizational thinking of those responsible for the business processes and the tools level, that is to say the IT systems used to support the business processes. For this reason, I approached SAP very early, with a view to convincing them of the advantages that their system documentation would reap if it were made more user-oriented with models. I had already developed a company data model consisting of about 500 data objects (entity types and relationship types) using the Entity-Relationship method in my book "Business Process Engineering", which was published in 1988. I presented the idea of clarifying the SAP system's integration content using data models to the managing board of SAP, which at that time, the early 90s, was itself deeply involved in questions of development. To begin with, I was greeted with skepticism, but with time the idea gained acceptance and a collaborative project was launched between SAP and the employees of my research institute, initially to carry out data modeling of the current R/2 system, and later for the R/3 system as well. With the successful introduction of the R/3 system in the US, the data models too were heralded as indications of the new thinking that characterized the system, as shown in figure 4, in which SAP cofounder and executive board chairman, Prof. Dr. h.c. Hasso Plattner, and Klaus Besier, then CEO of SAP America Inc., proudly introduce the data models on the cover of the magazine "Datamation".

Figure 4: Cover of DATAMATION, March 15, 1993

This early collaboration with SAP was also a driver for research activities at the Institute, particularly in the development of a suitable method of displaying processes, which culminated in the EPC method.

However, when describing a standardized software system like the R/3 system using its inherent business processes, there is one fundamental difficulty that must be overcome, and which we did not recognize at first. The R/3 system is a generic system, which can be modified to create one concrete solution by means of many parameter settings from a set of functions and procedures – Customizing. If all the possible parameters for business models contained in the system are formulated explicitly, the permutations of the parameters to be modified result in an enormous array of routine options that is virtually impossible to manage. Figure 5 is a small part of the R/3 system process model, showing an example of the complexity of the logical connections between the individual process paths.

But this diversity is of little use to the individual user, who may only require five to ten percent of these options for a specific application case. This wealth of choice tends to be confusing. In this respect, the documentation of the business processes included in the SAP system did not represent the benefit to the user we had hoped. On the basis of this realization, IDS Scheer then forged ahead alone, working on a solution whose chief emphasis was the rapid creation of a business process model for the user, without losing sight of the need to use only those

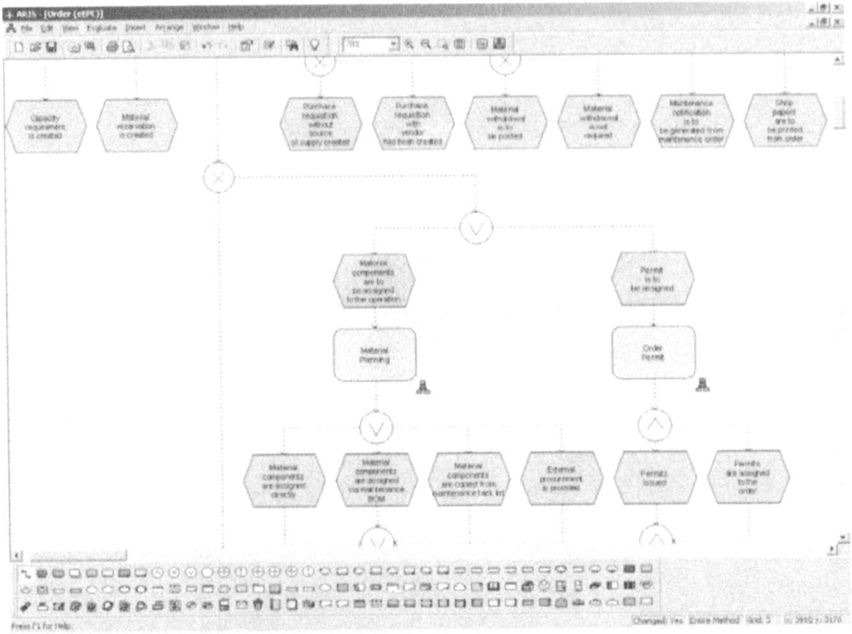

Figure 5: SAP R/3 reference model

functionalities that are also offered by the R/3 system. This approach is referred to as an R/3-oriented customer model. In this approach too, the ARIS Toolset is integrated very closely with the R/3 system, particularly with the repository, so that R/3 functionalities, such as displaying transactions or screen masks, are possible directly from ARIS models. At the same time, the structures of the functions contained in the R/3 system can be accessed for purposes of model creation.

The creation of an SAP-oriented process model may be effectively supported using SAP "best practice" models. These are produced for certain industries from the SAP system inventory and provide the user with ideas for his own model. Unlike the full SAP reference model, this already contains a selection of the total system possibilities that is more suitable for the user. Even so, it does not need to be updated immediately after every release modification, since it does not have the status of system documentation. IDS Scheer offers a number of SAP models for several industry sectors in ARIS.

Later, with the Business Engineer concept, SAP pursued the idea of developing a rule-based add-on that was designed to provide only the functionalities of the overall model that the user needed, as specified by the indication of a few descriptive features. This concept was subsequently abandoned.

As new developments of software architectures become available, the need to describe application systems using process models is becoming more pressing. The combination of components and their connection through EAI (Enterprise Application Integration) technologies is predicated on the existence of a unified road map for the business process. Accordingly, it is becoming even more important for the future to be able to describe these application systems methodically and associate them closely with the implementation level.

4. From Business Process Modeling to Business Process Management

The ARIS House represents a blueprint for describing business models, which the ARIS Toolset follows by providing corresponding support functions for graphic modeling. It soon became clear to us that the mere description of business processes was not enough to meet the needs of all aspects of business process orientation in companies.

Modeling serves to document a business process, and constitutes the basis upon which the business process is evaluated in terms of cost, time and quality, but its final function is to invest the business process with a definite structure. However, realtime control and monitoring of business processes is not considered.

Full business process management includes not only the design of the business processes, but also the control of functioning procedures and a feedback mechanism for processing results in the form of a continuous improvement process for the business processes. Therefore, in 1995 we developed the four-tier model of the House of Business-Engineering (HOBE), which was used to track a complete Life-Cycle model of business process management (see figure 6).

Process design is arranged on tier 1, and is supported in its entirety by the ARIS Toolset. Tier 2 is also oriented toward the business process owner, that is to say the person technically responsible for the design and flow of certain business processes such as Sales, Human Resources or Product Development. This person should be able to access status information on individual active business processes via monitoring functionalities. This allows him to provide a customer with information about the status of a customer order or a complaint, or make changes to a business process even as it is functioning if certain time or cost limits are exceeded. The set of business processes to be executed can be planned using time and capacity control techniques. Compressed information about costs, durations etc. is included in an Executive Information System for more strategic design questions. In all, this level serves for realtime control of processes and as the basis for organizational optimizations as part of Continuous Process Improvement.

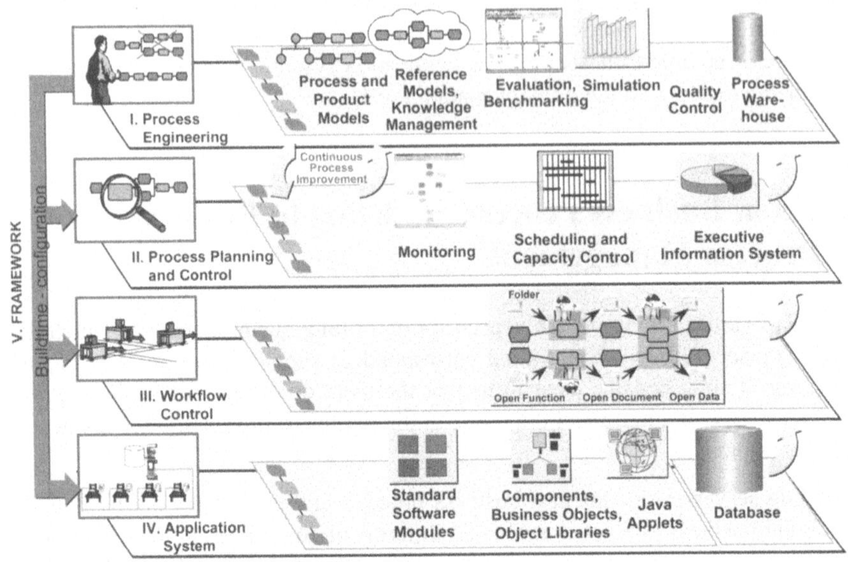

Figure 6: ARIS – House of Business Engineering

Tier 3 constitutes the connection with technical processing support. Process execution is controlled by workflow systems that access information from the procedural structure and transfer status information, e.g. completion of a function, to the next processing operation in the sequence and the organizational unit responsible for its performance. Workflows thus transport status information, references to documents to be edited, and in some cases the documents themselves. In ERP systems, procedural control is usually part of the programming system. In this case, there is no workflow component outside of the program code. Instead, the control logic is implicit in the program code in the specified form.

With the development of appropriate adapters, it is thereby possible to extract status information about completed business processes, e.g. from the document flow, and make this available to tier 2. The "ARIS Process Performance Manager (PPM)" system, an ARIS add-on component that is responsible for realtime evaluation of business processes, is designed along these lines.

The modules provided at tier 4 for functional support are then called from tier 3, the control tier. Tier 4 is where the software components are located that support processors in the execution of an order operation or invoice verification. These may be transactions from ERP systems or also components of office software systems, or even program modules that are accessed as Web services via the Internet.

The four-tier design of the House of Business Engineering has been adopted almost unchanged by other ERP manufacturers as the roadmap for their system architectures. The format that Wolfram Jost and I have refined in the course of many discussions is described in detail in the article "Business Process Management - A Core task for Any Company Organization" in this book.

This is a retrospective view of the experiences gained from 15 years devoted to the research, development and implementation of the ARIS method and business process management. The success of the product, with over 30,000 ARIS licenses sold, requires no further elaboration. Modeling of business processes with direct connectivity to the software configuration is becoming more important as component architecture and Web services progressively transform software architectures. Business processes that transcend company boundaries require that responsibilities be defined for reciprocal material and financial relationships, quality standards and time constraints. This can only be assured if a business process is known, which is to say documented. This, I believe, gives me good reason to remain highly optimistic about the continued success of ARIS in the future.

5. References

Chen, P.P.: Entity-Relationship Model: Towards a Unified View of Data, in: ACM Transactions on Database Systems, 1 (1976) 1, pp. 9-36.

Scheer, A.-W.: Principles of Efficient Information Management; Springer Verlag, Berlin et al.; 2nd edition, 1991.

Scheer, A.-W.: ARIS – Business Process Modeling; Springer Verlag, Berlin et al.; 2nd edition, 1998.

Scheer, A.-W.: ARIS – Business Process Frameworks; Springer Verlag, Berlin et al.; 2nd edition, 1998.

Scheer, A.-W.: Business Process Engineering – Reference Models for Industrial Enterprises; Springer Verlag, Berlin et al.; 2nd edition, 1998.

The ARIS Toolset

Wolfram Jost
IDS Scheer AG

Karl Wagner
IDS Scheer AG

Summary

In 1992, following the results of several research projects, IDS Scheer GmbH began development of a commercial product for modeling and analyzing business processes. Version 1.0 of the ARIS Toolset was presented for the first time at CeBIT 1993. It was the first marketable product to appear in this market segment. The following article describes the technical framework and the different methods and functions of the ARIS Toolset. We will pay particular attention to the general conditions and potential benefits of an ARIS project.

Key Words

Analysis, ARIS Repository, ARIS Toolset, Functions, Configuration, Methods, Metamodel, Modeling, Potential benefits, Process displays, Activity–based Cost Calculation, Publishing, General conditions, Reporting, Simulation, Technology

1. Early Factors for Success

The original thinking behind the ARIS Toolset dates from a period between 1990 and 1991 at the Institute for Information Systems of the University of the Saarland, under the direction of Prof. Scheer. The first protoypes were also produced at that time. In 1992, following the results of several research projects, IDS Scheer GmbH began development of a commercial product for modeling and analyzing business processes. Version 1.0 of the ARIS Toolset was presented for the first time at CeBIT 1993. It was the first marketable product to appear in this market segment. Since then, the product has been the subject of 10 major releases.

An important factor in the success of the ARIS Toolset has been the theme of Business Process Reengineering, which sparked many corporate initiatives to analyze and redesign business processes during the mid-90s. The reason so many companies were – and still are – willing to invest in projects of this kind lies in the realization that efficient business processes are crucial for the commercial success of the enterprise. A second factor was undoubtedly also SAP AG, which chose the ARIS Toolset as the carrier system for the R/3 reference model. In connection with the R/3 process models, the ARIS Toolset laid the foundation, as it were, for the entire area of process-oriented standardized software implementation, which would later be adopted as an implementation methodology by other producers also.

The term BPR has lost its currency over the course of time, and is now seldom used in public discussion; the modern term is Business Process Management. The profound changes that are presently reshaping the architecture of business applications (Web services, component orientation, collaboration) and the ever closer association of strategy, IT issues and organizational issues have placed the subject of business process management at the very top of companies' to-do lists.

2. Methods of the ARIS Toolset

The ARIS Toolset stands for a group of systems, the essential feature of which consists in the functions of documenting, analyzing and redesigning business processes. The term *business process* is intended to embrace not only the control flow, i.e. the chronological sequence of function execution, but also the descriptions of data, organizations and resources that are directly associated therewith.

Business processes are documented using models. In this context, a model is a simplified reflection of reality. The methodological background of ARIS models is provided by the architecture of integrated information systems (ARIS). The ARIS architecture is a conceptual framework developed by Professor A.-W.

Scheer that shows which of various views and levels can be used in general for describing companies and business applications.

Thus, the description may be performed from purely functional points of view. According to another option, the applications may be considered from the point of view of the data. At this point, the question arises of which data the system can manage, and how such data is structured. The third descriptive view is the organizational one. In this case, the organizational units and responsibilities are represented. In order to preserve the relational structure between functions, data and organization, the control view is introduced. The control view shows, for instance, which data is processed by which functions. At the heart of the control view is the connection between events and functions, which serves to describe the chronological sequence of function execution and thereby also the business process.

Appropriate description methods are needed in order to model the various views. Examples of description methods include the entity relationship model for mapping logical data structure, the event-driven process chain for displaying business processes, or the organizational chart for documenting organizational structures. These description methods are reflected in the ARIS metamodel. The metamodel comprises all information objects that are required to enable the mapping of the business affairs of a company by means of models. Besides the information objects themselves, the relationships among those objects are also defined in the metamodel. The quality of the metamodel is a critically important factor in the flexibility of the system, since it determines which contents can be mapped with the system.

The ARIS Data model is – in accordance with the ARIS architecture – divided into the four views functions, data, organization and control, the business processes representing the central element of the control view.

In the function view, objects are needed that are capable of describing the (technical) functions of a company. Examples of technical functions include: *Check customer creditworthiness, Calculate interest* or *Select supplier.* For this reason, the function is one of the central object types of the data model. Closely allied to functions are events. Events, such as for instance *Receipt of a customer order* or *Receipt of an invoice* are necessary in order to be able to map the temporal dependencies between the functions and thus the business processes. Functions can only be processed if the necessary events have occurred. For example, the function *Check invoice* can only be processed if the event *Invoice is received* has occurred. Besides events, the company data represents a further descriptive object. Examples of this include: *Customer data, Supplier data, Article data* or *Product data.* The organizational unit may be considered to be a fourth essential object type. Organizational units are needed to map the organizational structure of a company.

Thus functions, data, organizational units, and events represent the essential objects of the metamodel. Not only the objects themselves, but also the relationships between those objects are very important. These relationships, for example the relationship „is technically responsible“ between function and organizational unit, or the „activates“ relationship between a function and an event, are of fundamental importance in obtaining the truest possible mapping of the company's situation. These relationships express the business-based interdependencies of the objects. By way of example, the following figure shows an extract from a metamodel.

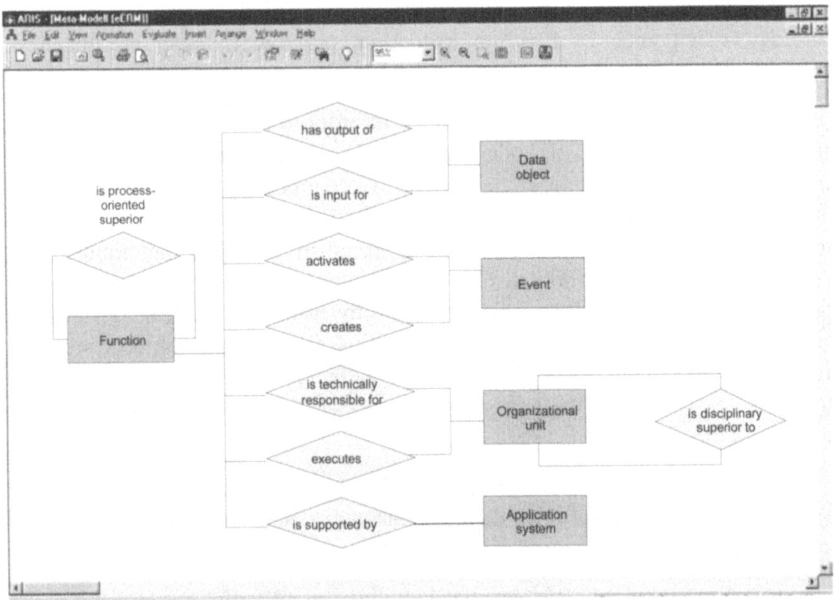

Figure 1: Example of metamodel representation

Besides the question „WHAT“, the question „HOW“ is also important. What form can descriptions take? The ARIS Toolset distinguishes at a fundamental level between table-based and graphics-based descriptive formats. To provide graphical description methods, graphical symbols are assigned to the objects of the metamodel. Figure 2 shows an example drawn from an actual practice.

3. Technology of the ARIS Toolset

3.1 Methodical Flexibility

The ARIS Repository's high degree of general applicability allows methods of the most various kinds to be integrated in the system. The conceptual strength of this approach is demonstrated by the fact that, while the nature and size of the problems and projects in which ARIS has been involved have changed radically since the first version became available, its data structures have undergone only very minor modifications. Whereas initially BPR was the primary focus for using ARIS, the list of fields in which it is used today includes e-business and e-commerce, Supply Chain Management, Customer Relationship Management, Balanced Scorecard (BSC)/Strategic Planning, process-oriented design of QM systems/ISO certification, Enterprise Application Integration (EAI), and more.

Even if these diverse subjects each require their own modes of representation, the substantive questions that they answer are very similar: Who does what? What data is input/output? What is the procedural structure? Which application software or transaction is used? and so on.

A simple example of this is included in *Collaborative business scenarios* for inter-enterprise relationships and the *Extended event-driven process chain (eEPC).* Your underlying metamodel essentially includes the same objects, that is to say roles, functions, and information objects. The various diagram formats only differ in their graphical presentation, i.e. different symbols, color scheme or layout.

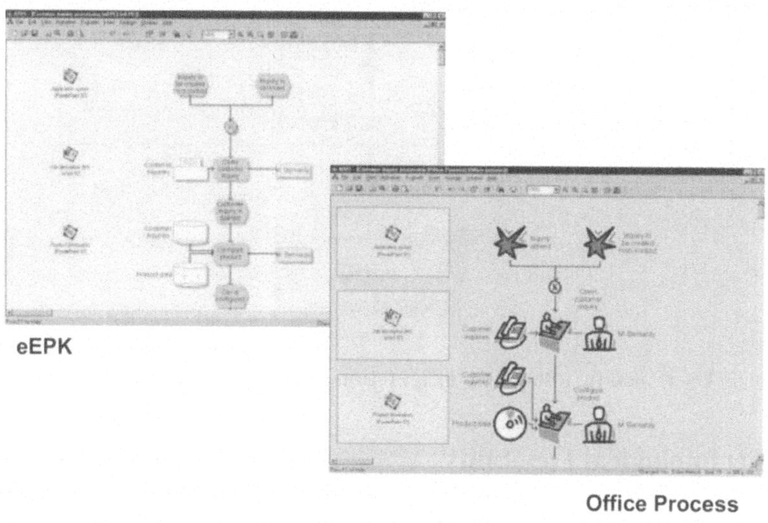

Figure 2: Examples of process representations: eEPC and Office process

The ARIS Toolset supports the various scenarios for use with specially defined method sets, which are fully integrated at the level of the metamodel.

Because the wealth of different scenarios for use yields such an abundance of methods, a filter level is also built into the ARIS Toolset. In this way, it is possible to provide each user in the project team with an interface which is specific to the problems that user is working on. This in turn leads to high acceptance and efficiency levels in the projects.

On the other hand, from the point of view of the corporation as a whole, it is an enormous advantage to have a fully integrated repository. The ability to allow other divisions of the company to reuse project results further enhances the return on investment. This flexibility in the thinking behind the ARIS Repository is the guarantee that ARIS users will continue to be well served, even as they face new technical and commercial issues that are as yet unimagined.

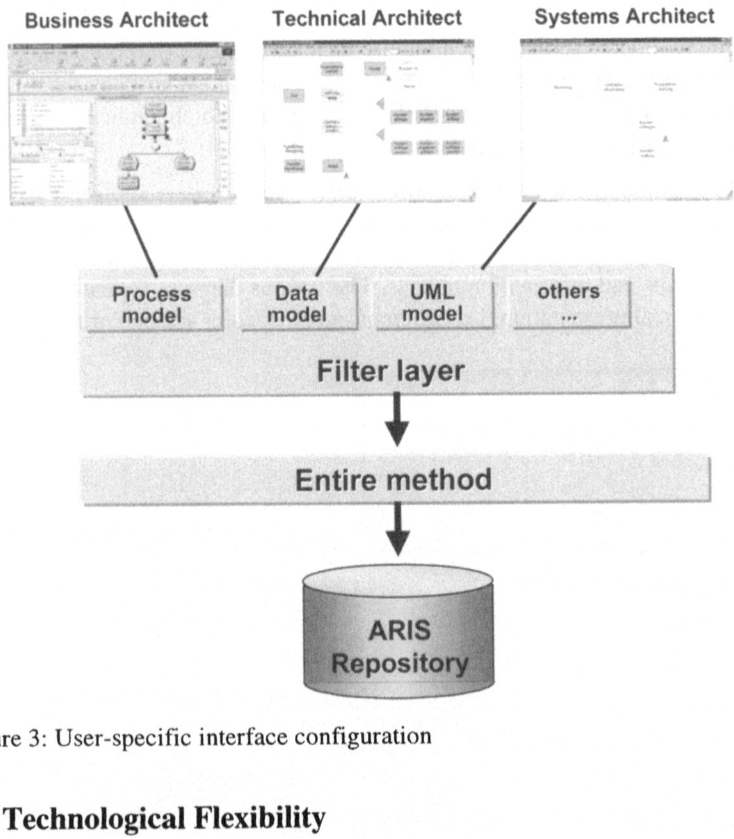

Figure 3: User-specific interface configuration

3.2 Technological Flexibility

Innovation and change cycles are getting shorter for companies all the time, due to both external and internal influences such as mergers, changes in the law, pressure from the competition, globalization etc.. In order to meet this challenge successfully, an increasing number of companies are making the transition from project-driven approaches to an integrated system of process management. However, this company-wide and to some degree global approach places enormous demands on the technology of the ARIS system itself. It must now provide the scalability described not only on a technical level (concerning method and content), but also in terms of technology: online/central, offline/decentralized, single user scenarios with Notebook, small workgroups on the LAN and larger implementation scenarios on the WAN, Internet, intranet or extranet.

As the demands on the technology have grown, so the system has evolved gradually from a standalone application into a multi-tier architecture: Client - Business Server – Database server.

Any of a number of relational database systems with different capability specifications can be used for data maintenance. ARIS Business Server accesses these and in thereby encapsulates all client accesses. To facilitate this, the Business Server provides user-friendly functions, such as „Load Model", wherein the logic for reading a model that is distributed among several tables in the database, is preserved centrally and ready for high performance operation. The load on the network between client and server is so reduced that an Internet connection with a simple modem is sufficient for communication. Communication is based on CORBA (Common Object Request Broker Architecture) and supports common security standards such as SSL (Secure Socket Layer). ARIS Web Designer includes a modeling tool that has been developed in Java and can be executed as a Java applet or a Java application. Taken together, these two features mean that the user now only needs an Internet browser, and can start work immediately, without installing, running a setup routine or spending time on administration: the slogan is „anytime, anywhere".

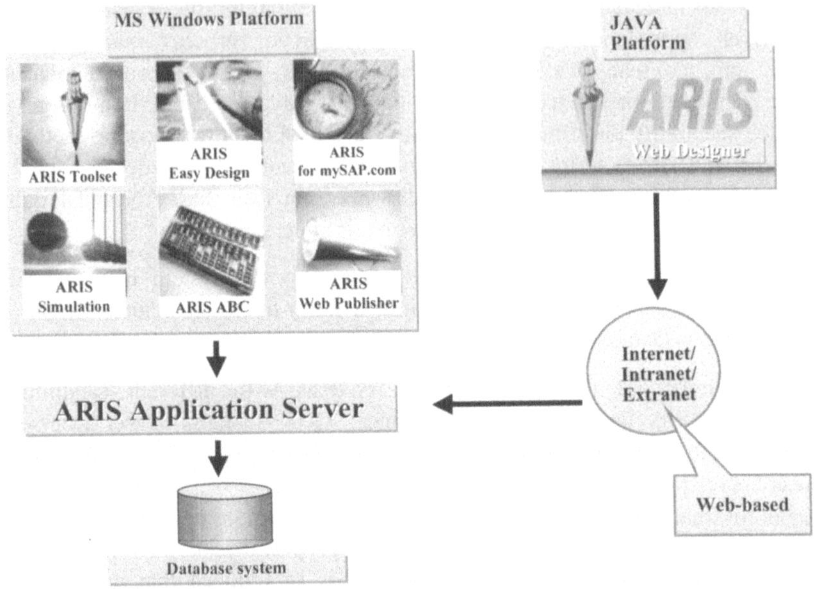

Figure 4: The technology of the ARIS architecture

The caching strategy in the Business Server is configured to enable free scalability, which in turn provides support for very large numbers of users. This part of the system has also been developed in Java, Unix platforms are available in addition to the Microsoft servers. Finally, large application scenarios – known as „ARIS sites" – also include supporting firewall solutions, security strategies and user-friendly administration functions.

Despite this very powerful architecture, the same system can still be used as a „standalone tool", running on a simple Windows Notebook.

3.3 Openness

Besides the methodological and technological flexibility, support for commonly applied industry standards and system openness is also of key importance.

Many technologies for accessing the repository are supported:

- Programming interface (API)
- OLE/COM interface for Basic
- Text export/import (file-oriented)
- XML

These bidirectional interfaces provide excellent data exchange capabilities. XML continues to gain acceptance specifically for automated configuration of EAI systems, Workflow and eCommerce platforms because of its evident advantages. Other possible areas of use include, for example, automated transfer to the ARIS Repository of diagram data from third-party systems, or of cost data from operational cost accounting systems. XML has become interesting particularly because of the efforts to standardize on the part of organizations such as RosettaNet, BPMI.org, or SCOR (Supply Chain Council).

4. Functions of the ARIS Toolset

The ARIS Toolset is made up of a number of different modules/components. These are: Modeling, Publishing (Navigation), Analysis/Simulation, Activity-Based Cost Calculation, Balanced Scorecard, Reporting and Configuration. The following section includes a brief description of each component.

4.1 Modeling

Modeling reflects the basic functionality of the ARIS Toolset. It contains the graphical model editor, database administration, user administration, model administration, object administration, and layout and model generation.

The graphical model editor shown in Figure 5 provides the core functionalities for gathering model information. It is used to create, modify and delete the graphical model objects and the relationships between them.

Database administration is used for creating, opening and deleting (logical) databases. Within a database, the consistency of models can be maintained at all times, since it is here that logical connections between the individual models/objects are constructed. On the other hand, there are no relationships between models of different databases. Databases therefore represent the highest structural unit within which models can be managed consistently.

In user administration, different users can be defined for each database, and these may then be assigned to certain user groups. Access privileges administration is closely associated with user administration. Access privileges administration provides the capability to assign certain access privileges to user groups as well as to individual users. This determines the mode (write or read) of access in which a user can access the models in a database.

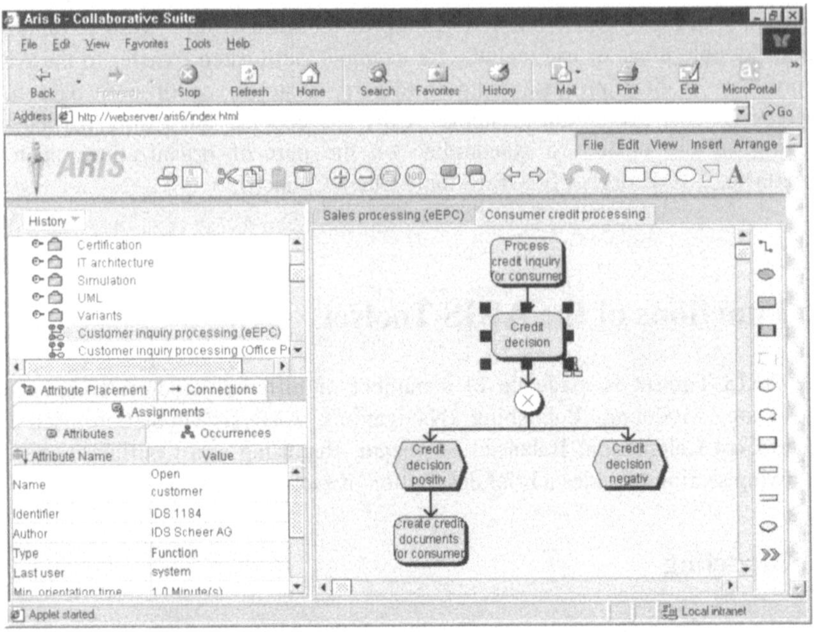

Figure 5: ARIS Web Designer

The essential functions of model administration are the creation, editing, storage, deletion, retrieval and printing of models. Model administration also provides the ability to collect thematically related models in groups. Object administration is closely allied to model administration. Object administration provides functions for creating, deleting, finding and copying objects (e.g. *Functions* or *Organizational units)*, and arranging them in hierarchies. Object administration is also the module provided for maintaining individual object attributes (e.g. *Name, Definition, Processing time, Wait time* in a *Function).*

Another important functionality of the modeling component is layout and model generation. Layout generation is used to automatically create an optimal model layout. Thus, the user is no longer obliged to refine the layout by hand. As a result, the modeling process is speeded up considerably. Model generation provides the ability to automatically create an overall model from a number of different submodels.

4.2 Publishing (Navigation)

Unlike the modeling component, it is not possible to manipulate models in the publishing component. This component provides read-only access to models. This is why navigation is also often referred to as a passive component. The purpose of this component is to render the relationship system within and between models transparent to the user, thereby making the model easier to understand. Navigation within a model includes functions that are used to show or hide individual objects and object groups on the screen. Accordingly, for instance, if necessary all the organizational units and/or data objects can be hidden in a business process model. This reduces the complexity of the models to ease concentration on a specific set of issues. Conversely, the models can also be expanded by stages after they have been hidden.

Besides business process models, the ARIS Toolset can be used to manage data models, organizational models and function models along the lines of the ARIS architecture. In this respect, it is important to note that these different model types are not disjunctive, that is to say they include some of the same objects. Thus, the organizational units of the organizational model are also a part of the business process model. The same is true of the data objects in the data model and the functions in the function model.

In order to clarify these relationship systems, the navigation component provides the capability to navigate between the various model types. This way it is possible, for example, to jump from a certain organizational unit in the process model to the corresponding organizational model.

The purpose of this functionality is to provide each user with access to the model information he requires based on his role in the company. Only when the contents of processes have been fully assimilated into „daily life" will their continuous further development be assured. Therefore, the publishing component also serves as a feedback instrument for users in the technical departments. In order to make access to relevant contents easier for the user with regard to technology, publishing is done via the Internet or intranet. This means that, from the point of view of technology, model contents can only be accessed via a Web browser.

4.3 Analysis and Simulation

The Analysis/Simulation component is provided for purposes of model evaluation. This refers essentially to the generation of certain key performance indicators on the basis of the business process models and the information included therein. Examples of this include: Throughput time, Capacity utilization, Wait time, Number of department changes, and Number of system changes. Armed with these key performance indicators, the user can evaluate the models. In principle, it is not possible to carry out a model evaluation without human intervention, because the interpretation of the calculated key performance indicators is strongly influenced by the specific environment conditions of the company.

Static or dynamic calculation techniques may be used to calculate the key performance indicators. Dynamic key performance indicator calculation is usually referred to as simulation, and is chiefly intended for use in calculating time and capacity key performance indicators. The difference between this and the static mode is essentially that dynamic calculations also take into account the time factor and the volume. With Simulation, it is possible to cycle through the progress of a business process chronologically under realtime conditions. This allows detailed statements to be made about, for example, capacity utilizations and cycle times. However, it is important to note that simulation entails devoting a significant amount of time to gathering data. Often the effort in terms of time is so great that a simulation is not practical from the point of view of cost-effectiveness.

This is where static procedures are useful. Static procedures basically return similar results, though with a slightly lower degree of accuracy in respect of times and capacities. Static time analyses are useful whenever a rough overview is all that is required. They cannot be used for analyses that must be accurate to the minute or even to the second. However, they are entirely adequate for calculating static key performance indicators that do not have a temporal dimension, such as the frequency of department or system changes.

Besides calculating process key performance indicators, analysis also includes functions for model comparison. The purpose of this is to use automated model comparison to identify the differences and similarities between models.

4.4 Activity-Based Cost Calculation

The aim of activity-based cost calculation is to provide an evaluation of the functions of indirect performance areas (overhead cost centers) with regard to cost. Activity-based cost calculation was developed from the routing costing existing in production. Routings may be seen as the business processes of the production area. They include descriptions of the processes in production accurate to the second, and evaluations of the processes for costing purposes using reference values and cost rates. Similarly, the activity-based cost calculation seeks to apply this thinking to business processes. Here too, the purpose is to determine the costs of a process. Cost drivers are used instead of reference values, and they yield process cost rates rather than cost rates.

The process cost rates calculated thereby are used on the one hand to evaluate the business processes in terms of their cost. But process cost rates can also be used for budgeting as part of the cost center calculation activity. Process cost rates can even be used as an element in product costing. This has the advantage for product costing that overheads can be charged to the individual cost objects with more accurate consideration for the source of the expense.

The ARIS Toolset offers a number of techniques for determining the costs of a business process. One example of these, the planning approach, is described briefly in the following.

Cost calculation for planning purposes is a top-down procedure. Starting with the costs of a cost center, this method attempts to allocate these costs to the processes that pass through that cost center. For this, first the cost categories to be charged (e.g. personnel costs and/or materials costs) are determined. Then the functions that are to be executed within the cost center(s) under examination are determined with their associated process performances. The process performance is normally measured in hours, i.e. the number of hours devoted to the function in question during the period under review is determined. The next step is to determine the cost drivers and the process volume. The cost driver represents the value that is used to determine the costs of executing a function. Let us take the example of the *Check quotation* function with the *Quotation items* cost driver. The process volume indicates the number of quotation items processed during the period under consideration. Then the process cost rate of the function is calculated on the basis of the three values 'process volume', 'process performance', and 'cost center costs'. Then, the costs of the business process are determined within the business processes on the basis of the function-specific cost rates, taking into account the usage factors (cost driver volumes).

4.5 Reporting

As business processes are modeled, a great deal of information is collected. The task of reporting is to analyze this information flexibly from various viewpoints, and to make it available in a form that is structured and easily understood so that it can be used in support of decision-making. Information that cannot be analyzed, even though it is in the database, is dead information. A flexible reporting mechanism is therefore crucial.

In the ARIS Toolset, the user can define different report types (evaluation types) to suit his purposes. In one report type, the relevant object types (e.g. *Functions, Events, Organizational units),* attribute types (e.g. *Name, Definition, Processing time, Execution mode)* and relationship types *(function creates event, organizational unit is technically responsible for function)* are specified. Besides the object contents, the report definition also comprises the associated layout information. No programming skills are needed to be able to define report types. The user compiles the report by selecting the information that is relevant for the problem at hand from a number of option lists. These settings can be stored for reuse whenever they are needed.

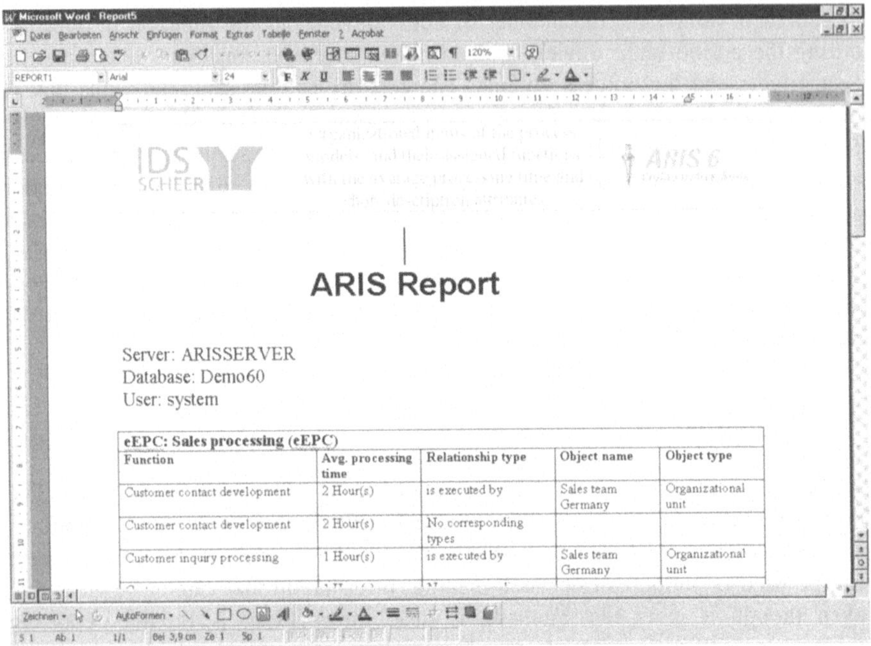

Figure 6: ARIS Reporting

Besides report definition, report output is also important. It is possible for the user to rearrange the sequence in which individual objects and attributes are output. Even the corresponding model graphics can be integrated in the report automatically. Report results can be output in table format or as text. For this, several file formats can be used, including XML and HTML. The most common Office programs can all be used as the output medium.

4.6 Configuration

The ARIS Toolset includes many different description methods (e.g. *Extended entity-relationship method, Event-driven process chain, Organizational chart, Function tree, Technical terms model, Value-added chain diagram).* This wide selection results from the range of problems the system is designed to handle. To simplify working with the system, the description methods needed for the task may be configured to suit the individual's needs. The configuration can be applied not only to the description methods, but also to the object types (e.g. *Function, Employee, Organizational unit)* and relationship types (e.g. *is input for, is output of, is technically responsible, executes)* they contain. Even the attribute types (e.g. *Name, Definition, Example, Frequency, Processing time)* of the individual object types can be defined according to requirements for a given project. In configuration, existing standard objects can be hidden and new customer objects may be added. Because they are able to configure the methods, employees are only confronted with the method information they must have in order to work on the project.

Besides the configuration of the description methods, project-specific consistency rules can also be defined. These consistency rules may refer to the consistency of different model types. One example of such is the rule that all organizational units in the business process model must also occur in the organization model. Or, these rules may refer to specific model types, for instance the rule that all business processes must start with an event and end with an event.

5. Prerequisites for Successful ARIS Implementation

It is fallacious to think that the success of a project can be assured by the use of a single tool. A tool is only as good as its operator. The ability to work with methods in this instance must always be given greater priority than knowledge of the functionality. It must also be borne in mind that business process modeling is a creative process, in which a system can be used for support, but can never fully replace the human element. Many project leaders refuse to accept this fact. The use of any tool entails certain overarching conditions. Only if these conditions are met can the benefits of the tool be exploited to the fullest advantage. Yet the benefits are significant. They include not only the enormous advantages in terms of time, and consequently costs, compared with conventional project management, but also the improved quality afforded by such an initiative and reusability of the project results, for example for workflow management and standard software configuration. The essential prerequisites for successful use of the tool include the following:

- Specification of modeling techniques
- Definition of a procedure model
- Specification of modeling conventions
- Specification of tool conventions
- Training of employees

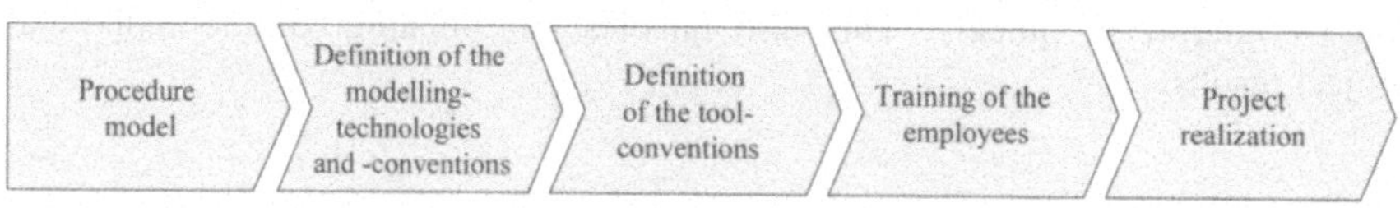

Figure 7: Essential prerequisites for efficient implementation of the tool

The tasks and activities to be performed as part of the project are defined and placed in their chronological sequence in the procedure model. Other components of the procedure model are the results to be achieved by the individual tasks and the documents required to perform the tasks. Even the project team members responsible for performing the individual tasks must be defined in the procedure model. Event-driven process chains can be used for the graphical documentation of procedure models in just the same way as for business process models.

Once the procedure model has been completed, the next step is to decide which description methods are to be used to document the results defined in the procedure model. For example, it may be decided that the target business process model is to be documented as the result of the „Define target business process model" task using the event-driven process chain (EPC) description method. In this way, description methods must be assigned to all the results provided for in the procedure model. Then these description methods must be defined in more detail. In practical terms, this means defining the object types, attribute types and connection types to be used as part of the description method.

When the description methods to be used have been specified in detail, the next task consists in determining conventions for the modeling activities. As part of the modeling conventions, for example, the system for assigning names to functions and events must be determined. Other determinations that must be made in this context relate to the level of detail in the models that are to be created and the use of decision rules when modeling processes. An important aspect of the modeling conventions is also the representation conventions. The display conventions relate to layout templates such as for instance the graphical positioning of objects or the spacing between individual symbols. Even the fonts to be used should be specified as part of these conventions.

In contrast to the modeling conventions, which are explicitly not tied to a tool, the tool conventions are defined with respect to the specific system that is to be used. The tool conventions describe which system functions are used, and in what way. Regarding the ARIS Toolset, these include, for example, the definition of standard reports, the specification of user rights and the determination of the group hierarchy for managing the individual models.

The specification of modeling and tool conventions is of primordial importance to ensure standardization and thus the ability to compare project results. These conventions ensure that the results returned by the individual project groups are uniform in terms of both technical content and structural and graphical organization. In this way, the results from employees even in other project groups can be interpreted quickly. This also enables consolidation of the individual project results.

6. Outlook

The functionality and technology of the ARIS Toolset are being constantly enhanced. Important developments are currently in hand in the areas of UML modeling (software engineering), process costs analysis, Web Services, Web Reporting and Enterprise Application Integration. Thus, a special graphical editor will shortly be available for generating UML models, and this will drastically reduce data collection times and provide close integration in the EPC models. With reference to activity-based cost calculation, a component dedicated specifically for use in this area is currently in development. Its purpose is to provide a simple but powerful method for calculating and analyzing process costs. Advances have been made with regard to Web Services so that in the future the existing interfaces will be extended to include the Internet standards SOAP, WSDL and UDDI. Web Reporting will enable users to evaluate the data of the ARIS repository from any location without the need for a client installation. In the area of Enterprise Application Integration, special methods are currently being developed to describe integration processes as well as the corresponding interfaces to prevalent EAI systems. In parallel with all of the above, the Web enabling project for the entire tool functionality is being pursued intensively.

Business Process Management : A Core Task for any Company Organization

Wolfram Jost
IDS Scheer AG

August-Wilhelm Scheer
IDS Scheer AG

Summary

Too much technology, not enough business: The first experimental forays into e-business may be reduced to this simple epigram. These days, in light of numerous disappointments, more and more companies are becoming aware of the fact that in the first instance, the emphasis of IT usage in general and e-business in particular must be concerned more with the "business", and less with the "E". Once this notion becomes clear, the revolution that is represented by re-engineering and the transformation of business processes is unmistakable. All the same, specifically in collaborative commerce, strategic and technical questions cannot be dealt with in isolation from one another.

Key Words

Business processes, Process transformation, E-business, Application architectures, Collaboration, Re-engineering, Strategy, Process integration, Business process intelligence, Business process performance measurement, Business process life-cycle

1. E-Business - From the Hype to the Reality

At the moment, e-business inspires an ambivalent response. On the one hand, the weaknesses in early projects are by now painfully evident, but on the other hand, business is now approaching the subject appropriately. Whereas until recently the smartest Website design and purely Web-based business models were seen as the keys to success, now much is being made of the integration of the frontend with the backend, and business models representing hybrids of the two. Whereas not long ago Web-enabling meant the same as "cutting-edge" when describing application software, now more than ever demand centers on process integration capabilities. And while the first faltering e-business initiatives relied heavily on electronic distribution channels, efforts are now afoot to breathe life into collaborative corporate strategies.

In short: The one-sided concentration on technical considerations – "E" – is being superseded by an emphasis on the "Business" aspects.

The inevitable consequence of this trend is that companies are evaluating their business processes more profoundly, and in the process are rediscovering the rather overlooked subject of re-engineering. And rediscover they must! Because until now this emphasis on the technical questions posed by e-business has hidden the need for a process-oriented approach. The same also applies, incidentally, for SCM, CRM, or ERP projects. Ultimately, all organizations, regardless of their size or the arena in which they operate, function by means of business processes. There is no such thing as a company without business processes. Companies that "refuse" to recognize or familiarize themselves with their processes, are in this ignorance missing the opportunity to actively promote their own effectiveness and efficiency. The reasons for the failures of many early e-business activities and dot-coms can also be determined by a consideration of their business processes. For example, what use is the most alluring portal to a company if the downstream logistics process is not integrated with the online ordering system?

2. Paradigm Shift in the Architecture of Standardized Software

Companies are being forced to adopt a more concerted approach to business processes relating to technical considerations too. The replacement of closed ERP systems with open, loosely interconnected application modules goes hand-in-hand with a loss of integration in general and of process integration in particular. For example, all the various mysap.com applications, and the SAP portal software offer their own repositories. Providers point out the greater flexibility and release-independence of the individual modules, characterizing them as advantages of these new software architectures. What they neglect to mention, to their shame, is this: The advantage for integration due to a single repository, which ERP software hitherto honored, is lost. But with this high degree of integration, when companies bought the ERP software, at the same time they were purchasing business processes embedded in the software. For the receipt and transaction based structure automatically triggered process chains – from quotation to order to delivery and invoicing, and so forth.

This integration effort has now been shifted to the companies themselves. It is true, software providers do offer integration technologies such as EAI modules, but technical process integration is not supplied by the manufacturers. So customers are finding themselves confronted with questions such as where and how a purchase order should be maintained - in the SCM, in the CRM, in Finance? – and so on. When the individual software modules are provided by different manufacturers, the problem becomes even more vexing. Only when they refer to the business process perspective will they find the tool they need to grasp and control even intercompany processes.

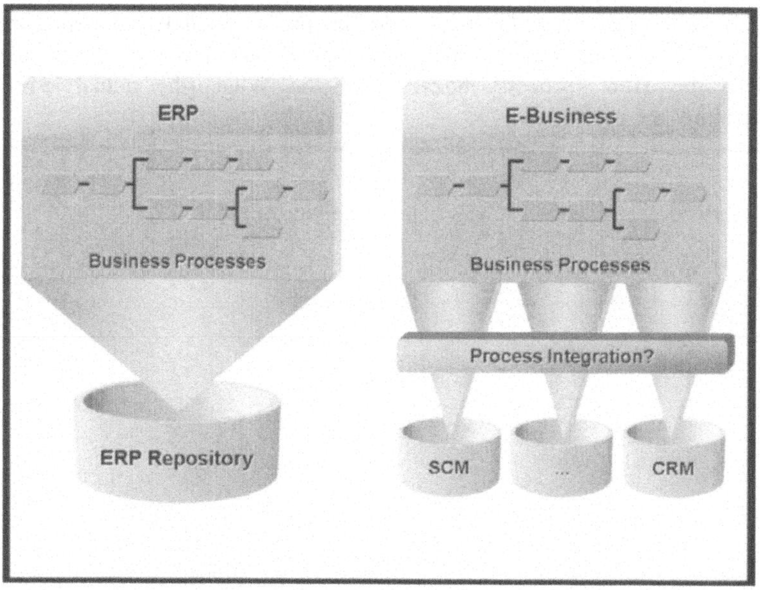

Figure 1: The problem of integration

3. Business Process Transformation

The question of business processes aside, the e-business initiatives in question are conducted with no organization applied to the transformation, a situation criticized notably by the Gartner Group in a current research note. Yet the very transformation of a company into an organization adapted for e-business itself constitutes a process. A glance at current efforts shows how much difficulty even prestigious companies are encountering just in organizing the transformation process. BMW and Siemens, for example, have set up their own subsidiary companies, while Deutsche Bank struggles with the task internally.

The e-business activities themselves are imbued with the pioneering spirit. One must have the courage to try new things, and if these prove unsuccessful, to regroup or make modifications without succumbing to distractions. Trial and error. The fact that modifications must be considered constantly even during runtime naturally translates to a high degree of complexity and also naturally entails grave misgivings about the effectiveness of the strategy that has been adopted.

It is entirely reasonable to be skeptical about the existence of a golden bullet, yet another conclusion drawn from previous e-business projects. For this reason, the importance of establishing a valid e-business framework and an architecture that is suitable for the company cannot be overstated. This is where the strategic objectives, the process and IT architecture, the process models and responsibilities are defined in terms that are still very general, and the Who (organizational model), the How (process model), and the What (the actual e-business architecture) are determined.

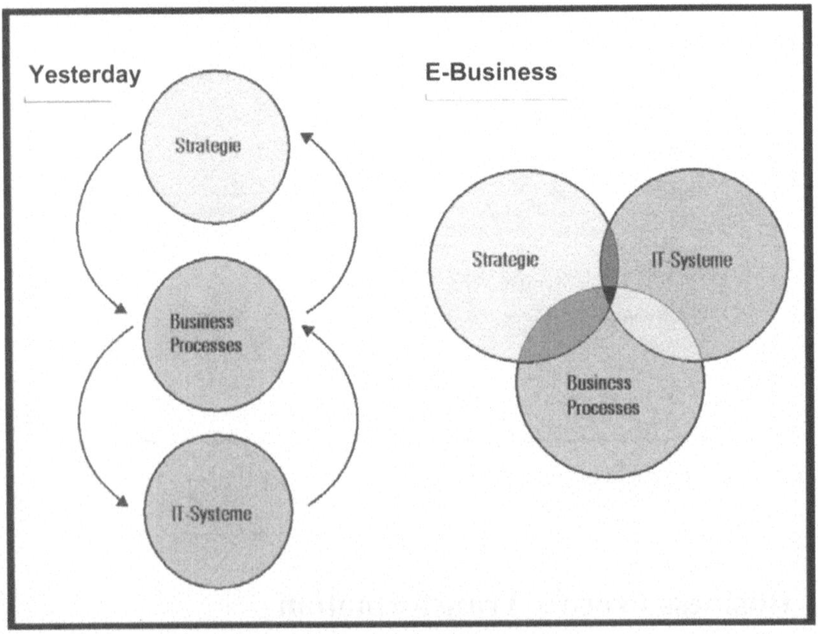

Figure 2: Change in strategic corporate planning

In connection with this framework, it is important to understand that: Contrary to the previous situation, corporate strategy, business processes and IT systems can no longer be treated in isolation; in fact, each aspect has very profound implications for both of the other two. The simple answer to the question of which processes are to be considered core competencies, and so do not extend beyond the limits of the company, and which may be shared with or entrusted to external partner companies, can be significant in determining the establishment of a portal or connection to a digital marketplace. Participation in an e-marketplace such as Covisint can in turn entail extensive cooperation among companies, in design for instance, thereby necessitating reconfiguration of business processes, even to the extent that the company must reevaluate its own core competencies.

The parameters on very general terms in the e-business architecture provide the necessary spaces for such decisions. For this reason, it should also not be compared with the company data model of the 70s, in which subsequent modifications were precluded by technical descriptions that were carved in stone. On the other hand, the existence of an e-business architecture that is implemented throughout the company is imperative, since otherwise it would not be possible to provide a shared foundation for the range of different activities.

The individual e-business projects themselves should rather be tackled in smaller, manageable steps. The question of which business processes are instituted in substantive terms is most simply deduced from the general business process model, which at the abstract level complements and extends the internal company processes at the boundaries by adding relationships and activities relating to suppliers and customers. In the early e-business scenarios, companies will concentrate on business processes that involve close interaction with customers and/or suppliers. Purchasing processing (e-procurement, perhaps) or sales processing (for instance determination of reliable delivery dates) would be examples of this. On the other hand, internal processes such as Finance would probably not be chosen as the starting point for a company's e-business initiative. However, forecasts can be made with much greater accuracy, and uncertainty regarding supply and demand reduced to a minimum if major clients automatically communicate their plans with the manufacturer.

Collaborative process scenarios can also be drawn up, in which subcontractors take it upon themselves to find out whether partial deliveries will be helpful for filling an order in the event of supply bottlenecks.

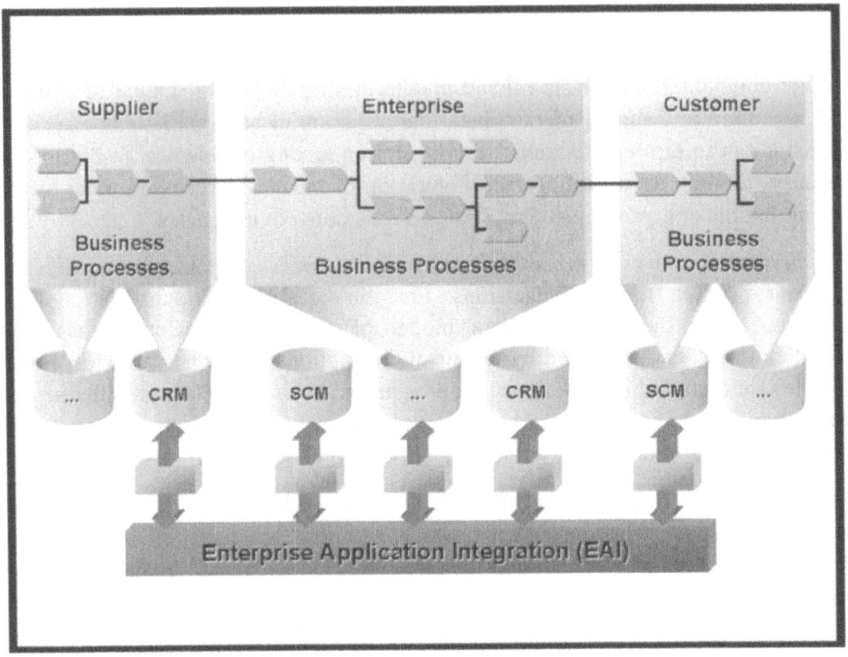

Figure 3: Integrated business process development

4. Business Process Excellence

However, one should not be misled into thinking that changes on the "boundaries" of the company have no effect on internal processes. Indeed, many e-business initiatives have fallen into this very trap, and failed as a consequence. For example, in order to be able to set a reliable delivery date and make an availability check (available to promise), it is essential to have full access to all information on the production and supply capacities of the manufacturing facilities. No less important: If the process is to be executed collaboratively, external partners must be involved from the outset, so that the process design can be undertaken jointly. After all, collaboration inherently entails the exchange of information and mutual reciprocal authorization of access to systems. The interplay between process and technology indicated previously is evident here, as aspects such as a portal, a public or private marketplace etc. are included in considerations.

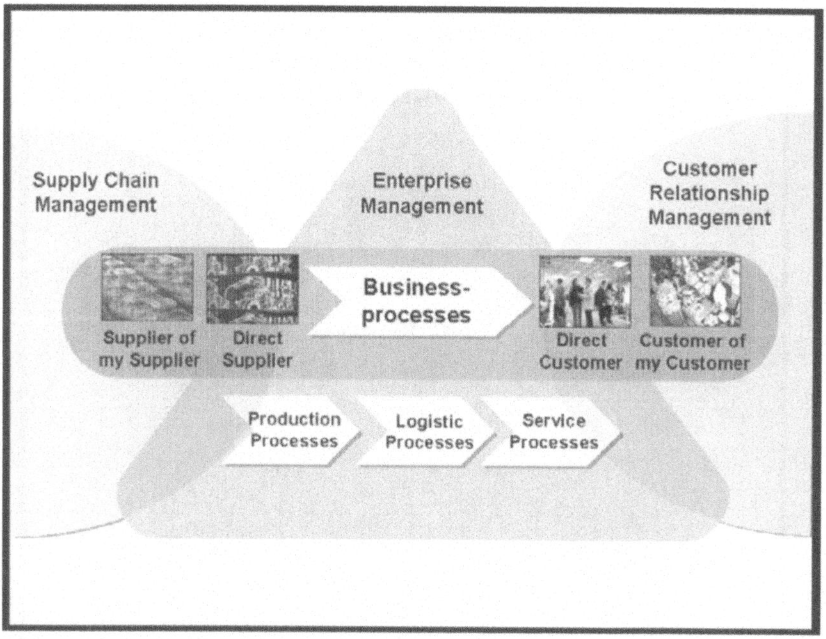

Figure 4: Process management across company boundaries

However, the business process design and the associated technological implementation usher in only the first stage of a successful e-business strategy. As was mentioned in the introduction, trial and error - within certain limits - are integral features of the associated projects. On the basis of such trial and error, companies are challenged to compare their objectives with the results of the implementation constantly, and to strive unceasingly to optimize their activities. As a consequence, the level of business process intelligence, at which the company's procedures are drafted, analyzed and measured assumes greater significance and importance. In recent years, companies have invested very heavily in automation for their operational business processes. The success of the big ERP manufacturers is linked very closely to this fact. In this "implementation mania", questions of process design and process measurement have frequently been neglected. The initial introduction of systems is the "compulsory program", but continuous optimization is an "optional" exercise. The profound changes in software architectures (component formation, Web services) and the constantly shortening change cycles in the business processes mean that the importance of the Process Intelligence level is constantly increasing. The growing importance of business process management is also evident in the debate that is now under way concerning the role of the Chief Information Officers (CIO), and possibly restructuring this position as the Chief Process Officer (CPO). The innovative power of the Process Intelligence levels (levels 1 and 2) illustrated in Fig. 5 are critical in determining the efficiency and quality of the operational business processes, and thus also of the economic success of the company. These days, it is no longer enough to redesign business processes once and for all, a continuous Process Lifecycle Management must also be established.

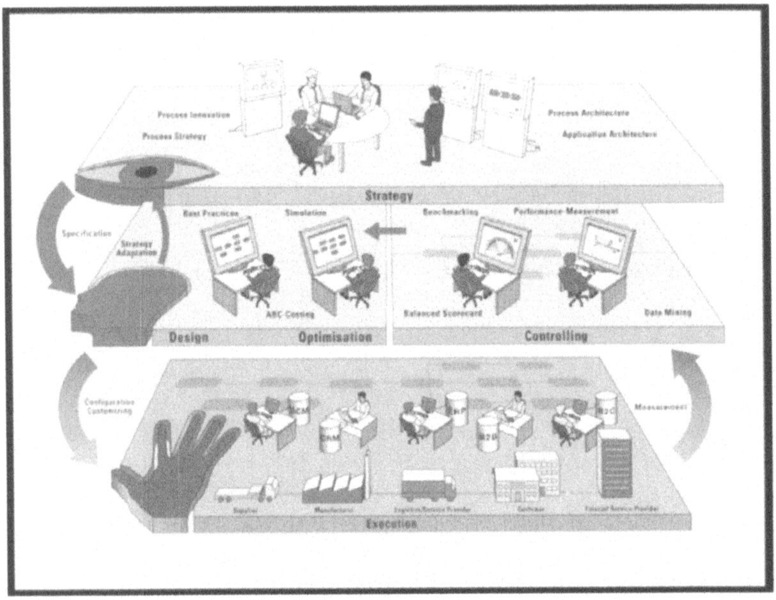

Figure 5: Business Process Excellence ARIS

5. Learning from Formula 1 Racing

An analogy from formula 1 motor racing may help to explain the development: Even in the supreme class of motor racing, analysis of race data, telemetry, is assuming a decisive importance for the outcome of a race. Thus at every pit stop, besides the visible activities like tire changes and refueling, information is also extracted and analyzed on fuel consumption, braking behavior, tire wear and so forth. The appropriate strategy is adapted constantly according to the progress of the race. Victory or defeat is no longer decided purely by the ability to drive fast, but also by the strategy developed in the pit.

Figure 6: Pit stop in a formula 1 race

Incidentally, the pit stop is a classic example of the conflict of interests that exists between process optimization and resource efficiency. The formula 1 racing teams buy the optimal process with a "profligate" use of resources (personnel, materials etc.). Companies are hardly able to afford this approach. At the same time, they cannot do without the "telemetry data" of their e-business processes if they wish to use process efficiency to improve the company's success.

Until now, management has derived its knowledge about the business situation from indicators such as the trend in sales revenues, cashflow, profit, contribution-based accounting, sales volume figures, etc. It has relied on information that is rooted in the past. Important incidents, such as a serious deadline overrun due to quality deficiencies, which occur at short notice and require immediate countermeasures, are recorded too late, if at all, in quarterly, monthly or weekly reports. When the incident is finally revealed, valuable time has already been lost irretrievably. To return to the analogy from formula 1 motor racing, companies are still analyzing lap times after the race has been won.

6. Business Process Performance Measurement

As a consequence, new measurement units need to be selected and set up to provide a reliable basis for the evaluation of efficiency in near real time.

Conventional Business Intelligence tools are a source of valuable information on this point. Generally, however, they are not equal to this task because they are based exclusively on operational data. But this data is not correlated with business processes. An analysis of customer behavior on a regional basis from current sales data or calculation of opportunities for cross- and up-selling may not have required any linkage to business processes, but questions like the following certainly do:

- Are some customer orders completed late, or even lost?
- How cost- and time-effective are individual procurement and distribution channels?
- Where are the weak points and bottlenecks in the procedures?
- How good was deadline reliability for a certain product line in July?
- What was the average throughput time for this product line and what were the outliers?
- How successfully have improvement actions been implemented? Have the processes improved since the last quarter?

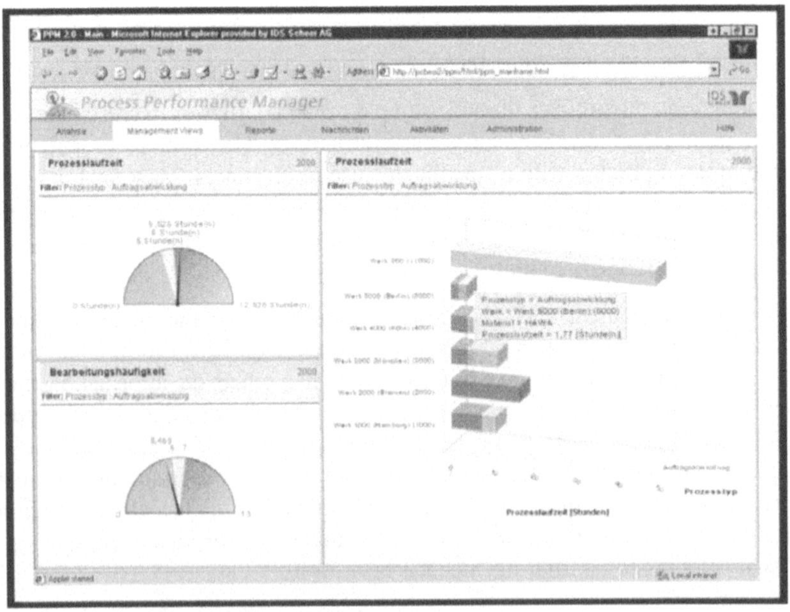

Figure 7: ARIS Process Performance Manager

The questions cannot be answered using just document-based, transaction oriented applications. So, a transparent process view must first be superimposed on the affected applications and then meaningful Key Performance Indicators (KPIs) must be defined. Data (documents, log files, timestamps for transactions, custom settings etc.) from the applications involved form the basis for determining KPIs.

To measure process performance, the individual activities of a procedure (order receipt or similar) may be linked together for example using event chains. In principle the business process and its indicators is thus generated in reverse from the operational applications, with the additional use of tools.

The process orientation of these performance measurement tools suggests that they be identified as Business Process Intelligence (BPI) tools. As with BI tools, the use of BPI tools in and of itself is no guarantee that business processes are immediately optimized. This evaluation must (still) be made by the management.

But the following basic principle applies: What cannot be measured, cannot be improved! And by measuring Business Process Performance, companies are creating an important prerequisite for establishing a Business Process Lifecycle view. In a closed system, processes can be administered from design and development, through processing to monitoring and optimization. This congruence of purpose between the analytical and the operational applications enables those responsible in the company to monitor the effects and implementation of their strategic measures constantly, and to evaluate them in near real time with the process metrics they have put in place. The high degree of uncertainty in e-business scenarios makes this an absolute imperative.

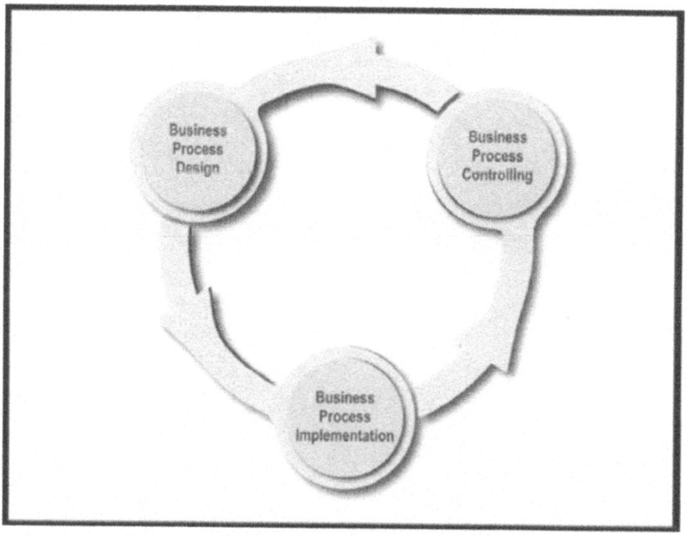

Figure 8: Business Process Lifecycle

But – and it is important to note this – no effort to improve business processes can succeed unless the participants "do their part". For process changes are always and inevitably linked to behavioral changes on the part of the people. The technical variant, replacing system A with system B, is much easier, because the prevailing situation can be preserved almost unchanged. This approach worked for the introduction of ERP software. But for e-business, there is no getting round a consideration and evaluation of business processes.

[illegible]

Figure 2: Business Process [illegible]

But [illegible] it is important to note that no [illegible] business processes can succeed unless the participants do their part. The process changes [illegible] and necessarily linked to behavioral changes on the part of the people. The technical [illegible]

Using SCOR and Other Reference Models for E-Business Process Networks

Mathias Kirchmer
IDS Scheer, Inc.

George Brown
Intel, Inc.

Herbert Heinzel
Siemens AG, SBS

Summary

While companies in the 90's focused on the design and implementation of their internal business processes to overcome functional barriers, the 00's are about the integration between enterprises, about inter-enterprise processes. Key in that field is the improvement of supply chain management processes. Major enabler is the internet. That's why the resulting processes are called e-business processes, connected to entire networks of processes.

In order to design and implement those inter-enterprise e-business processes efficiently and effectively, more and more organizations use available industry standards in form of reference models like the Supply Chain Reference Model (SCOR), developed by the Supply Chain Council, the RosettaNet Standards, or software reference models. Unclear is for many enterprises, HOW to use those standards.

Goal of a joint initiative between Intel; Siemens AG SBS; IDS Scheer and various technology partners, has been to develop a comprehensive methodology for the use of reference models, especially SCOR and RosettaNet, to define and implement inter-enterprise collaborations within supply chain networks. The methodology leads to fast and reliable results in supply chain improvement. It increases the performance of the implementation as well as of the resulting processes.

Key Words

ARIS, ARIS Toolset, e-Business, eBPI, inter-enterprise business processes, intra-enterprise business processes, reference models, RosettaNet, SAP reference models, SCOR, Y Model

1. Background

Businesses face many challenges that require fully leveraging information to enable individuals to quickly respond to increases in the speed of business cycles, the need to optimize resources and relationships, the need to increase business processes' efficiency, and the need to interact effectively across the entire business network. As always, at the fore of these imperatives is the ceaseless effort to decrease costs while increasing revenue to meet profitability and expected financial earnings—these are the bottom-line mandates with which everyone must align and focus their efforts.

By the end of the millennium, companies were engaged in a frenzied effort to improve intra-enterprise application integration through technology that facilitates a loose coupling of applications with integration infrastructures, based usually on messaging. The EAI technology addressed the need to unify the interaction between disparate applications, but on a point-to-point basis. The vision was to move the enterprise to an application service-based architecture, but often failed to get traction because service requirements were ill-defined. The new millennium ushered in a wave of interest in e-Business, perceived to be the essential means to maintain competitiveness in the new Internet era.

Concurrent with heightened interest in doing business on the Internet, industry partners sought agreement on what messages were to be used for process interaction across the enterprise boundary. For example, the semiconductor industry threw its weight behind RosettaNet as a consortium to define protocols appropriate for inter-enterprise processes. The rapid transition to e-Business solutions shifted interest in EAI technology to Business-to-Business Integration technology as companies grappled with the implementation of the point-to-point protocols defined for public processes. Implementation of EAI technology had been a major investment, but public protocol implementation proved to be even more problematic than anticipated and required a minimal level of readiness on the part of each partner involved. In addition, point-to-point solutions did not resonate with the business groups that were trying to improve the effectiveness of their processes across the enterprise boundary within a particular community of business, like third party fulfillment.

Overlaid on the rush to e-Business solutions has been a growing interest in leveraging supply chain management to gain or maintain competitive advantage. The virtual enterprises of today and the future will be increasingly complex and dynamic both in the changing of partnerships but also in the multiplicity of roles each partner may play. These dynamic supply networks are strongly influenced by the "internet speed" with which customer demand changes and also by the shortened product life cycle made necessary by competitive positioning. Much work has gone into making the supply networks more responsive and to designing different portions of a company's supply network to ensure the required degree on flexibility, all with reasonable cost and little, if any, excess inventory at the end of a product life cycle.

Key is the concept of an "universal model". From a business perspective, it is important that the business process be defined in terms of business goals, functions, and constraints rather than in terms of the resources that implement the process. Success in realizing these business management goals is dependant on making sure that all your enterprise processes have integrity. One fundamental tool in ensuring integrity in enterprise processes is the concept of a universal model which can provide a framework for integrating various lines of business.

In order to design and implement inter-enterprise e-business processes efficiently and effectively, more and more organizations use available industry standards in form of reference models like the Supply Chain Reference Model (SCOR), developed by the Supply Chain Council, the RosettaNet Standards, or software reference models. Standardization organizations like e.g. the Supply Chain Council consist of hundreds of member companies, developing reference models that reflect industry best practices. Other reference models are developed by solution vendors, e.g. application software vendors or consulting companies. What is unclear is for many enterprises is *how* to use those standards.

Consequently Intel and Siemens stepped up to define and implement a joint project to develop a methodology and framework for the design and implementation of inter-enterprise business processes, which will add value by aligning the SCOR methodology to the RosettaNet standards. The methodology leads to fast and reliable results in supply chain improvement. It increases the performance of the implementation as well as of the resulting processes. IDS Scheer was chosen as a strategic partner for the initiative. This ARIS Toolset was used to serve as a proof of concept and presentation tool to Siemens, Intel, the SCC, and RosettaNet.

Using SCOR as a foundation ensures a focus on inter-enterprise-processes in the supply chain area and the use of a generally available and accepted reference model. The RosettaNet standards are used to specify detailed inter-enterprise interactions, integrated to processes based on standard application software reference models.

2. Use of Appropriate Reference Models

Vital to the initiative has been the design and integration of the supply chains of the involved companies. Therefore, the Supply-Chain Operations Reference–model (SCOR) had been selected as the reference model to be used. This reference model is widely used in industry and is already known to Intel and Siemens. Using this industry standard should facilitate a broad use of the developed approach.

In order to specify the detailed interactions between involved companies, the RosettaNet models were chosen. These standards are very common for the high tech industry.

2.1 SCOR

The Supply-Chain Operations Reference-model [1] has been developed and endorsed by the Supply Chain Council (SCC), an independent not-for-profit organization. The SCC was founded in 1996 in the USA and has now branches all over the world.

SCOR is a business process reference model that contains all supply chain activities from supplier's supplier to a customer's customer. This includes

- All customer interactions from order entry through paid invoice
- All product (physical goods, services, etc.) transactions including equipment, supplies, spare parts, bulk product, software, etc.
- All market interaction from the understanding of the aggregate demand to the fulfillment of each order.

SCOR contains three levels of process detail. The top level (process types) defines the scope and content. It consists of the five top level processes

- Plan
- Source
- Make
- Deliver
- Return

The second level of SCOR, the configuration level (process categories), contains 30 process categories, like "Make-to-stock", "Make-to-order", "Engineer-to order" or "Production execution". These process categories can be used to configure a company's supply chain. Companies implement their operations strategy through the configuration they choose for their supply chain.

The third SCOR level, the process element level (decomposed processes) is used to fine tune the operations of a company. It consists of

- Process element definitions
- Process element information inputs and outputs
- Process performance metrics
- Best practices
- System capabilities necessary to support best practices

- Systems/tools to be used.

Companies implement their supply chain solution on level 4 (or even more levels of detail). Level four, called implementation level (decomposed process elements), defines practices to achieve competitive advantage and to adapt to changing business conditions. This level is company specific and not in scope of SCOR.

The structure of SCOR is shown in figure 1: Structure of SCOR

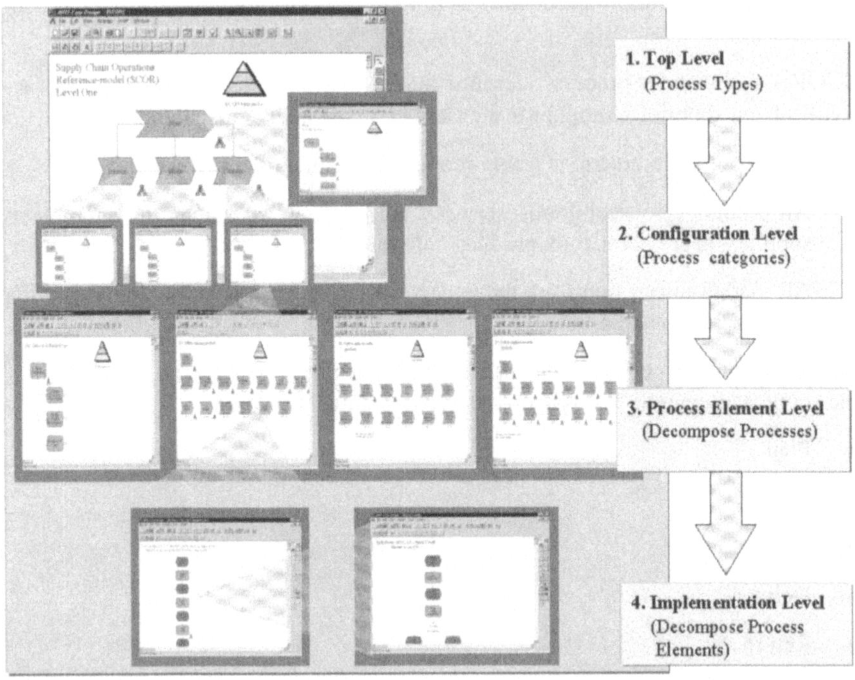

Figure 1: Structure of SCOR

SCOR also includes a methodology that enables companies to analyze and improve their supply chain operations by helping them communicate supply chain information across the enterprise, measure performance objectively, identify supply chain performance gaps and improvement objectives. The SCOR methodology has essentially four steps:

- Analyze the basis of competition
- Configure the supply chain
- Align performance levels, practices and systems
- Produce a plan for supply chain improvement backed up with projected ROI.

The methodology is applied to produce supply chain improvement project proposals backed up with sound business cases and high-level specifications of proposed solutions. It has also been used in the initiative described here.

2.2 RosettaNet

The RosettaNet group is an industry organization that drives collaborative development and rapid deployment of internet-based business standards, creating a common language and open e-business processes that provide measurable benefits and are vital to the evolution of the global, high-tech trading network [2]. RosettaNet has been founded in 1998 in the USA and has now also achieved a global presence.

The RosettaNet standards consist of a three level business process architecture that supports inter-enterprise e-business interactions:

- Partner Interface Processes (PIPs)
- RosettaNet Dictionaries
- RosettaNet Implementation Framework (RNIF)

Of foremost relevence for the context of the initiative described in this article is the business view described in the PIPs. However, it is an important aspect that the use of the PIP standards also ensures the technical implementation of the defined solutions.

A PIP describes activities, decisions and interactions necessary to fulfill an entire inter-enterprise business transaction. They also define the structure and format of business documents.

An example of a PIP process definition is shown in figure 2: Example for PIP process definition. It is an excerpt of an event-driven process chain [7].

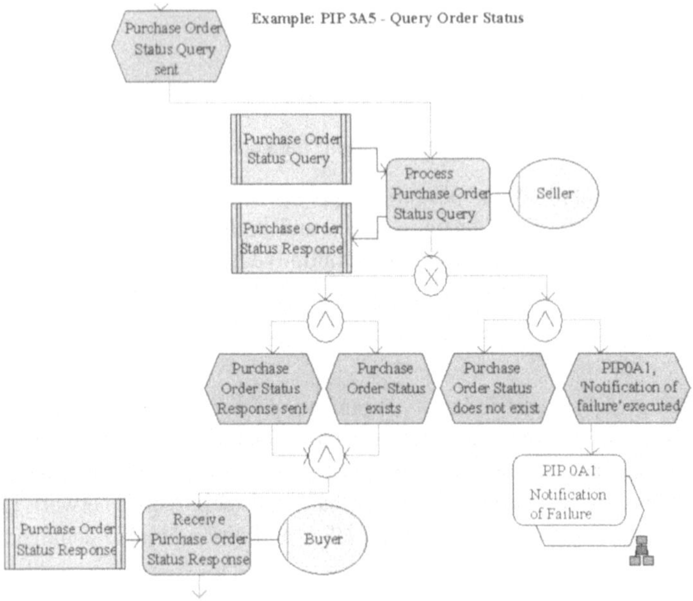

Figure 2: Example of a PIP process model

2.3 Others

In order to identify the relevant inter-enterprise supply chain interactions between companies the Y model developed by Scheer [3] [4] has been used. It includes all relevant business processes of a company, including planning and execution activities.

Each involved company can be represented by one Y model based upon which the interactions can be easily defined. Since it also includes activities that are not in the scope of SCOR, e.g. research and development, the Y model can be used both as a complement to the SCOR model as well as to identify the areas that will be specified using SCOR. The use of the Y model is especially important to create a high level entry point into the inter-enterprise process definition activities.

On the implementation level software reference models can be added to the mentioned reference models [5]. Since Intel and Siemens are users of SAP software the SAP reference models were chosen and included in the developed approach. However, business process models based on other software solutions can be used in the same way.

3. Development of a Procedural Model

After selecting the reference models to be used, a procedural model had to be developed, describing *how* the business reference models for the design of inter-enterprise e-business process networks could be used. The ARIS Architecture provides the basis for process description and the eBPI approach provides the framework within which the SCOR methodology is extended.

3.1 ARIS Architecture as Basis for Process Description

The "Architecture of Integrated Information Systems" (ARIS), developed by Scheer [6] [7], can be used as a framework to describe business processes efficiently *and* completely, thus managing knowledge about business processes. Using ARIS, a process can be examined from five different points of view (see figure 3: ARIS Information System Views):

- Organization view (Who takes part in the process, which companies, departments or people?)
- Function view (What is done in this process?)
- Data view (What information is produced or needed?)
- Output (Result) view (Which outputs/results/deliverables are produced?)
- Control view (How do the four other views interact? Who works on which functions using which data and in which operational logic to produce which deliverables?)

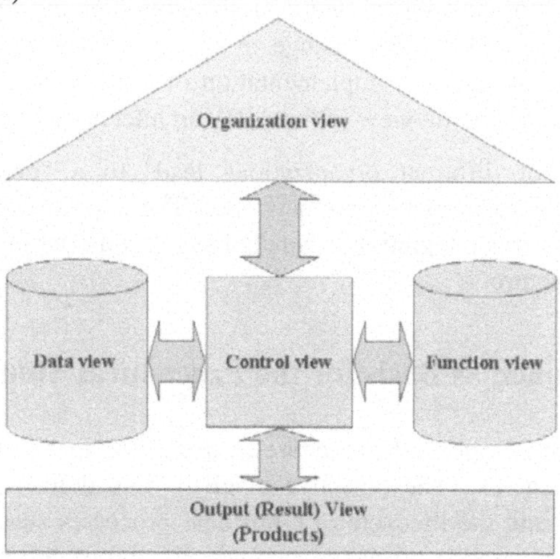

Figure 3: ARIS Information System Views

If it is possible to answer the questions concerning the various views, then a business process is adequately described. All the knowledge necessary for an efficient and effective business process lifecycle management is gathered. The control view, in particular, plays a central role, as it brings together the individual views and thus forms the foundation for successfully functioning business processes. The different views can be described on a pure business concept level, an information technology (IT) specification level (defining IT solution types, e.g., supply chain management (SCM)) and an implementation level (defining concrete IT solutions, e.g., a specific SCM system).

Every view of the ARIS architecture can be described by various modeling methods. They can be used to answer and communicate the mentioned questions, as well as a structure for information modeling methods. A big advantage for the practical use of the ARIS architecture is the availability of a software tool based on this architecture, the ARIS Toolset.

The ARIS architecture is especially suited for the use in inter-enterprise environments [8]:

The use of the Internet allows companies to change and extend their offerings. Instead of selling CDs, music files can be downloaded directly from the web, for example. Or packages in transit can be tracked through the internet – as additional customer service. Therefore the examination of a specific "output (product) view" of business processes, as suggested by the ARIS architecture, is extremely important in an e-business inter-enterprise environment.

E-business processes enable the efficient and effective collaboration between enterprises, directly or through "e-marketplaces". This means that responsibilities are shared between organizational units of the collaborating enterprises. As a consequence the examination and change of organizational structures becomes vitally important for design and implementation of e-business processes—again, an aspect handled in a specific view of the ARIS architecture.

The collaboration of different organizations leads to a "process-to-process" integration, and to e-business process networks. The coordination of all aspects necessary to achieve this integration is handled as a key aspect in the control view of the ARIS architecture.

3.2 eBPI Approach as Basis for the Procedural Model

The eBPI approach is a general procedure to use ARIS in an inter-enterprise e-business environment [8]. The objective of eBPI is to deliver, on one hand, a structure for managing the lifecycle of e-business processes successfully. On the other hand, it's imperative to leave enough flexibility to adapt procedures continuously to changing environments, typical of an e-business initiative. eBPI is an information model-based approach to e-business, combining aspects of efficiency and effectiveness.

The eBPI approach is structured into four major phases:

- Development of the e-business process vision
- Specification of the resulting e-business processes
- Realization of the e-business processes
- Continuous improvement of the e-business processes

The starting point eBPI is the elaboration of an e-business process vision. Core deliverables are e-business process scenarios—high level descriptions of the envisioned collaboration of organizations. These scenarios are further specified in the following phase of eBPI. This specification phase includes the definition of inter- and intra-enterprise processes necessary to realize the defined scenarios. It also includes the selection of the required e-enablers, such as application software products. The selected e-enablers are used to realize the e-business processes in the following phase of eBPI, which combines software implementation and e-integration activities. The realization phase triggers a continuous improvement of the implemented e-business processes (CPI). Key is here the definition of an effective business process performance management. The CPI can then restart the whole eBPI procedure in order to reflect customer, new market and technology developments.

While the e-business process vision focuses on complete e-business scenarios consisting of one or more processes, the specification phase focuses on individual e-business processes, and the realization phase on sub-processes or functions to ensure rapid results. Those sub-processes or functions are reassembled to complete business processes, which lay the basis for the continuous process improvement.

The phases of eBPI are not just in a "process sequence" with a defined beginning and a defined end. The continuous improvement will trigger – sooner or later – another visioning phase. Also, the different phases influence each other, which may cause changes in preliminary eBPI phases triggered by activities in the current phase.

The structure of eBPI is shown in figure 4: Structure of the E-Business Process Improvement Procedure (eBPI).

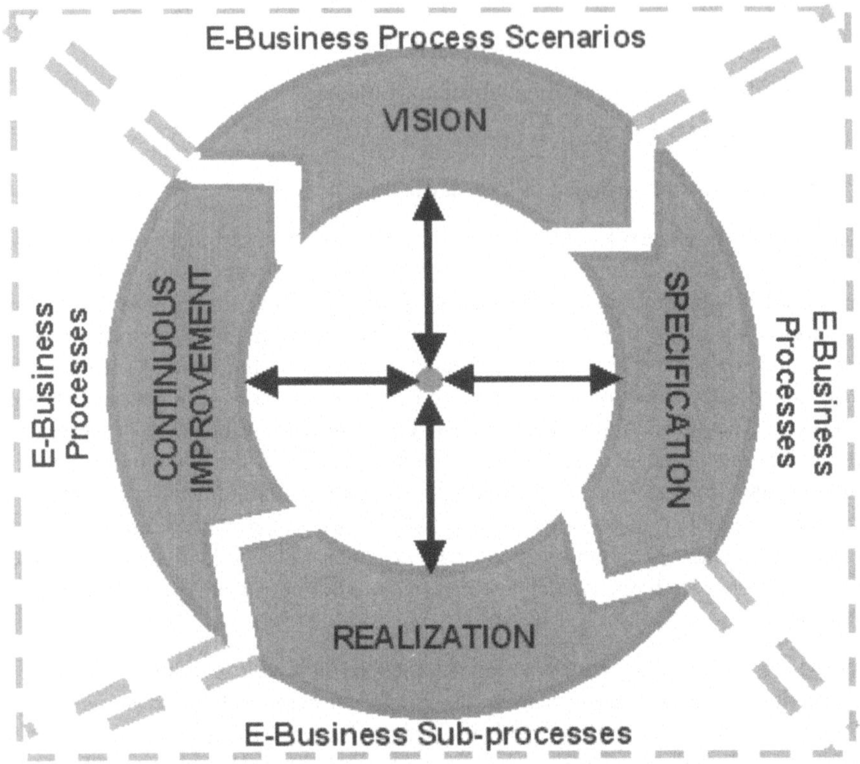

Figure 4: Structure of the e-Business Process Improvement Procedure (eBPI)

3.3 Modeling Procedure for the Integrated Use of the Selected Reference Models

The selected reference models reflect all ARIS views of the relevant inter-enterprise business processes. Focus of the modeling procedure to be developed is on the Vision and Specification phases of the eBPI approach.

The SCOR methodology is used to analyze an extended supply network in the Vision phase of eBPI. The starting point of the eBPI procedure is the elaboration of an e-business process vision, which in this case equates to the results of the SCOR methodology as used to identify and prioritize supply chain improvement projects. Core deliverables from the SCOR analysis within the Vision phase are e-business process scenarios in the form of a high level description of the envisioned collaboration between organizations of the extended supply network.

Therefore a first modeling step is the identification of scope, both for the relevant process and chosen products (goods, services, others) [9]. The relevant activities of each company can be either identified using SCOR, or on a broader base, using the Y model. Since the described initiative focuses currently on the improvement of supply chain networks, the relevant processes could be identified using SCOR.

The standard elements of the top level of the SCOR definition (the process types "plan", "source", "make", "deliver", and "return") have been found to be too general. Therefore, one usually starts the supply chain configuration by defining the roles within each tier of the supply network (e.g., Manufacturer at facility x, Distributor, Customer, etc.) and the major activities using a value added chain diagram (VACD) as method. An example for a level 1 supply chain definition using the VACD structure is shown in figure 5: Example of a supply chain definition. This representation is actually one level above the configuration model of SCOR which would reveal the process categories (e.g. Source to Stock, Make to Order, Deliver to Order, etc.) for each role.

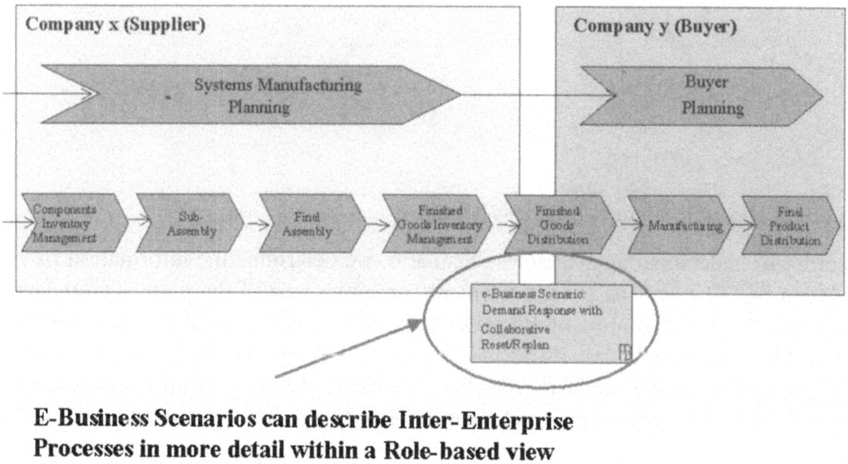

Figure 5: Example of a supply chain definition

As a result of applying a SCOR analysis to the supply chain, an inter-enterprise e-business scenario can be identified and prioritized based on best practices and specific patterns of the supply chain definition. These patterns can be aligned with performance objectives (at the moment the possible development of a reference model concerning these patterns is being explored).

The "model object" encapsulating the scenario model is positioned on the supply chain VACD as shown in Figure 5 which refers to an example scenario: "Demand Response with Collaborative Reset/Replan" from the Intel-Siemens project. It can then be specified using SCOR level II and III elements as a guideline. This means the scenarios are defined using the SCOR structure, but the process elements are specified according to the specific situation. The scenarios are role-based, so that they can be used in all similar situations. The scenario models define how business processes are distributed between the various roles and which business documents are exchanged. They cover all ARIS process views. An example of an e-business scenario model is shown in figure 6: Example of an e-business scenario.

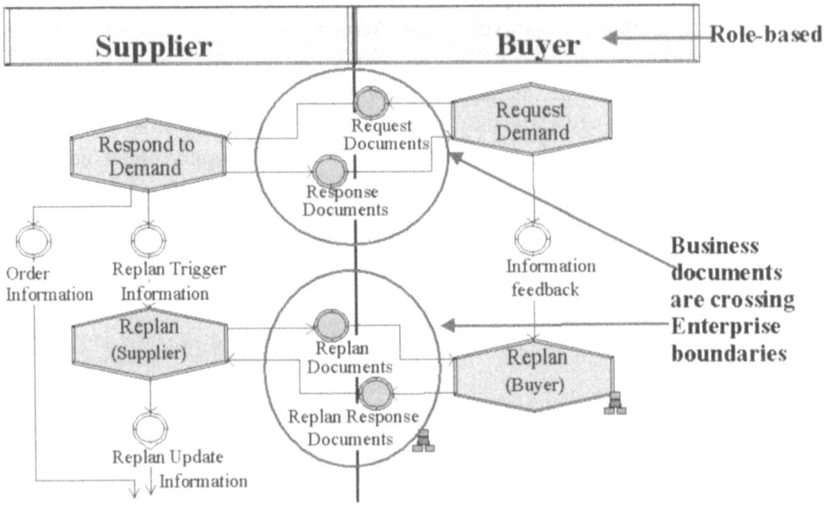

Figure 6: Example of an E-Business Scenario

In order to understand an e-Business Scenario, we determine the information flow between SCOR Level III process elements on either side of the partner boundary in a particular community of business partners for some segment of a supply chain. The information flow as defined by the SCOR in/out data elements defines the interactions of the scenario, e.g. the "Demand Response with Collaborative Reset/Replan" scenario of the Intel-Siemens supply chain.

The in/out data elements coupled with the semantics implied by the participating process elements at level III of SCOR can be used to identify protocols that correspond to public protocols as defined in RosettaNet. Careful inspection of the interactions required to span a particular scenario reveals a clustering of interactions around easily recognized business functions, e.g. planning and scheduling, that appear in multiple scenarios. These clusters of process elements involved in re-occurring inter-enterprise interactions constitute what we have labeled "collaborations". This aggregation of functionality in level III SCOR models has allowed us to use a simpler model type, the e-Business Scenario models which contain objects that encapsulate the clusters of process elements making up the collaborations. The collaborations thus have links to the process definitions that were created before. The process elements, in turn, provide linkage to public protocol specifications defined by RosettaNet. A summary of representations and model types utilized in the methodology is summarized in Table 1: Summary of models employed within the eBPI procedure.

eBPI phase	SCOR methodology	SCOR modeling	e-Business scenarios	Reference models	ARIS Arch. tier
VISION	Basis for Competition	SCORcard			(spreadsheet)
		Products			Product
		Organizations			Organization
		Locations			Organization
		Material Flow			Process
	Configure the Supply Chain	Level II Process Flow		SCOR	Process
		Level II Metrics		SCOR	Process
	AS/TO BE Align Performance	Level III Process Flow		SCOR	Process
		Data Flow in/out		SCOR	Data
		Level III Metrics		SCOR	Data
	Prioritize Alternative Solutions	Ranking Table	e-Business Scenario template		Process
SPECIFICATION			e-Business Scenario		Process
		Level III Process Flow		SCOR	Process
		Data Model			Data
				RosettaNet PIP Specification	Process
				ERP Reference Model	Process
				Legacy Process Model	Process
REALIZATION			e-Business Scenario transport		BPML

Table 1: Summary of models employed within the eBPI procedure

Note that The Business Process Modeling Language (BPML) is a meta-language for the modeling of business processes, just as XML is a meta-language for the modeling of business data and is under consideration for the transport of specifications into the Realization phase.

The process parts of the e-scenarios exchanging documents between roles and, therefore, between enterprises can now, be further specified using elements of SCOR level three and the RosettaNet PIP specifications. Again, all ARIS views are covered. Figure 7: "Process definition using SCOR and RosettaNet elements" shows an example of such a process specification.

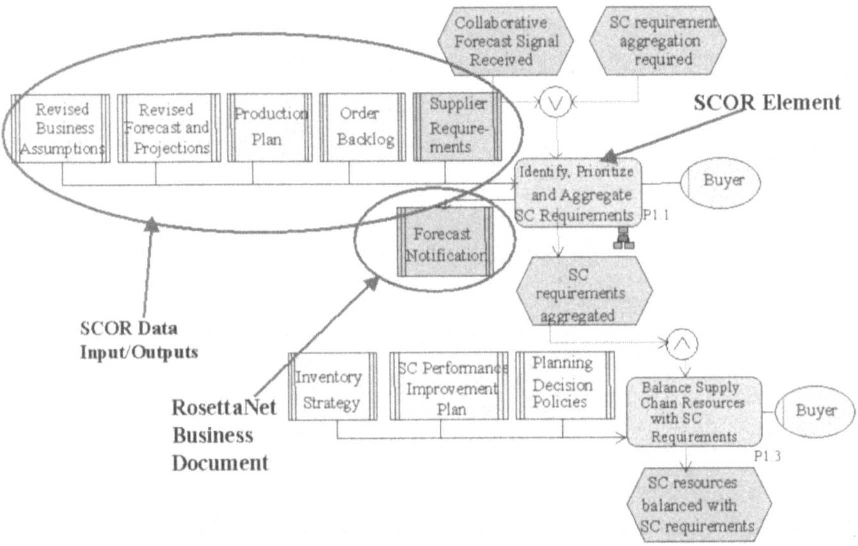

Figure 7: Process definition using SCOR and RosettaNet elements

Further RosettaNet PIP elements, especially the detailed process models, can be used on levels four and above, in conjunction with software reference models. The use of SAP and RosettaNet reference models has been positively tested. This highest process specification can now be implemented based on identified application software packages and the technical components of the RosettaNet standards in the Realization phase of eBPI.

The Realization phase triggers a Continuous Improvement phase for the implemented e-business processes, but this fourth phase is out of scope for our methodology development so far. The eBPI framework, as simple as it is, has helped us organize and relate the modeling that supports SCOR to the B2B modeling used to define the e-Business Scenarios down to the level of public protocols.

Figure 8: "Defining e-business process networks with SCOR and RosettaNet" shows the described approach in an overview.

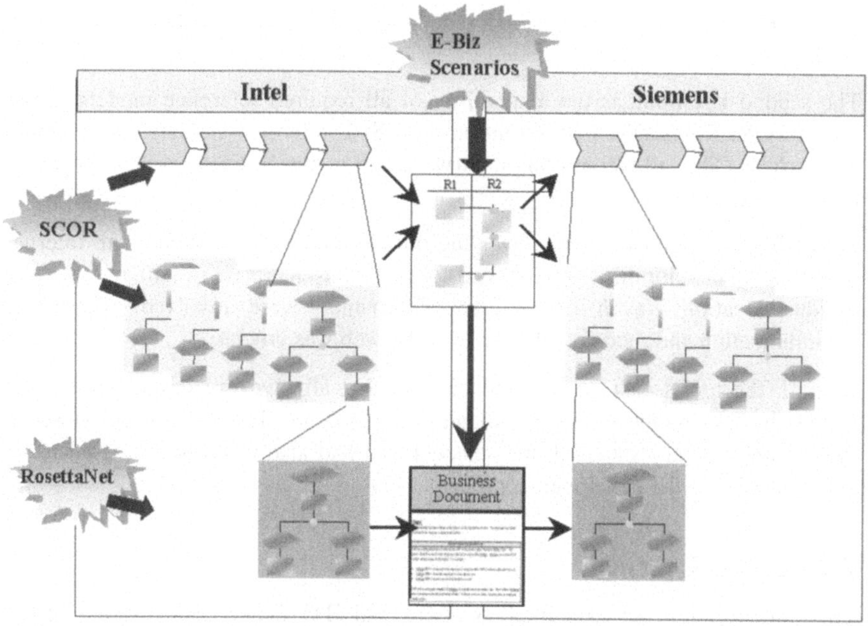

Figure 8: Defining e-business process networks with SCOR and RosettaNet

4. Application of the Defined Approach

The vision of the joint project with Intel, Siemens and IDS Scheer was to develop a methodology for the design and implementation of inter-enterprise business processes, which will add value by aligning the SCOR methodology to the RosettaNet standards. Workshops were organized to provide realistic examples of the SCOR to RosettaNet mapping methodology in the ARIS toolset as applied to the Intel-Siemens supply chain.

4.1 Key Tool Functionality

Since the ARIS architecture had been chosen as the basis for the process description, the ARIS Toolset (ATS), a set of software tools based on ARIS, was a natural fit for this initiative [11]. However, several characteristics were especially important for the final selection of the tool.

Of fundamental imporatnce is that the described methods are supported. But it is also important that the ATS allows UML modeling and interfaces to software development tools. Therefore developed requirement definitions can be used as a basis for necessary software development very efficiently, without any double work.

The second key point is the availability of all required reference models in the tool: SCOR, RosettaNet PIP definitions and SAP reference models are available in the ATS. This allows a straight forward use of the business content of those industry standards.

Possibilities to publish models over the internet and even to support an internet based model development were crucial for this inter-enterprise initiative. People at various locations—even of different continents—were involved. Therefore, communication and model exchange over the web was crucial.

Overall, the tool's ease of use and the fact that all involved organizations had already been using the ATS was another decision factor. Just as the used reference models are industry standard, the selected tool had also to be widely used to be able to duplicate the developed approach easily.

4.2 Lessons Learned

This collaboration between Intel, Siemens and IDS Scheer has resulted in the alignment of independently defined modeling initiatives to form a pragmatic, understandable business process modeling approach based on SCOR and the mapping of SCOR to RosettaNet standards. All parties involved were enabled to efficiently and effectively communicate the value of the SCOR to RosettaNet mapping methodology to companies and organizations involved and affected. The results were incorporated in the IDS Scheer eBPI approach.

The following benefits have been achieved:

- A single integrated repository of SCOR models, standard e-business scenarios, and RosettaNet PIP information enables the support of future Supply Chain Projects dealing with inter-enterprise processes.
- The SCOR models provide the overall framework of the ATS database. The addition of general e-business scenarios at the level 2 and possibly level 3 will enable project teams to utilize a pre-defined set of e-business scenarios within the SCOR framework. In addition, through linkage to RosettaNet PIPs from the e-business scenarios, project teams will be able to focus on a pre-selection of applicable PIPs with regards to specific inter-enterprise process steps. The project teams will be able to access the documentation for the PIPs directly from the ATS database.
- Once a solid meta-architecture is developed for the SCOR to RosettaNet mapping effort, other standards can be incorporated easier.

- Based on these standard models, project teams then will be able to model their specific processes at the levels 3, 4, and 5 as necessary. Selecting complete reference models or just specific parts and elements of those will expedite their efforts and lead to a much higher standardization across project teams working off the same reference database.
- The outcome new projects based on this approach will be additional templates based on the SCOR reference structure, incorporating standard inter-enterprise processes, and utilizing RosettaNet process standards for document transfer.

The result? A "business process warehouse" of reference models has been built which creates, together with the defined procedures and the enabling ARIS tool a "business process factory". This combined software and tool environment enables an efficient and effective design and implementation of e-business process networks.

6. References

[1] cf. Supply-Chain Council (ed.): Supply-Chain Operations Reference-model – Overview of SCOR Version 5.0. Pittsburgh, 2001.

[2] cf. RosettaNet (Ed.): RosettaNet Overview. On: rosettanet.org. 07/2000.

[3] cf. Scheer, A.-W.: CIM – Computer Integrated Manufacturing. 3rd edition, Berlin, New York, and others 1994.

[4] cf. Scheer, A.-W.: Business Process Engineering. 2nd edition, Berlin, New York, and others 1994.

[5] cf. Kirchmer, M.: Business Process Oriented Implementation of Standard Software – How to Achieve Competitive Advantage Efficiently and Effectively. 2nd edition, Berlin, New York and others 1999.

[6] cf. Scheer, A.-W.: ARIS – Business Process Frameworks. 2nd edition, Berlin, New York and others 1998.

[7] cf. Scheer, A.-W.: ARIS – Business Process Modeling. 2nd edition, Berlin, New York and others 1998.

[8] cf. Kirchmer, M.: e-Business Processes – A Complete Lifecycle Management Approach. White Paper. Berwyn 2000.

[9] cf. Kirchmer, M.: Market- and Product-Oriented Definition of Business Processes. In: Elzina, D.J., Gulledge, T.R., Lee, C.-Y.: Business Engineering. Norwell 1999, p. 131-144.

[10] cf. e.g., Jost, W.: Mit innovativen Loesungen zum dauerhaften E-Business Erfolg. In: IDS Scheer AG (Editor): Documents of ARIS Processworld. Duesseldorf 03/2000.

[11] cf. IDS Scheer AG (editor): Business Process Management – ARIS Toolset Products. White Paper, Saarbruecken 02/2000.

Strategy and Processes. Two in One Project at ZEC Bydgoszcz SA

Witold Horowski
IDS Scheer Polska

Paweł Olsztyński
IDS Scheer Polska, Pl.

Róza Czarnecka
ZEC Bydgoszcz

Summary

Working together at ZEC Bydgoszcz, management and employees came long way in 2001. The project conducted in Bydgoszcz concerned more than designing and implementing new business processes. The goal – although this was nowhere directly defined – was also to bring about a change in the way of thinking about our company. It resulted from the sector specifics as well as from company's organizational culture. Because of this, our story about the joint project will start with a description of the economic background, which is crucial for understanding essence of the project.

Key Words

Company reorganization, business process management, Balanced Scorecard, Value Based Management

1. Project Background

1.1 Changes in Polish Industry

For Polish industry – as for other Central European countries – the beginning of the nineties was the most important challenge to development we had ever confronted. In the centralized economy – although many areas were uncertain – sales was often among the most stable business elements. The changed operating environment forced many companies to make a complete reorientation. Those that could not adapt mostly went out of business. Marketing, sales, client, and quality – these are the key words in the strategies of Polish companies that were formulated in the first half of nineties. The second half of the decade was marked by increasing of managerial interest in subjects connected to effectiveness (e.g. business processes) and modern forms of financing developments. Throughout this period, known in Poland as the system transformation, importance of the privatization process cannot be overestimated. In many cases it meant a change of ownership but also in the management philosophy of the company, financial development, a new organizational culture.

1.2 The Energy Sector

The energy producing sector was considered to merit special consideration in the economy all over the world. Of prime importance to the economy, the added value chain is very sensitive to fluctuations in the economic situation, and on the other hand it is often the subject of political manipulation (central as well as local authorities). The Polish energy sector is no exception, and may even be seen as an archetypal example. With its monopoly status, the power industry in the first half of the '90s was plunged into stagnation – at least compared to the revolution in its economic environment. Later years brought a liberalized Energy Law based on the Scandinavian and British solutions.[1]

The principal objective of creating the energy market in Poland is to develop competition and so to increase the efficiency of entities operating in the energy sector and minimize prices for final consumers, as well as to provide the energy sector entities with the revenues they need to make return payments and develop the technical and business infrastructure.

The Energy Law provides the conditions for a gradual introduction of market mechanisms. These include the development of competition in generating and supplying electrical energy, with the assumption that the transition from wholesale electrical energy trade competition to retail trade competition will not last more than eight years from the date the law becomes effective. The basis for the promotion of competition in these two areas will be the effective regulation of enterprises described as natural monopolies, which are engaged in the transmission and distribution of electrical energy, and the inclusion of a provision for third party access to the grid (Third Party Access principle), which means opening the electrical energy market to the level of final consumers. Depending on the quantity of energy purchased, certain consumer groups will have access to the grid between 1999 and 2005.

The Energy Law provides for careful and gradual introduction of the TPA principle, the process being designed to ensure that the necessary reliability of supply and quality of fuels and energy be maintained. The provisions of the Law make it clear that this principle is limited to the fuels extracted in Poland and the energy produced from them.

The following groups are operating on the domestic energy market:

- Power generating plants (power plants);
- System power plants connected directly to the power transmission grid;
- Over 270 local power plants and thermal power plants connected to the distribution network (of which ZEC Bydgoszcz is one);
- Entities operating the transmission grid (at voltages of 220 kV and 400 kV) - PSE S.A. (Polish Power Grid Company);
- Entities operating the distribution network (at voltages of 110 kV and below) - currently 33 utility companies;
- Entities dealing with energy trade - currently the same 33 utilities.

With respect to the scope of operations, the energy market is divided into: system and local markets. The system market is part of the electrical energy market in which trading is done within the framework of the transmission grid, that is the network at voltages of 220 kV and 400 kV. Approximately 67% of energy is generated on the system market. The local markets are part of the electrical energy market in which trading is done within the framework of the distribution network, that is the network at voltages of 110 kV and below. Approximately 33% of energy is generated on the local markets.

The process of sector privatization is being carried on concurrently with the process of developing the ultimate structure of the electrical energy market. According to the program and conditions for energy sector privatization, the document approved by the Komitet Ekonomiczny Rady Ministrów - KERM (the Cabinet Economic Council) on July 2, 1998, all energy enterprises will be privatized individually. The first meaningful privatizations in the energy sector took place in 1999. It was anticipated that the privatization process would be completed by 2002-2003.

Conclusion: The energy sector in Poland has already undergone many changes, but this is just the beginning of transformation; the rest of the economy is much closer to the client, the market, and modern management. As a consequence, companies in this sector are often forced to try to "catch up" with their business environment by introducing complex adapting programs.

1.3 The Company

The group of Heat & Power Combined Plans of Bydgoszcz, a joint-stock Company in Bydgoszcz, is a single joint-stock company of the State Treasury. The plant was set up as a state-owned enterprise in 1971, and was transformed into a state company in 1994. The origins of the company date back to 1929, when the Municipal Electric Power Station in Jachowice, Bydgoszcz (today's Heat & Power Plant Bydgoszcz I), began operations.

ZEC Bygdoszcz S.A. is made up of three thermoelectric power stations. The company was established as a result of transforming the state-owned company and by decision of the Regional Court in Bydgoszcz.

The production capacity of the company's thermoelectric power stations provides the city of Bydgoszcz with:

- 70% of the municipal heating demand
- 90% of the industrial heating demand
- 60% of electrical energy demand

Yearly demand for energy from ZEC Bydgoszcz S.A. is estimated at 8,000-9,000 TJ of heat energy and 600-700 MWh of electrical energy. The downward trend in heat energy sales since 1995 calls for action to increase production of electrical energy in an associative cycle. Use of a new 13UP55 turbine set in EC II and appropriate control of production economics enabled the company to achieve a positive financial result in spite of a drop in heat production.

Obtaining a license from the president of the Power Industry Regulatory Office allowing heat transmission and distribution until 2011 enabled the company to provide transmission services and deliver process steam to four companies.

A next step is to upgrade a back-pressure turbine into a condensing turbine in EC II. This will lead to a 60% increase in sales of electrical energy outside the heating season.

The company produces heat in heating water for communal needs and in process steam for industrial needs and electricity in combination.

1.4 The Project

The IDS Scheer project at ZEC Bydgoszcz S.A. was initiated by an interest in business processes, and quickly exceeded its initial terms of reference. Subjects in which the company's Supervisory Board was interested in were a wide understanding of the process of adapting the company to the demands of competition, clients, and suppliers as well as the reorganization and increase in company's value. For us, the challenge was to create a project methodology that included strategic diagnosis as well as process mapping. The objective was to harness the synergy of such an approach in the common planning of final solutions: a new processes map, organizational structure, and Balanced Scorecards' system for increasing the value of the company.

2. Initial Stage – "Strategic Reconnaissance"...

...in our projects this is the name we give to the preliminary stage which allows us to become better acquainted with the client's company. Usually, within the terms of strategic reconnaissance (which lasts for a few days) we determine the company's overall situation and key management problems. It allows us to better prepare workshops for the company's Supervisory Board. In Bydgoszcz – because we knew the sector well – it was enough to conduct two interviews and an analysis of the organizational-financial documentation.

2.1 Strategic Workshops

Two objectives were set for the first day of the workshop: first, the Board and key management staff were introduced to the topic of Value Based Management, and the IDS-preferred methodology of VBM implementation (i.e. Balanced Scorecard) was presented. The next step was a discussion of the strengths and weaknesses of the company and the impact of these elements on its market position. This allowed us to present the strategic position of the company in the SPACE matrix (Strategic Positioning and Action Evaluation). The conclusion was – and this was not convergent with the opinions of some of those present at the meeting – that the position of the Company was not encouraging, either from the point of view of balanced weighted strengths and weaknesses or with regard to the opportunities and threats facing the company. Initial assumptions have not been optimistic: the suggested strategy was the defensive approach with gradual rebuilding of the competitive position by using strengths and fighting weaknesses. After the analysis of those results and the reasons for this situation it was possible to determine that, in the short term (about one year), the restoration program would be possible to implement, which could assure a consistent foundation for permanent improvement of the company's market position. The second day of the workshop was devoted to visualizing the strategy map according to the Balanced Scorecard (BSC) methodology. The management of the company declared that the presented VBM concept should be the guiding scenario for ZEC Bydgoszcz. This meant the subordination of all main targets to one superior goal: the value of the company. The philosophy of formulating company strategy according to BSC and VBM clearly determined the planned strategic investments in ZEC.

2.2 Organization of the Project...

... according to our – more and more often used – methodology, this refers to the step that follows profound familiarization with the customer and the strategic workshops. Why? With this approach, the defined basic project (detailed range, schedule, assignment of tasks to assets, etc.) can take into account the changes for which the customer can decide. In short, in the introduction phase, it is often necessary to correct the previously planned scope or schedule of the project. During the project in Bydgoszcz we:

- Pointed out the issues to be thoroughly examined during the strategic diagnosis,
- Agreed on the need to adjust the methodology to the potential BSC implementation process;
- Defined the organization regulations document of ZEC, based on the ARIS system, as the main tool for the implementation of process-managed organization.

Of the other goals of the company, the need to prepare the exclusion of secondary operations (e.g. repairs and supply of coal) is the main activity. The project was split into two clear phases: the diagnostic phase and the project phase. The first was aimed at building the proper platform enabling a correct decision-making process.

3. Diagnosis – Searching for Problems

3.1 Process Mapping

As was indicated earlier, company restructuring is an important and expensive undertaking. Accordingly, the organization of activities in an appropriate "cause and effect" sequence represents an opportunity to take complete control of the completed project. Michael Hammer in his book "Reengineering and its consequences" indicates recognition of business processes as a method of researching all activities and discovering essential connections between them. During the restructuring process, a properly modeled and designed business process allows the establishment of responsibilities and sequences of those activities.

As opposed to the traditional approach to restructuring, in the ZEC project the full set of advantages of the process approach was to be used. The goal of process mapping was primarily to identify the functioning rules of the company. This is why the architecture of the processes had a general character enabling:

- Understanding of the flow of the processes
- Identification of the barriers in process flows
- Definition of the responsibilities for the processes – identification of the key organizational units
- Identification of the information flow on the basis of the flow of significant documents

In the process of gathering information about processes, the whole set of organizational documentation was used, e.g. internal regulations, job descriptions, internal procedures of the units. In addition, the members of the Board as well as the key managers representing different areas of the business were involved in the work of creating process maps. The interviews conducted by the IDS consultants acted as a very important source of information about the actual process flows, the employees interviewed pointed out the needs for change and possible changes and improvement opportunities. This had a direct impact on the level of engagement of the key employees in the project and identification with its results.

The implemented project methodology enabled a quick transition to modeling of the overall target state. The tool assisting the tasks of different project groups was the reference model for the companies from the energy sector developed on the basis of some years' experience within IDS Scheer Polska. This model proved to be a source of profound knowledge about processes assisting ongoing acitivities as the overall target state was projected.

The activities produced a process map, which served as a main tool for developing and optimizing the rules of functioning of ZEC Bydgoszcz S.A. When projecting the overall target state, the direction of restructuring was also associated with the break-up of the group of secondary processes to the new business units (companies). As a result, it was now possible to set the framework for the functioning of the planned capital group ZEC BYDGOSZCZ. The modeling methodology chosen was also determined by the stated objectives of the project. With the Value Added Chain Diagram models it was, revealed that there was a need to define and analyze the value created by processes (for the customer and for the company). The "eEPC column display model" connected with the "VACD model" showed and allowed us to evaluate the level of complexity of the processes from the point of view of the flow through the structure and the need to break the organizational barriers. In addition to this the methods chosen directly affected the capability to create reports and the new organizational documentation of the company.

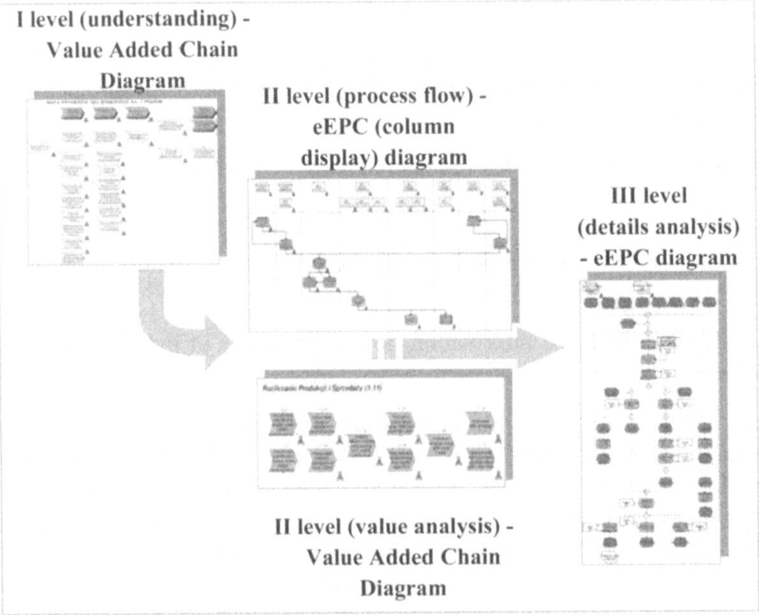

Figure 1: Process Mapping used in the project

3.2 Organizational-Financial Diagnosis

The challenge that was accepted by the project team called for a thorough examination of many dimensions of the company. The diagnosis of the processes alone could not fully visualize the picture of the company needed for projecting the organizational structure, restructuring recommendations, development and exclusion of the secondary activities. On the other hand, a full diagnosis taking into account all main areas would be too expensive and would negatively affect the schedule of the project. This is why the approach was adopted of analyzing only the key areas, which have crucial importance for the project, i.e.:

- The competitive environment of the company (customers, suppliers, competitors);
- The organizational structure (the degree of centralization, formalization, coordination, configuration and specialization);

- The managerial potential (the area of potential knowledge, skills, approach to the changes and the ability to accept and implement the changes);
- The human resources (the area of personnel structure and the quality of the motivational system);
- The system of planning and control as a key-management function in the company;
- The financial condition of the company, with particular focus on the ability of the company to generate operational profitability.

4. Solutions – New Management Fundamentals

4.1 Optimization of Processes

Process identification, before the implementation of changes, is made on the basis of branch models and internal documents gathered in the company. The best way to collect information is to conduct direct interviews and analyze a company's documents, which in restructuring projects provide first-hand information based on the experience and qualifications of company's employees. The next step is to create a process map functioning in the company, which will be progressively modified and optimized.

Based on the overall model of the objective state, a multi-standard and complex process analysis was done. In all the analytical works conducted, following criteria were used:

- Process structure analysis
- Added value analysis
- Decision path analysis
- Evaluation of the boundaries between processes, range of implementing activities, connection between the parts of process
- Information flow analysis
- Connection of documents with process elements, the method of documenting the process flow
- Benchmarking

- Comparison of boundaries between processes, range of implementing activities, connections of the process to the reference model for branch companies
- Organizational barriers in the process flow
- Assignment of process elements to organizational units coordinating its implementation.
- Indication or observation of malfunctions
- Indication of problems in the workflow and information flow

Based on the process analysis, a general set of conclusions that directly influenced the process improvement was drawn up. The following conclusions were made:

- Emphasis of process orientation on production, not on customer service
- Limited orientation to external and internal clients
- Considerable gaps in information and document flow
- Lack of monitoring of process results. Some need for organizational improvement
- Numerous organizational barriers and process duplication

The general conclusions of the analysis translated directly to the range of changes in process improvement. First, the need to develop, formalize and standardize currently non-existent or dispersed processes was determined. The processes, which were present in several places in the organization, were excluded. Exact process flow was defined, simultaneously showing unspecified ranges of the responsibilities of organizational unit owners. Many processes were integrated and redesigned with a destination in the new organizational units.

In the evaluation of process improvement proposals, the Board members and key specialists took an active part. The objective range of the analytical meetings included the verification of the solutions proposed by IDS Scheer Polska consultants for increasing process effectiveness. The basic criteria of the evaluation determined the correctness of the changes made, the correct allocation of tasks to the appropriate organizational units, the maintenance of standards and work safety specifications in effect for a company that produces energy and electricity.

The following may be added to the significant effects brought about by the process improvement activities:

- Definition of divisions between basic and supporting processes, thus showing business priorities
- Creation of the new model of Strategic Planning processes

- Creation of the new model of Client Service processes (before and after sales)
- Creation of the new model of Strategic Management processes
- Simplification of the Property Management process model
- Elevation of management and process coordination efficiency by organizational arrangement determining the range of responsibilities of the organizational units

In the course of the organizational changes, close cooperation between ZEC Bydgoszcz employees and IDS Scheer Polska consultants developed the new look for the company as an entire organization. Underlining the hierarchy of importance of some fields defined as basic (business) lent a new dimension in organization in the range of assigning priorities for strategic decisions. This is particularly true for the processes hitherto seen as secondary or marginal (Customer Service, After Sales Service).

The result of the consultations was a high level of knowledge about the approach to management issues, an increase in awareness of correct process organization and the need for its optimization and the role and place of particular units in the Company processes. All the above represented the necessary foundation for organizational and cultural changes and a preparation of all resources for planned process management implementation in a systematic approach.

4.2 Project for New Management System Rules

Analytical activities within the scope of strategic consulting led to the following recommendations regarding system management changes:

- The new organizational structure taking into account the plans to exclude certain external activities.
- The planning and control system at ZEC Bydgoszcz Group (at the strategic and operational levels)
- The motivational system at ZEC Bydgoszcz Group (changes to the motivational system at ZEC Bydgoszcz S.A. and its subsidiary companies)
- Definition of the owners' relations in the capital group
- The project of assigning functions among ZEC Bydgoszcz S.A. and its subsidiary companies (based on the new process map)
- The rules of financial management in ZEC Bydgoszcz Group (consisting of all financial conditions, taxes and accounting operations in the ZEC Bydgoszcz Group

Some of the proposed solutions were instructional in nature, supporting the process of further decision making. Others related to implementation documents. Together with the client, IDS Scheer Polska consultants made decisions about the integration of basic, traditional organizational documentation (Organizational Rules) with the process platform in the ARIS system. Technically, this required that the consultants provide a specific methodology of process management at the second level of the process map as well as designing a special report for ARIS in which specified functions were assigned to the organizational units with a definition regarding a leading or supporting role. This was significant from the technological (easier control of overall documentation) and, more importantly, the communications point of view. This effort required that all employees pay attention not only to processes but also to ARIS and the IDS Scheer methodology of process definition from the outset. At the same time, IDS Scheer consultants made general improvements to the existing organizational rules and supplemented basic management rules by adding the elements of typical process approach to management. These will be presented in detail in the following chapter.

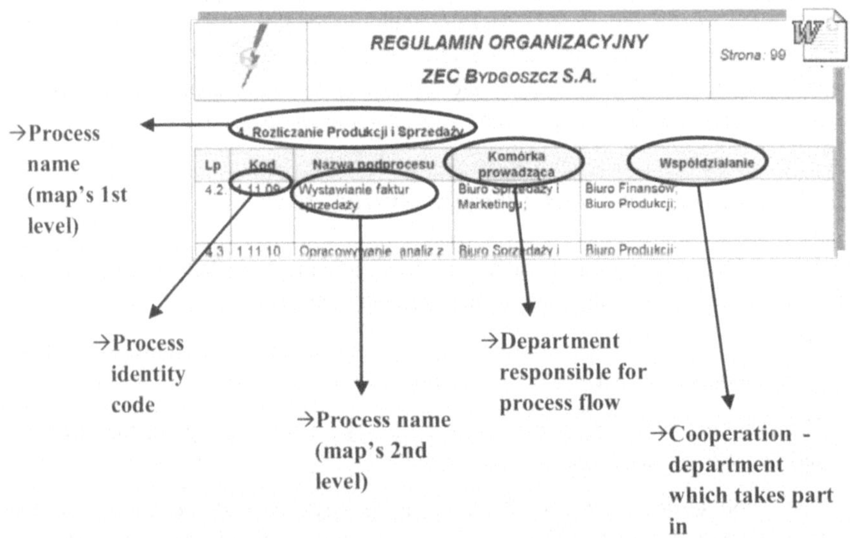

Figure 2: Organizational Rules based on the ARIS – structure of a document.

5. Interactive Process Improvement System

The company's Board and the IDS Scheer Polska consultants were both aware that maintaining the accepted model for managing the company couldn't be limited to one-time tasks planned for the project.

In process orientation, a very important element in successfully completing tasks in preparation for achieving real success is to work out and implement the system of continuous improvement for the company. This focuses the attention of the organization on the range of requirements primarily connected to the ability to approach the problems of the current company's functioning in a new way, and consequently to constantly make proposals for new and better solutions. In addition, it is important to bring ideas to the attention of those responsible for change management units and for implementing those improvements. This mechanism for organizational improvement in its mature form becomes the basis for change process management, engaging ideas and competencies from the widest possible group of people. Attention was paid to a new organizational culture, which means new definition of the roles and attitudes that are expected from company employees. The essence of the motivational system was specified as the active tool supporting staff participation in the processes for change. Therefore, ZEC Bydgoszcz S.A. Board recognized that a basic priority for full implementation of the company's process management project would be to achieve independence in management and continuous improvement of processes.

In the project development methodology proposed by IDS Scheer Polska consultants, the Interactive Process Improvement System (IPIS) was presented, which is based on Internet technology. It was accepted that the format of Internet pages is presently the most frequently used method of transferring and presenting information, assuring quick implementation from the technical side whilst assuring ease of access for its users. Moreover, it was very important for the Board to be able to assure flexibility and possibility of continuous development in accordance with the company's needs and users' expectations. The added value of this project was the fact that the prepared IPIS concept would also constitute the basis for significant development of corporate intranet as a basic communication platform at ZEC Bydgoszcz S.A. This was essential to ensure that all project participants made full use of the existing project effects, including the process maps and organizational structures that had been created. In these terms, the functionality of ARIS tools was used to the full. These tools provide the means to convert project tasks to Internet page format while retaining all informational content. The following figure is a graphical interpretation of the technological scheme presented to the Board.

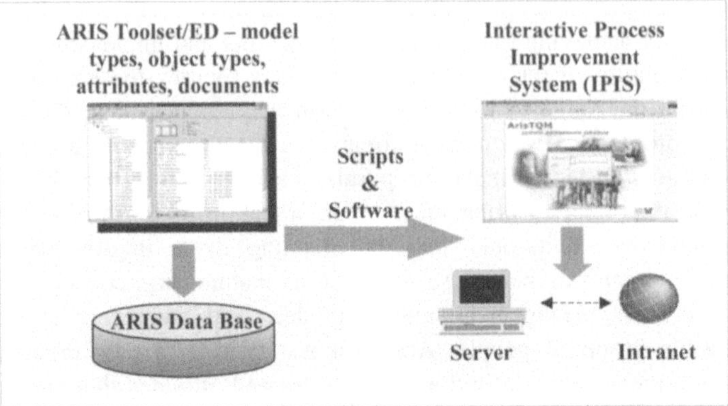

Figure 3: Technological scheme on of IPIS diagram.

The conversion of the company's model to Internet pages allows knowledge about the company, including those models, to be presented in a clear and intelligible graphic image. Every detailed model modified and generated by ARIS will be seen connection with the other models and easy to review. IPIS as a corporate, technical and organizational undertaking allows cooperation via the intranet, serving as the company's internal computer network. One of its basic functionalities is the immediate transfer of new ideas via e-mail to the appropriate project groups or units that are responsible for process management. Afterwards, the information is collected, analyzed and implemented in the company's current activity. IPIS technical support for this change management process is presented in Figure 4.

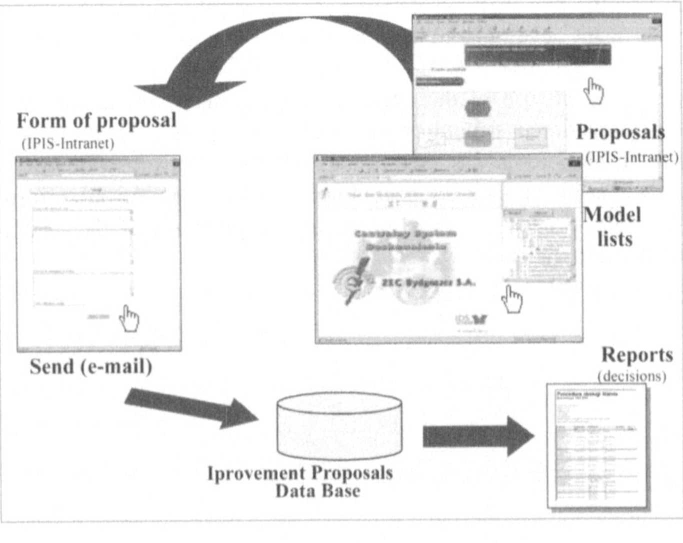

Figure 4: Structure of IPIS operational scheme supporting process management

The implementation of an intranet can definitely surpass the goals associated with this project of implementing a system of business process management. In a context of realized internal projects, an intranet service can be used in preparing, implementing and supporting an Integrated Information System (quality, ecology, safety and hygiene of work). Thus, overall access to the company's required quality standards, with an easy structure for change implementation and audit system management is guaranteed.

In connection with the replacement of the company's paper-based organizational documentation with electronic records, financial considerations are also essential. The project experiences of IDS Scheer Polska presented to the Board of Directors indicate the opportunity of significant financial savings associated with the support and operation of process management systems, including quality systems.

Elementary Portal Functionality

- Operation of optional structure and process management system form
- Publication and facilitation of process documents on the intranet
- Possibility of selective access to process description documentation
- Full access to forms and documents supporting process flow
- User participation in shaping the process management system
- Complete fulfillment of change management conditions and improvement of process management system

At the same time, it was observed that even the best technology could not guarantee full implementation of process management without the active participation of the employees. Because of this, the essential element of the proposed methodology is also defined and designed:

- Structures managing processes
- Adequate procedures steering change management
- The range of responsibilities, authorities and roles assigned to particular groups of employees for the completion of projects.

The conditions thus defined influenced the establishment of units responsible for process management and its improvement not connected with the functional organizational structure.

Based on organizational records, the decision regarding the establishment of the following process management levels was made:

- Process Council – coordinating the process management system, stimulating, and evaluating the process improvement range
- Process Owners – person responsible for process management, accomplishing assumed indicators and effectiveness measurements, influencing changes in the process
- Process Management Team – team responsible for detailed parts of the process, coordinating realized tasks in the process, group of advisors for the Process Owner
- Process Performer – direct, operational participant in the process, responsible for proper realization of basic activities, engaged in notification of changes and improvement proposal.

Besides employee selection, activities in this area include the development of detailed, specific ranges of responsibility, activity procedure, and cooperation models. All these elements are included in the proper documentation, regulating the basis of process management rules and responsibility structure. Basing on functional IPIS assumptions, the division of roles and authorizations in the company's process improvements was defined. Figure 5 below presents the elementary connections structure.

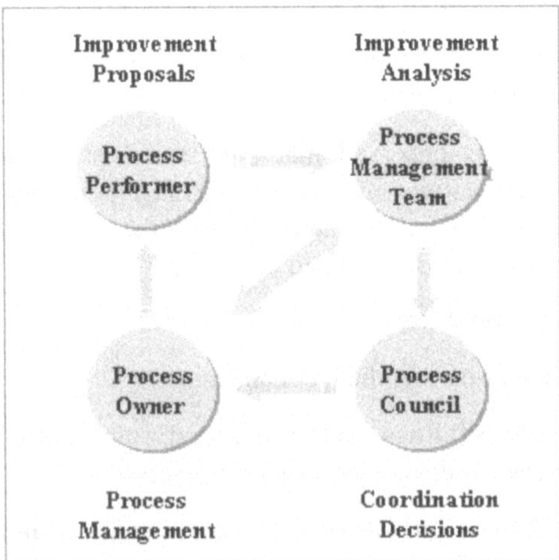

Figure 5: Elementary connections structure

The fundamental element determining the success of the process management implementation project would be the assurance that the results achieved would be sustained in the future. The introduction to the organizational culture of adequate mechanisms that engage employees in the improvement of effectiveness and organization represents one of the primary tasks of the process improvement system. It will require appropriate design of such a system, supported by IT tools for including the positive attitude of employees in change process management: Process Council, Process Owners, Teams Managing Processes. Particular importance will be attached to the Process Owners, whose task will be to maintain the correct process structure, ensure its highest quality and efficiency, and to initiate and schedule improvement programs.

Base of Portal Functionality

- Operation of any structure and forms of process management system
- Publication and accessibility of process documentation on the intranet
- Possibility of selective access to process description documentation
- Complete access to forms and documents supporting process flows
- User participation in shaping the process management system
- Change management and process management system improvement

Advantages of Portal Functioning

- Use of intranet allows reduction in time to prepare and implement process management system in organization
- Lower costs of preparation and distribution of system's documentation
- Lower costs of system modification and development
- Increased effectiveness of process improvement
- Increased participation by employees in system's development
- Greater control over actual practices with quality system
- Basis for preparation portal supporting communication within the company

6. Balanced Scorecard System

We have referred to the reasons for developing the project along the lines of the Balanced Scorecard. The most important value of the system was the introduction of process management governing other perspectives: Finance, Clients, and Development. It is the simplest method by which the initiatives of business process improvement can be integrated into the company's strategy. It also allows the presentation of cause and effect relationships between them.

It was determined that the monitoring strategy tool will be Strategic Enterprise Management, part of mySAP system, and that the system will consist in the first phase of about 5 cards (Corporation, Property Management, Production, HR, and

Supply). In the next phase, the following 13 departments were included (project implemented by IDS in cooperation).

6.1 Balanced Scorecard Architecture

In the initial phase of the project, the emphasis was placed on defining the Balanced Scorecard architecture. It met the planning of the company's goals map and organizational units, and the strategy measurement system. In this project phase, consultants agreed that ARIS BSC is very helpful for designing the architecture. The ARIS tool enabled cards to be designed that were dedicated to prototype, clear, easy to coordinate, and especially friendly for users who knew little about the BSC concept. The models used were: BSC Cause-and-Effect Diagram and Key Performance Indicator allocation diagram. The following figures show some examples of ARIS BSC use. Not all the capabilities of ARIS BSC were used because of initial assumptions about strategy modeling based on the simulation model because ARIS BSC specifics were not sufficient for this project.

6.2 Strategic Modeling

BSC architecture is – according to our methodology, a kind of hypothesis. Targets, indicators, and initiative systems are the net of connections, which are not quantitatively defined yet. Within the framework of strategic modeling, a simulating decision model was created in which specific indicators are assigned planned and target values and the mutual relations are examined. Sometimes the wrong assumptions from the previous project are verified. A well-designed strategic model fulfill three functions: a strategic business plan for the company from which the company's' value evaluation flows (Economic Value Added®) simultaneously being the tool for strategic decision making. Presently, IDS Scheer Polska integrates the traditional methodology of planning in an Excel spreadsheet with the advanced technology of dynamic simulation in the Powersim tool. In the ZEC Bydgoszcz project, the use of MS Excel proved to be sufficient.

6.3 Strategy Communication

Strategy communication is defined by the authors of the Balanced Scorecard as a key, but not the most important element of their methodology. Probably before final implementation of BSC, an evaluation of its effects and advantages seems not to be conclusive, but it would be a worthwhile exercise to learn the initial impressions of the customer's managers involved in first stage of the project.

"In my opinion the implementation of the Balanced Scorecard system is important for anyone who comes to his/her company to work, and not just to mark time until it is time to go home at 3 pm… I guess that all management staff can be included in this group. The implemented Balanced Scorecard system lets us set the goals we should be aiming at. Reaching these goals, or even just getting closer to them, should give us satisfaction (every employee should identify himself with the targets of his company). But to reach those goals, they must be properly defined. And here comes the most difficult part of the project (at least for those, whose responsibilities have changed). It is rather hard to set measures when the scope of responsibility changes. Additional complications are those connected with the change in the organizational structure and in the changes to the operations of the company when business units are excluded outside the company. However, I am sure the setting the goals, even if they will have to be changed, updated in the future, will allow us to fulfill market requirements much faster. A special kind of "art" but also courage is required to set up the goals in such a way that they will make us look for new, better ways of dealing with our tasks at the job. And this is the only approach, that will let this tool make our job easier and bring quantitative benefits to our company."

Sławomir Serafin, Warehousing Manager

"The process of creating the Balanced Scorecard system in the initial phase was incomprehensible to me, especially in the financial area, which is not really my field. From my point of view and with my experience I can say that the most useful is the realization of the strategic initiatives from the employee perspective. The set of measures will allow us define some very hard measurable ranges of our activity, and will help us finally perform the employee evaluation process. Implementation of a tool like BSC in our company is undoubtedly an innovative action. I see future possibilities and how this tool will be helpful in my everyday job, but I also see complications in the early stages of the implementation process. After implementation of the BSC, it will no doubt be a useful tool for managing the company's affairs."

Alina Giza, HR Manager

"I hope and I am sure that the implemented scorecards will be a great tool for examining the effectiveness of the activities of given business units. They also create a synchronized and correlated program of activities of all organizational units. Bringing the activities of all the units together will allow us to achieve a synergistic effect, which in our case is the growth of the company's value. I am fully aware that we still have much work to do, because we are still implementing the scorecards and we will have to develop them as well as create new scorecards for the next organizational units, but we can see right now that the activity of creating and developing the scorecards helped us to understand and take into consideration many factors, which would be missed without proper analysis.

Róża Czarnecka, Controlling Manager, BSC project manager

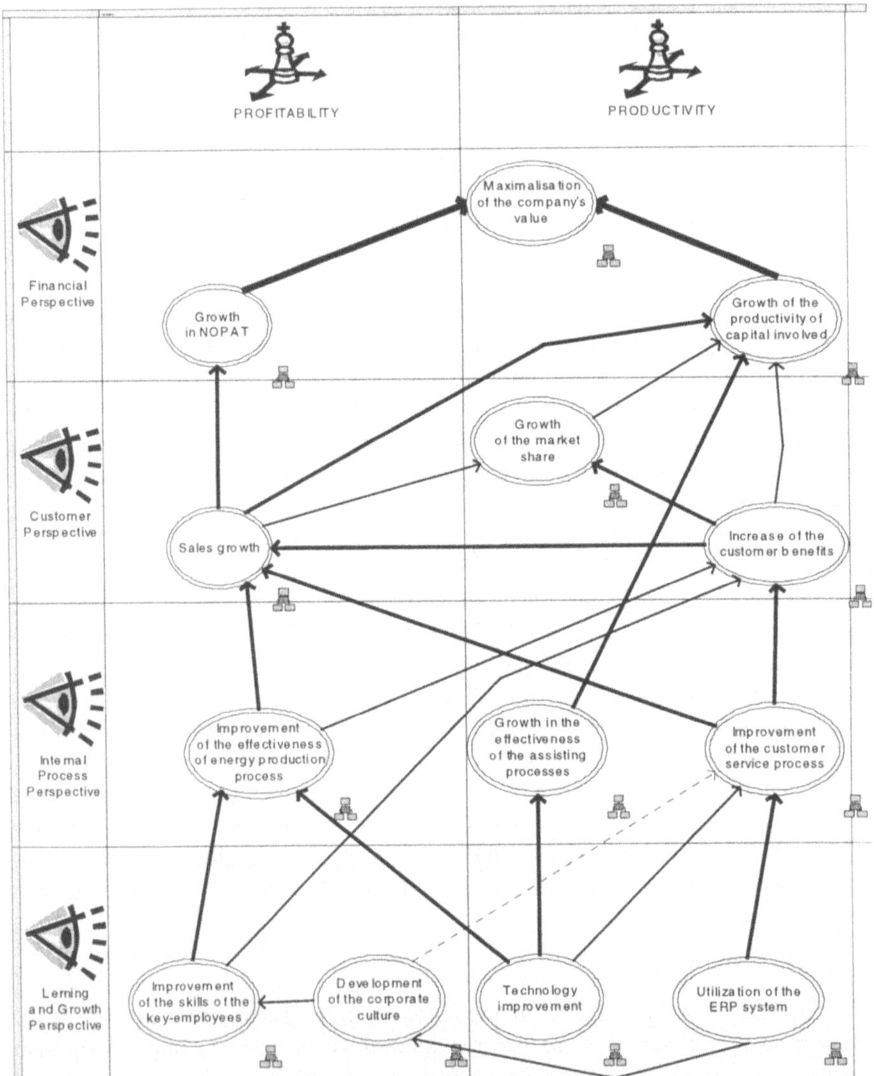

Figure 6: Corporate Balanced Scorecard (version changed due to confidential restrictions) (BSC Cause- and- Effect Diagram)

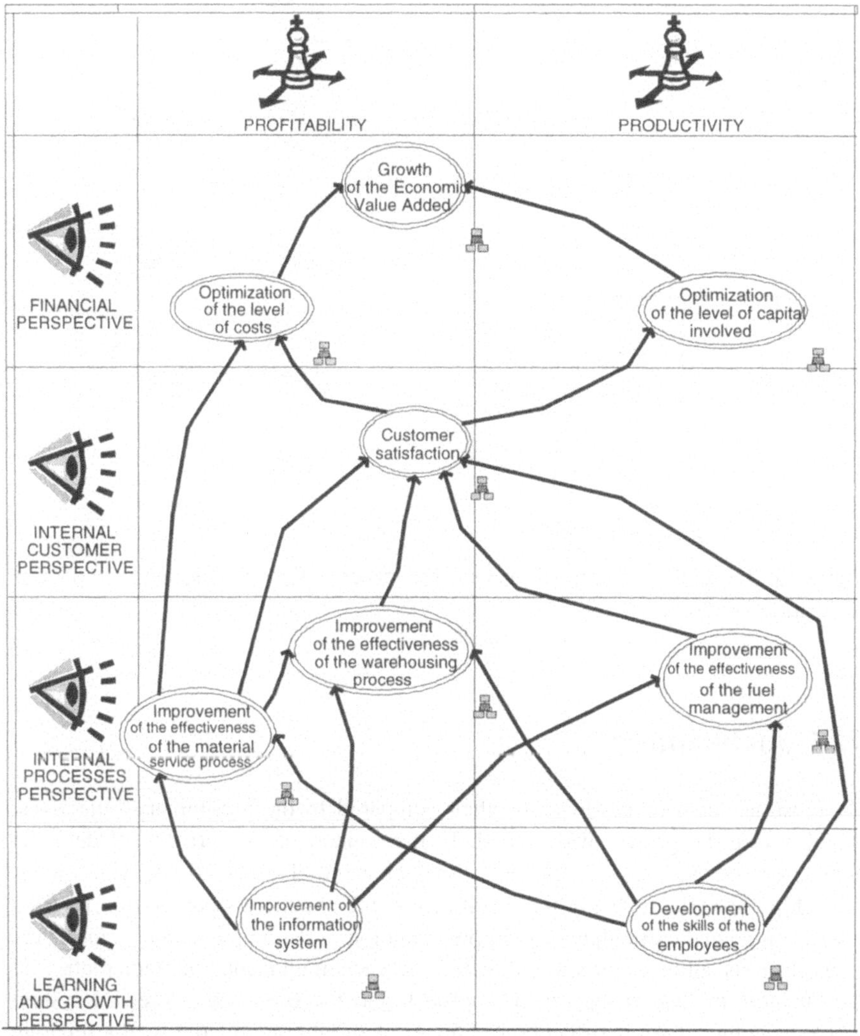

Figure 7: Warehousing Department Scorecard (BSC Cause-and -Effect Diagram)

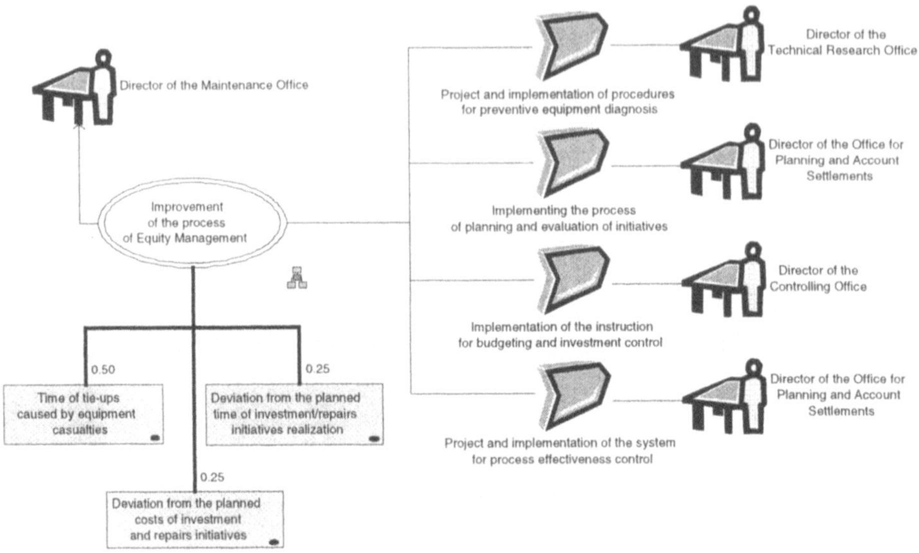

Figure 8: Example of part of measuring system (Key Performance Indicator Allocation Diagram)

7. Conclusions

Conclusions seem to be difficult when compared to the preliminary objectives, stated before the project was started. In the context of this project all declared goals were positively realized, even surpassing initial expectations. This means that additional effects, being the result of e.g. the company's preparation for ISO certification and simultaneous implementation of complementary measures supporting its solutions. It was estimated that the simultaneous implementation of the business process management approach and the Balanced Scorecard system yielded savings of approximately 35% in terms of labor compared with a separate implementation of these undertakings. The most important advantages are those measured with the greatest difficulty, being the result of the synergy between Business Process Management & Balanced Scorecard, mutually intensifying their implementation.

For IDS Scheer Polska, the ZEC Bydgoszcz project also has another, symbolic dimension. It is the first project in which the three basic fields of the consulting company's activities: were integrated: strategy consulting (analyses, structural design and BSC), business process consulting (mapping, optimization, BPM) and implementation services (mySAP SEM-CPM).

Using ARIS to Manage SAP Interoperability

Thomas R. Gulledge
George Mason University

Georg Simon
IDS Scheer, Inc.

Rainer A. Sommer
George Mason University

Summary

SMART and SIGMA are projects that were initiated in 1999 under the Navy Enterprise Resource Planning (ERP) pilot program. The project boundaries were delineated in 1998, and the software solutions were selected as SAP R/3 in 2000. The project teams are now approaching critical milestones, and it is timely to revisit interoperability issues. While many aspects of the current projects can proceed independently, certain business processes that are shared by the tow projects require additional attention. At the request of the Program Director, we focused on understanding, documenting, and analyzing the SMART and SIGMA solutions as the SAP software enables them. This paper demonstrates how we used the ARIS methodology to analyze inter-project interoperability.

Key Words

Standard Software, SAP, Interoperability, Defense Enterprise Solutions

1. Background

SMART and SIGMA are two projects that were initiated in 1998 under the Navy ERP pilot program. At conception the software solution provider was unknown, and there was no business process architecture for ERP. The project boundaries were delineated in 1998, and the software solutions were selected in 2000. Both projects selected the SAP R/3 standard software solution, and after two years of implementation progress, both projects are approaching critical milestones.

The SIGMA project was originally scoped as a Program Management solution, while the SMART project was scoped as an Aviation Supply Chain Management & Maintenance solution. In the early stages of implementation, it was realized that these arbitrary boundaries caused problems for integrated enterprise software, so the projects were extended to include other functionality that ensured an integrated solution. Over this same period, it was discovered that the SMART and SIGMA projects had a special relationship, because shared functionality provided the potential for a complete integrated solution across the Naval aviation value chain.

This study was initiated at the request of the Program Director of the Enterprise Solutions Program Office. Inter-project Enterprise Resource Planning (ERP) system interoperability is an issue as the Navy coordinates the rollout of multiple ERP solutions. This study is focused on two of the projects:

1. SIGMA [a Naval Air Systems Command (NAVAIR) project], and
2. SMART [a joint project between NAVAIR and Naval Supply Systems Command (NAVSUP)].

The Program Director desires the best solution for the Navy; hence, any enhanced SIGMA and SMART interoperability that delivers additional value to the Navy is desirable. This project was undertaken in that spirit.

As the SMART and SIGMA project teams are approaching critical milestones, it is timely to visit these interoperability issues. While many aspects of the current projects can proceed independently, certain business processes that are shared by NAVSUP and NAVAIR require additional attention. These shared business processes are prominent in the maintenance processes that will be enabled in future phases of the SAP implementations. We focused on understanding, documenting, and analyzing the SMART and SIGMA solutions as the SAP software enables them. The study provides a pure technical assessment from an SAP R/3 perspective of the interoperability of the SIGMA and SMART solutions and how they may be improved.

In order to accomplish such an assessment, an unambiguous baseline for comparing the solutions is required. Since different contractors and contracting methodologies were used across projects, the raw project documentation is not comparable.

However, the projects do have one thing in common, the R/3 software. Hence, we mapped the disparate documentation from both projects to the R/3 reference model, constructing business process architectures for SIGMA and SMART. These business process architectures form the comparable baseline for our analysis. We know we are comparing "apples to apples," since both projects are mapped to the R/3 reference model.

As another feature, we provided two ways for displaying the architectures:

1. High-level overviews for executives in the form of SAP solution maps,
2. Detailed business process models for the business teams, to support configurations workshops, interface analyses, master data comparisons, etc.

Since the business process models are mapped to the R/3 reference model; the detail is complete to the R/3 transaction code level. We believe that this is the only comparable documentation of the two projects, and hence the planning baseline for the Naval aviation value chain.

Finally, we provide a technical strategy for using our methodology. A project plan in the form of a business process architecture does not guarantee success, but one is more likely to succeed with a plan than without. We show how the business process architecture can be used to document the scope of the transition of all maintenance business processes into a single aviation instance, and how the Program Executive and his team can use the architecture to monitor implementation progress using consistent and comparable documentation.

While no study of this type is better than the data that is used to support it, this study is based on actual project data. Even if the data is only 90% correct, we feel confident that we have recommended a good technical solution that aligns with the R/3 software.

2. Procedure

2.1 Methodology

SAP project details, including business process scope, are usually documented in the Q&Adb. Our approach uses modern tools, provided by IDS Scheer, Inc., to "reverse engineer" the Q&Adbs from the Navy pilot projects, revealing their Solution Maps and C-Business Scenarios for the project scopes that were defined during the ASAP implementation phase by the implementation teams.

The above approach is only approximate, since the architecture is derived from the project Blueprints as opposed to the configured software. However, this level of detail is sufficient to support an objective discussion of functionality overlaps and gaps.

Project documentation is produced during all ASAP phases. If one strictly follows SAP's recommended methodology, this project information is stored and managed in the Q&Adb. For example, in the Blueprinting Phase the consultants lead interviews or construct models to document project scope. Once the scope information is stored and analyzed in the Q&Adb, a macro is executed that generates a Business Process Master List (BPML), which is a first cut at transactional scope (i.e., the business processes to be included in the implementation as well as the SAP transactions that are enabled by these business processes).

In reality, the process is never so pure. Consultants have adapted the ASAP methodology to meet their own needs, and it is often the case that the Q&Adb is never fully populated. In short, the BPML is often generated by other means, which is precisely the case for the SMART and SIGMA implementations. We had various data sources, including BPMLs for both projects. We loaded much of this information into the Q&Adb to support our analysis.

Once the project information is in the Q&Adb, we used the ARIS methodology and the ARIS for mySAP.com toolset to analyze the information. We used the ARIS toolset to "reverse engineer" the Q&Adbs that we constructed for the SIGMA and SMART projects so that we could produce two types of project documentation:

1. Solution maps for easy summary presentations to senior executives, and
2. Business process models for detailed study and analyses by implementation teams and others who need to understand the details of SAP enabled business processes.

Each of these presentation formats is described below.

The approach that we selected has major advantages over paper-based documentation of drawing tools, such as Visio. Since ARIS for mySAP.com operates directly on the Q&Adb, all documentation is precisely linked to the R/3 reference model. That is, since the business functional scripts are mapped at the transaction level, the resulting solution maps and business process models are directly related to each other, as well as the R/3 software. This provides a precise view of business process scope relative to what has actually been configured by the project teams.

The second advantage has to do with configuration management and consistency of documentation across SMART and SIGMA. Since all documentation is stored in a repository, changes are immediately reflected across all business process and other views. For example, if an object is contained in 10 business processes in multiple organizational views, a single change to the object is immediately reflected in all views where that object occurs. This is in direct opposition to drawing tools (like Visio), where each drawing that contains the object must be manually updated. Also, since both SMART and SIGMA are documented using the same methodology, and both are directly mapped to the R/3 reference model, unambiguous comparisons across the projects are possible.

Analysis of alternatives still requires manual input. For example, if there is documented business process overlap across the two projects, someone still has to make a decision about how the overlap will be resolved. But, with this approach, at least you know that you have overlap, and you can also analyze the implications of various resolution strategies. In short, there is no "silver bullet" for resolving project boundary issues. In the end, the senior executives must understand the boundary issues and the implications of resolving one way versus another, and finally someone has to make a difficult decision. This approach only provides documentation to support that decision.

2.2 Business Process Architecture

2.2.1 Business Process Architecture Justification

This section focuses on SAP implementation in the US Navy and customer-mandated extensions, whether they be packaged or legacy. The objective of the section is to provide a justification for maintaining a SMART/SIGMA business process architecture, as was developed as part of this study. To obtain maximum long-term benefits from SAP, the Navy must understand and manage its cross-functional business processes over the complete system life cycle. Configuration never ends as extensions and upgrades are continually executed. Future business processes must be configured so that they leverage the current investment in SAP by adding maximum value (in terms of products and services) to the customer. This requires business process documentation, configuration discipline, configuration management, ongoing testing, and continuous training.

So, why document and maintain a business process architecture in an enterprise repository? The answer is straightforward - You cannot properly configure a business process in SAP unless you understand it. Since modern business processes are cross-functional, multiple stovepipes are spanned. Hence, documentation and agreement among process owners and configuration teams are essential. For upgrades, reworks, and extensions, the repository is the configuration baseline. Without the repository, the organization is constantly creating and realigning diverse documents and drawings to support required ongoing activities, and there is a high cost associated with re-creating project details that were not documented while executing the ASAP methodology. The management and enterprise systems literature is clear on this point, and the assembling of the documentation to support this study across SMART and SIGMA reinforces the point.

So, why not document using Word, Excel, and drawing tools (such as Visio)? Again, the answer is straightforward. You cannot maintain business process configuration in a drawing tool with linked Word document descriptors. A change in one business process object is often reflected in many places; hence, configuration management is almost impossible with drawing tools. Drawing tools are used when there is no requirement to manage over time; i.e., a one-shot quick-use requirement. The engineering literature is clear on this point.

2.2.2 How Should Business Process Repository Be Used?

This point requires additional discussion. The following argument is often used by consultants to discourage the creation of a business process repository in the SAP environment: "The processes are embedded in the software, and documenting these processes in a repository results in unnecessary additional work." This logic is faulty for the following reasons.

If the project is simple with no unusual aspects, then one could argue for a rapid implementation with minimum documentation. That is, if we are implementing the discrete manufacturing model for the 25th time, and there are no unusual aspects of the 26th implementation, and if rapid implementation is the ONLY objective, the quick approach is tempting. However, DoD implementations do not fall in this category. The implementations are complex, and the DoD is making the FIRST attempt to align commercial business processes with its organization. Certainly, a SMART/SIGMA solution where two organizations intersect with very complex maintenance requirement is not a candidate for rapid minimum-documentation methodologies. There are too many overlaps, gaps, and unresolved issues that require study and agreement before significant money is spent on consulting services.

As previously mentioned, if the implementation is routine, with no additional changes (i.e., upgrades) or extensions (e.g., Supply Chain/Customer extensions), then perhaps a business process architecture would not be needed. However, the software and its extensions are continuously evolving, and the implications of these changes must be understood and managed. Hence, the primary benefits of a business process repository are realized over the long-term as the extended enterprise integration environment evolves. The business process architecture is used as follows:

1. The business process architecture is the agreement with the consultants on requirements and scope. It is the build-plan, and any deviations (scope creep or de-scoping) must be justified.
2. The business process repository documents the agreements between SMART and SIGMA on what will be configured and how it will be configured.

Without agreement, endless high-level meetings and configuration re-work is almost guaranteed.

3. The business process architecture is used to compare the business process change implications of moving from R/3 4.6c to future versions of the R/3 software. The existing business process architecture is the baseline for any additional configuration that may be required.
4. The business process architecture is used to understand the implications of extending the R/3 solution with extensions, B2B solutions, CRM solutions, legacy interfaces, etc.
5. The business process architecture is used to support training for transmitting the implications of all configuration decisions to Business Process Executives and other managers, super users, and users.
6. The business process architecture is used to maintain interface and B2B configuration control.
7. The business process architecture is used in conjunction with the technical architecture for future documenting and planning for maintenance and continual retesting.

The answers to the following questions summarize the main points.

Why Have a Business Process Architecture?

Answer: You cannot maintain business process configuration in a drawing tool. Business process objects are shared across business processes. A change in one object is often reflected in many places. Drawing tools are used when there is no requirement to manage over time; i.e., a one-shot quick-use requirement. The engineering literature is clear on this point.

Is a "Complex" Tool Needed?

Modern organizations are complex, and the DoD is even more complex. Business processes are complex and cross-functional in nature. The systems that support the processes are complex. It is amusing that some organizations will spend $100s of millions on an industry leading packaged software solution (like SAP R/3), but they try to manage their ongoing environment in a drawing tool, or a tool that every independent analysis considers to be inferior. If you select the "best" ERP solution, why would you consider inferior tools, basing the decision on information that is selected from marketing presentations or the vendors' web sites? It makes no sense? Implementing organizations should pay close attention to the independent studies and invest in the training that is necessary to leverage the tool for maximum benefit. The management and technology literature is clear on this point.

2.2.3 Repository Tools

Business process documentation is more than depicting the time-ordered sequence of events and functions that define business process procedural steps. Other "objects" should be linked to the extended event-driven process chains and managed in conjunction with the business processes. Critical objects for inclusion are organizational units, systems, data clusters, and eventually data models. For the Navy projects, these should be documented and managed using the language of SAP.

This leads to a key point. Legacy architectural documentation frameworks, such as CIMOSA, PERA, GERAM, or Zachmann, are not capable of documenting in accordance with the required business process structure, since their locus of integration is not the business process. These legacy architectural frameworks were designed to manage IT/IS resources from a data-centric point of view, and were not designed for business process management. These frameworks are implemented in various documentation tools that are used by the Navy. For example, BPWin and ERWin are implemented from the CIMOSA point of view, using an IDEF-like non-integrated structure, while PTECH's Framework is a generalization of the Zachmann framework. This is not a criticism of these approaches and their associated tools, but as the independent studies have noted, these are niche players for business process management. The tools do not have a dominating business process view, because they were designed for purposes other than supporting complex SAP implementations. Superior solutions exist.

It goes without saying that drawing tools (such as Visio) or process modeling tools (such as SIMProcess or Intellicorp's LiveModel) cannot meet the repository requirements. They can document business process steps, but they can't handle dataflows, system linkages, data clusters, or models that are required in a true repository. In addition, their configuration management, Web publication and modeling, and report generation capabilities are severely limited.

Data modeling tools that are capable of documenting information system processes[1] should not be considered. These tools were designed to support the design and development of information systems. With SAP, the data models are purchased. They were developed by SAP and they were used to support the design, development, and testing of R/3. Tools such as ERWin, IDEF1x, and others are data-centric, focusing on logical dataflow and software processes. Not

---

[1]This difference is noted in the process management literature. Business process modeling is distinctly different from information systems process modeling. The two concepts have been widely confused, especially by IT/IS professionals, and especially in the US Department of Defense. Business processes have an explicit and dynamic process flow, while information system process models may be dynamic with respect to dataflows, but static with respect to time sequencing. IDEF is a good example of a static IS process modeling methodology.

only are the approaches inconsistent with the business process orientation of SAP, they are used primarily to support software design and development as opposed to implementation and configuration.

Other methodologies and supporting toolsets, as indicated by the Gartner Group [Kleinberg (1997)], are more appropriate for the Navy's ERP environment. The ARIS solution [Scheer (1998, 1999)] is completely integrated with SAP and is the dominant industry leader.

2.2.4 The Architecture of Integrated Information Systems (ARIS)

ARIS does not have the limitations of the previously described frameworks and models. It offers a complete set of object-linked views and is capable of supporting more than 100 modeling methodologies. Hence the ARIS Toolset [Scheer (1994)] is a meta-tool. The following is a subset of the benefits that are offered by ARIS:

1. When an object is modified, the effects are reflected throughout the enterprise in all views; i.e., business process, function, data, organization, and output. The tool is completely object-linked and consistency across views is maintained in the object repository.
2. The ARIS methodology integrates around business process, using the documentation of SAP. This integration is complete, since ARIS was used to develop the business process reference model for SAP R/3[2].
3. ARIS is completely network capable and Web enabled.
4. Report generation flexibility is guaranteed through integration with Microsoft Office.

2.3 The SMART/SIGMA Business Process Architecture

The objective was to develop and execute a business process architecture to support the analysis of the gaps and overlaps across the SMART and SIGMA SAP projects. The constraints on the problem are the following:

1. The results must be presented so that senior management can easily understand the choice of alternatives and the implications of the recommendation.
2. The results must be presented at a level of detail that is technically precise, enabling support for new scoping or configuration decisions.
3. Lengthy interviewing and design efforts are not allowed. The analysis must be accomplished using existing project data (i.e., reports, models, drawings, etc.).

---

[2]See Jost, et al. (1991), Jost (1993), and Nüttgens (1995)

The selected Business Process architecture was used and tested by re-engineering the current pilot blueprint and by executing the methodology on the SIGMA and SMART SAP projects. The key of this analysis is the shift from a function-oriented view on various software instances to a business process-oriented view across the physical boundaries of the software. The developed business process models are therefore the basis for a process-oriented completion of projects.

Hence, we have developed a full representation of the SMART and SIGMA projects at various levels of detail. Each view is more disaggregated, and hence more precise. The lowest-level view is at the transaction code level in the software. Hence, if providing a management overview is the objective, then solution maps would be used. If the objective is to resolve a configuration issue in a business process workshop, then a lower-level view would be used. The levels of the deployed Business Process Architecture are the following:

Level I – Solution Map

1. View I – Overview
2. View II – Detail

Level II – Business Process Blueprint

1. View I – Scenario
2. View II – Business Process
3. View III – Business Process Transaction

Each level is discussed below.

2.3.1 Level I - Solution Map

SAP's Solution Maps are designed as a methodology to help visualize, plan and implement a coherent, integrated and comprehensive information technology solution within an organization. The solution map outlines the scope of an organization's business. The solution map also shows how various business processes areas are covered, including the processes supported by SAP and its partners. Solution Maps are developed with customers, partners, and SAP experience. The concept was developed to support pre-sales and sales in a customer interaction environment, with no specific linkages to the R/3 standard software solution.

The SAP Defense Solution Map was selected as the highest level for the Business Process Architecture. The Defense Solution Map illustrates the coverage of the SAP defense solution as viewed by SAP's defense customers. The defense solution map is the conceptual basis for strategically defining a defense solution design that is enabled by the R/3 software solution. The defense solution map helps senior executives to focus on core processes and key functions as they are defining the requirements for their specific SAP solutions[3]. Our contribution is that we have linked the defense solution map to the R/3 software, so we can use this format as an unambiguous presentation level for senior management. The Defense Solution Map is the ideal baseline to show the scope of each project as well as the coverage within a defense organization.

There are two views of a Solution Map:

1. View I – Overview

2. View II – Detailed

The Overview (presented in Figure 1) gives a broad picture of the major business processes within a comprehensive defense solution. These business processes are arranged in process categories and represent the critical business processes (e.g., Program Management) for the defense establishment. As indicated in Figure 1, the heads of each row represent industry specific process categories while the colored rows consist out of the critical business processes within each category.

The detailed view (View II) provides the more detailed aspects of the specific functionality required for each business process area. This view also uses the language and terms of the defense industry. A typical View II – Detailed (e.g. Acquisition) looks as follows is presented in Figure 2.

The top row of Figure 2 describes the critical business processes for the specific business process category (Acquisition), while the items within each column represent a solution to support the business processes. The "bullet" associated with each item indicates the product coverage by current SAP, future SAP, or partner products.

[3]From a requirements point of view, there is no restriction that focuses only on SAP. These are general defense requirements and they could be examined relative to Oracle, PeopleSoft, or any other solution. SAP has supplemented the requirements matrix with an indication of whether or not the functionality is supported by SAP, future releases of SAP, or third party products. If one is willing to complete this mapping for other products, similar statements could be made about their ability to meet defense requirements.

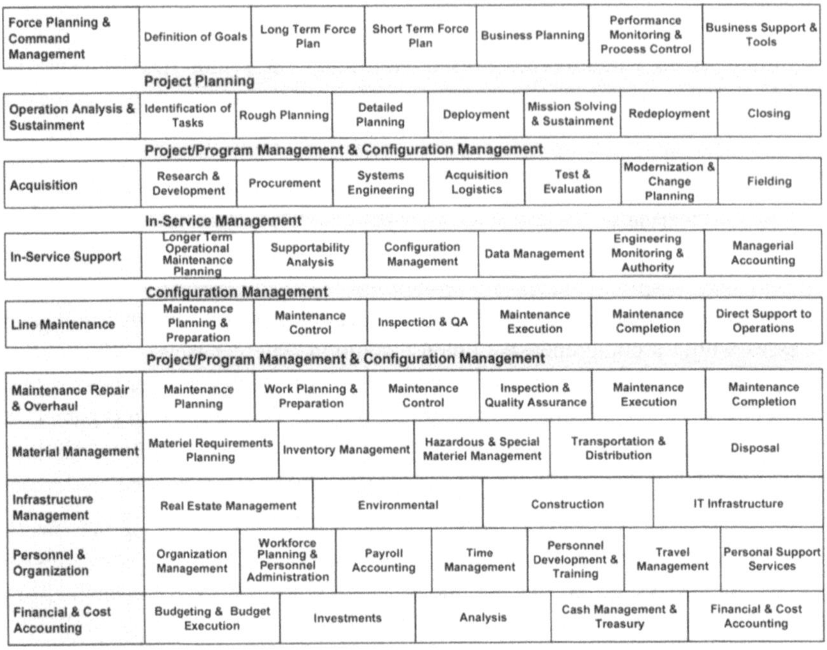

Figure 1: Defense Solution Map - Overview

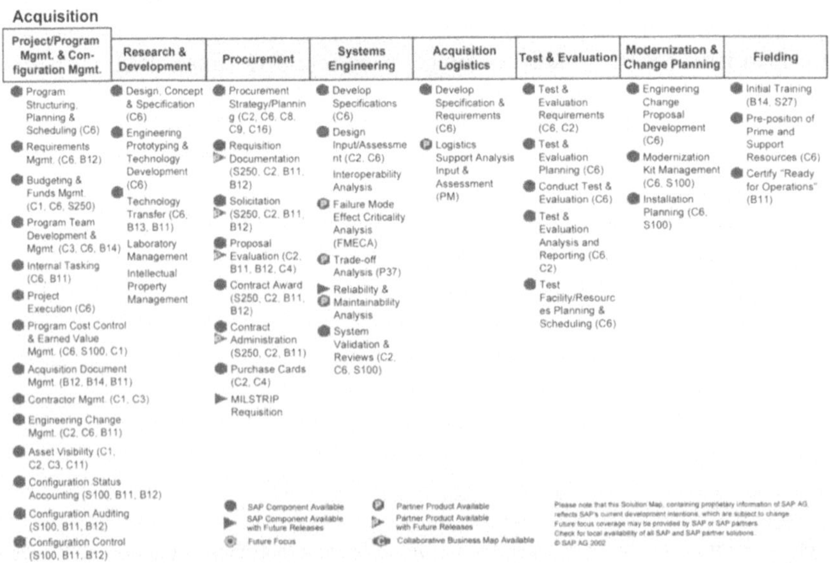

Figure 2: Detailed view - Acquisition

2.3.2 Business Process Blueprint

In an industry-specific implementation project, value chains and business processes are used to define the Business Blueprint. SAP provides these value chains in the Business Process substructure within the standard SAP R/3 reference structure. The reference model structure is presented in different views. Value chains describe all key processes for a specific industry, across all enterprise areas. They are structured hierarchically and consist of

1. View I – Scenarios
2. View II – Business Processes
3. View III – Business Process Transactions

The Business Process Blueprint is the bridge between the top-level business requirements and the technical transaction level. To support any implementation decision it is important to understand the business processes from an end-to-end perspective down to the transactional integration[4]. Business processes defining the context for each transaction. The same transaction may occur in multiple processes, different departments or even in different SAP instances, but starting point to identify gaps or overlaps is the context provided by a process flow and the involved data and organizational elements. Business processes are also the bases to identify any impact BEFORE making system or organizational changes.

View I – Scenario View

A scenario is a composition of business processes that reflects a typical way of doing business in the related enterprise area. Scenarios represented as an end-to-end Value Chain describe all key processes for a specific industry, across all enterprise areas. A typical Scenario is presented in Figure 3.

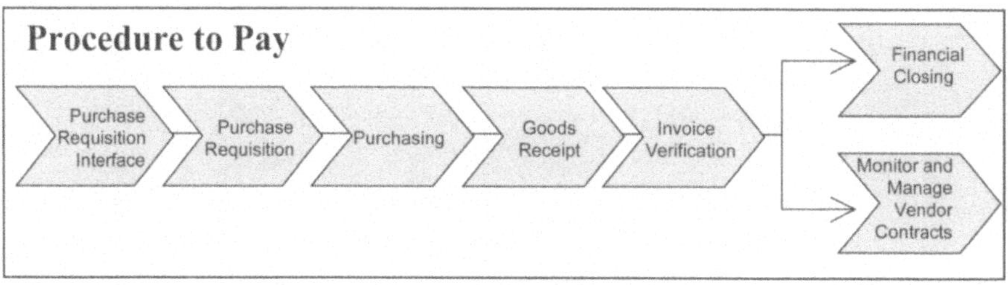

Figure 3: Scenario view of a business process architecture

View II – Business Process View

A business process by SAP's definition is a sub-process that is assigned to a step within a scenario. A business process defines the procedural sequence of business

[4]For example, the SAP transaction codes are included on the SIGMA business process scripts. This level of detail must be documented before the software can be configured.

process transactions as they are visually illustrated as "event-driven process chains." In this context, the starting and ending events of every business process is specified. Events trigger functions, or can be results of functions. The events and the rules define the specific flow of a scenario instance. This is standard SAP documentation, and a good review is included in Keller and Teufel (1998). The basic elements of a business process are presented in Figure 4, and a typical business process is presented in Figure 5.

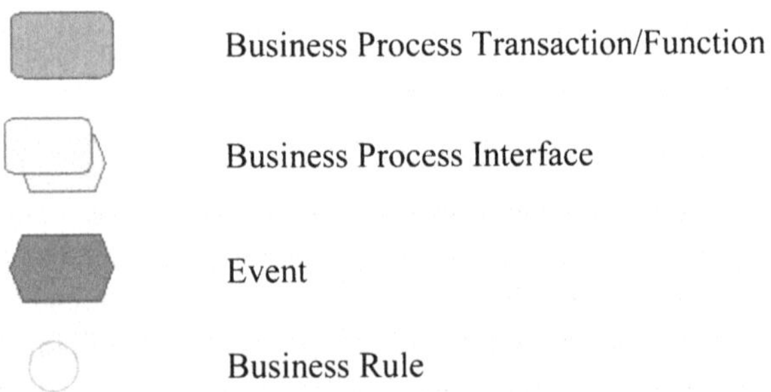

Figure 4: Objects in an SAP business process

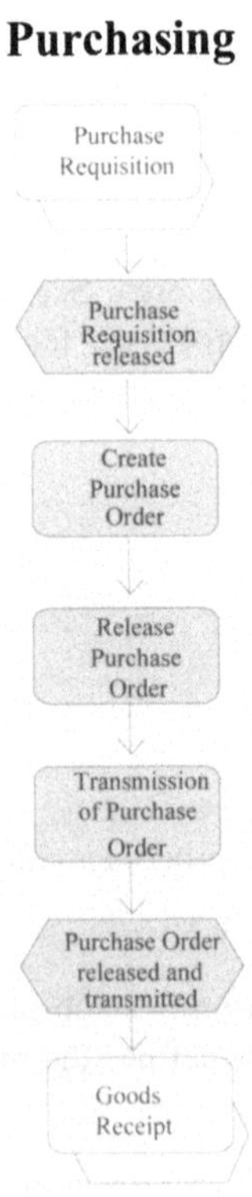

Figure 5: Business process representation in SAP

View III – Business Process Transaction View

A Business Process Transaction is the description of the smallest, self-contained business task in the R/3 Business Blueprint, where SAP transactions usually represent business process transactions. The basic elements of a business process transaction are presented in Figure 6, and a typical transaction is presented in Figure 7.

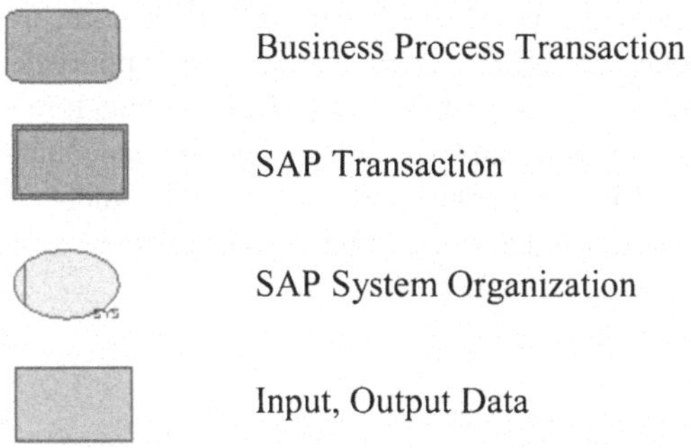

Figure 6: Basic elements of a Business Process Transaction

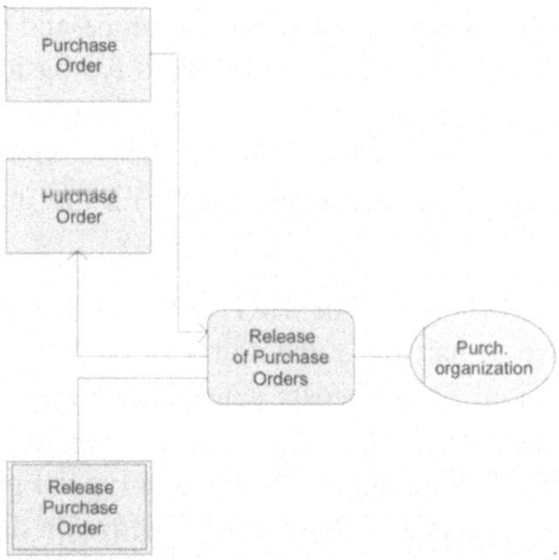

Figure 7: SAP Transaction Code Level

The business process blueprint provides a standardized documentation across multiple projects to facilitate communication and problem resolution. Functional overlaps can be identified and resolved, reducing duplicative configuration efforts. Business teams can document and study the business processes prior to configuration, eliminating costly re-work. The business process architecture is documented relative to the SAP reference model, and it defines the basis for the IT architecture. Scope and configuration are documented in a single repository in a consistent format as opposed to multiple data sources and formats. This documentation allows resolving issues before configuration begins as opposed to post-configuration.

2.3.3 Using the Business Process Architecture

We did not develop an analytical tool that analyzes alternatives (e.g., simulation, optimization, or cost-effectiveness analysis). Our tool documents the requirements of a complete SAP solution as defined by SAP's defense customers, and it provides an accurate documentation of the SMART and SIGMA solutions relative to the SAP solution. Hence, one can use the documentation to support decision from a position of complete information. The business process architecture can be used in the future to manage (monitor and document) the implementation. It represents the agreement reached by all parties, and it documents where you are going in much detail (i.e., all the way to the transaction level). It is the "plan," and it is up to the Navy to study, update, and enforce the plan.

3. Analyses and Results

Data is hard to find, because the workload depends on scope and complexity. The dollar figure varies widely, from a few thousand dollars for basic data extraction to millions for a full message-broker-plus-tools complement. Since the SMART/SIGMA maintenance implementation is large and complex, the interfacing cost would be significant. However, even with the impreciseness, we note the following.

One rule of thumb is the 10:1 rule. For ERP implementations, the cost of consulting & training relative to hardware and software is about 10:1. Gonsalves (1999) notes that "typical initial project costs can run as much as $530,000 for software, maintenance and support." This is implies a "typical" implementation cost of $5,000,000. Of course, this number is based on a typical project, and there is nothing that is typical about NAVAIR/NAVSUP. Then, one must consider the maintenance cost of the interface over the life to the project. The cost is significant.

3.1 Incomplete Defense Solution

SAP's defense customers constructed the SAP Defense Solution Map to document a complete defense solution. There are parts of this map that are not relevant for SMART and SIGMA. For example, there are certain functionality areas that are associated with Headquarters-level functionality. Still, if one is designing a defense solution using SAP, the Defense Solution Map is a good baseline.

For this project, we have constructed a complete document of SIGMA and SMART, and we have mapped the documentation to the Defense Solution Map. There is no expectation that either project should define a complete defense solution. However, the projects are somewhat fragmented in their coverage, and the details of the coverage are not completely visible until one explores the lower levels of the maps. There are some things that are worth noting. On the overview level, there is not much overlap. There is some overlap in finance and other overlap in some of the configuration management details, but all in all, the projects are quite dependent. Even in areas of functionality overlap, the context of the functionality is quite different. For example, a procurement transaction in SIGMA could originate from a project request, while the same transaction in SMART could originate from a maintenance order. This provides a clue as to why the business process detail must be included.

3.2 Example of Interface Complexity

To demonstrate the complexity of the maintenance interfacing under the current implementation plan, we were asked to map an example to the current solution and document the interface complexity. The particular reparable item that we were asked to examine is a gyroscope. We were provided with all of the materials related to the gyroscope LEAN map study[5].

This is a typical repair flow for an avionics component that has been determined to be beyond capability of maintenance (BCM) at the local I-level maintenance facility (AIMD). Approximately 70% of the repairable components that fail at the O-level are successfully repaired at the local I-level. The gyroscope flow is typical of what happens the other 30% of the time. One could argue that this particular gyroscope bounced back and forth more than usual between the Naval Depot (NADEP) and the Defense Logistics Agency (DLA), but there is sufficient evidence to make our point. We have mapped the flow to the SMART and SIGMA configurations, and we have documented that at least five complex interfaces could be eliminated if all of maintenance was in an aviation instance.

The LEAN map study tracked the item through a standard O-, I-, and D-Level[6] maintenance process, and documented the flow using LEAN mappings. LEAN mapping shows the path of a specific part as it moves from task to task, with the intent of capturing the "life experiences" of a specific part. While LEAN maps are useful for understanding flow, they do not map to the SAP software, so it is impossible to define the interfaces between SMART and SIGMA, as well as well as external interfaces. To examine the complexity of processing the gyroscope

[5]We have not been able to locate a written document that describes the study; however, we were provided the source data, map diagrams, and high-level analysis in the form of Power Point slides (EDS and Deloitte Consulting, 2001)

[6]Operational, Intermediate, and Depot define the levels of maintenance in the Navy.

under the current SMART and SIGMA configurations, we mapped the example to the as scoped solution maps. This mapping provides insight into the complex inter- and intra organizational process flows that support O-, I-, and D-Level maintenance.

The maintenance process crosses several Naval (NAVSUP, NAVAIR) and DoD (DLA) organizational domains. Since these organizations are in the process of implementing the SAP system, the analysis also provided a high-level estimate of the type, and the number of R/3 system transaction codes that would most likely be executed if the SAP system were to support the complete gyroscope repair process. The results follow, along with our interpretation of the results.

3.2.1 The Gyroscope Repair Process Analysis

Our analysis was based on tracking the gyroscope as it was transferred across organizational domains over its life-cycle. This flow is represented in Figure 8.

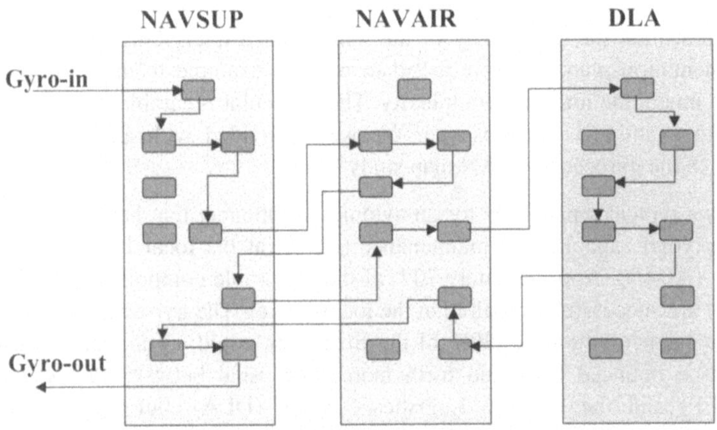

Figure 8: Gyroscope organizational Hand-off concept

The gyroscope "Hand-off" concept would be analyzed from three different views:

1. Organizational hand-offs (includes all organizations that "touch" the gyroscope),
2. Project hand-offs (hand-offs between SIGMA, SMART, and BSM[7]), and
3. Application System hand-offs (all systems, including legacy).

The organizational hand-offs are summarized in Figure 9. This figure shows how the gyroscope is passed back and forth among 18 Naval organizational units that

[7]Business Systems Modernization (BSM) is the acronym for the DLA SAP implementation project.

are involved in the maintenance process. It also shows how many tasks and how many organizational changes are involved in the complete repair process. This data demonstrates the complexity of the business process.

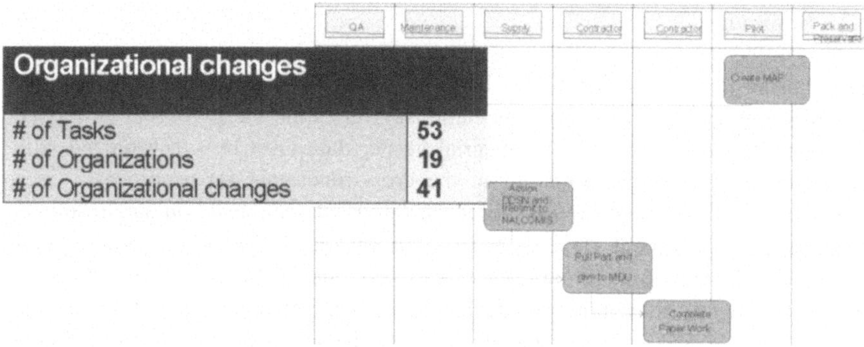

Figure 9: Organizational Hand-off Summary

We also documented the project hand-offs. There are five hand-offs between SIGMA and SMART domains, and four hand-offs with outside vendors and BSM. To manage the gyroscope in the SIGMA and SMART R/3 instance as it is passed from one domain to the other would require the EAI interface consider material, financial, and document flows, significantly increasing the cost of the interface. Hence, the five interfaces between SMART and SIGMA could be avoided if the maintenance processes are move into a single aviation instance.

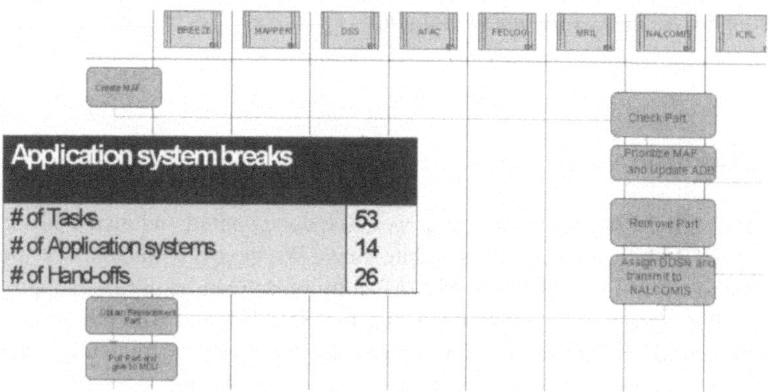

Figure 10: Application System Hand-off.

Figure 10 presents application hand-offs. This figure shows how many systems are currently interacting with the gyroscope maintenance process. We don't know if these legacy systems will be replaced by SAP functionality, but if we assume that

SMART and SIGMA are implemented as planned, the split maintenance process will require more complicated legacy interfaces to both the SMART and SIGMA R/3 instances.

3.2.2 Summary

The business process hand-offs between SMART and SIGMA will have considerable impact on the implementations. Every time the gyroscope is moved from one domain to another the material master data must be synchronized with the systems that are participating in the cross-functional repair process. Each transfer potentially requires the synchronization of technical, human resource, financial and document flow data and thus makes the interface requirements among the systems very complex. Given that interfacing is a very expensive proposition it would be more practical to have all maintenance related data reside in just a single R/3 instance, and thus reduce the need for complex interfacing requirements. A single instance would impact the gyroscope example in the following ways:

1. Eliminate hand-offs among systems,
2. Reduce inter-system transactions,
3. Possibly reduce the number of outside interfaces,
4. Standardize the numbering system (i.e., material numbers),
5. Streamline scheduling and capacity planning, and
6. Reduce the complexity of matching spare parts supplies with demand while increasing the accuracy of demand planning.

4. Conclusions

At the request of the Program Executives, we have documented and analyzed the SMART and SIGMA business process architectures. We have also shown how the ARIS methodology and the ARIS for MySAP.com toolset can be used to support the analysis. We have also recommended that the SMART and SIGMA project adopt architectural planning as an approach for project planning and implementation monitoring. Not only is this good business practice, it demonstrates to external sources that the Program Executives are taking all necessary steps to produce a solution that is best for the Navy. That is, it is an indication that the projects are not proceeding independently, but there is a plan for eventually integrating the aviation value chain. With time, the same approach should be extended to the maritime value chain, and the Navy as a whole.

Finally, we argue that consistent documentation practices be applied across all Navy projects. Use the newly developed business process architecture as the guide. This architecture extends the reference structure in the newly populated Q&Adb to included sequenced business processes that may be used to support the business teams and training. It also demonstrates to the leadership that the projects are following SAP's recommended implementation methodology.

1. References

EDS and Deloitte Consulting, E-2 LEAN Mapping (Power Point Presentation), 2001.

Gonsalves, A., EAI: Buy Now, Pay Later, *PC Week*, April 12, 1999.

Jost, W., EDV-Gestütze CIM Rahmenplannung. Wiesbaden, 1993.

Jost, W., Gehard Keller, and A.-W. Scheer, Konzeption eines DV-Tools im Rahmen der CIM Plannung, *Zeitschrift für Betriebswirtschaft*, Vol. 61, 33-64, 1991.

Keller, G. and Thomas Teufel, SAP R/3 Process Oriented Implementation. Harlow, England: Addison Wesley Longman, 1998.

Kirchmer, M., Business Process Oriented Implementation of Standard Software. Berlin: Springer-Verlag 1999.

Kleinberg, K., BPR Tool Functionality: What You Need, What They Have, Gartner Group Strategic Analysis Report, R-600-106, 1997.

Nüttgens, M., Koordiniert-dezentrales Informationsmanagement. Wiesbaden, 1995

Scheer, A.-W., ARIS: Business Process Frameworks. Heidelberg: Springer-Verlag, 1998.

Scheer, A.-W., ARIS: Business Process Modeling. Berlin: Springer-Verlag, 1999.

Scheer, A.-W., ARIS Toolset: A Software Product is Born, Information Systems. Vol. 19, 607-24, 1994.

Business Process Improvement and Software Selection Using ARIS at a Mid-Market Manufacturing Company

Ed Brady
American Meter Company

Marc Scharsig
IDS Scheer, Inc.

Summary

During the 1990's, many companies who undertook initiatives to implement ERP systems followed one of two paths of conventional wisdom. The first was to select standard software, and force business processes to conform, with the understanding that standard software has the advantage of best practices from many clients. The second was to clearly define functional requirements and modify standard software solutions in accordance with those requirements.

An emerging scenario is Business Process Oriented Standard Software Implementation, wherein core or critical business processes are defined in sufficient detail to select and optimize standard ERP software solutions. This scenario has two distinct advantages. Post implementation "rework", a common side affect of forcing business processes to conform to standard software, is minimized and ROI measures are realized quicker. The highest time, cost and implementation risk assiciated with customizing standard ERP software is reduced, ensuring implementation project success. This case study describes the Business Process Oriented Standard Software Selection of American Meter Company.

Key Words

ARIS, ARIS Toolset, BPI, BPR, Standard Software Selection, ERP, Business Process Analysis, Business Process Modeling, Business Process Design

1. Project Background

1.1 American Meter Company Background

American Meter (AMCO) has been a leader in the measurement and control of natural gas since the very beginning of the industry. Today, AMCO continues to fulfill that role as a member of ELSTER-AMCO. This global organization brings the latest technology and best practices from leading European and American manufacturers of gas measurement and control equipment to markets around the world.

AMCO has a history of designing innovations that have consistently improved the accuracy and the service life of gas meters, and has established the industry standards for long-term accuracy and reliability.

This organization has several world-class manufacturing facilities around the nation for their broad-based product lines.

Looking to the future, AMCO continues to invest in the development of innovative products and services for the natural gas industry. These investments will assure that they are able to continue to provide their customers with the very best value in gas measurement and control.

1.2 Motivation for the Project

1.2.1 Business Conditions

Market dynamics in the utility industry have driven virtually all major players to refocus on cost efficiency, which represent both a risk and opportunity for American Meter companies to streamline administrative business processes and to introduce additional services, which provide value and increase satisfaction of their customers. A considerable amount of manufacturing optimization has already been accomplished to satisfy these objectives. The fact that most of the core business information resides in several different Enterprise Resource Planning (ERP) systems, which are inherently closed, has rendered their replacement with one integrated ERP system as the next high leverage enabler of continuous improvement.

1.2.2 Project History

Several projects have been undertaken to study the strategic information technology options and feasibility of an enterprise-wide deployment of an integrated ERP system to consolidate core business information and to leverage common business processes. The ERP initiative was selected on the basis of total cost, risk, and flexibility with respect to strategic business plans. The executive board approved a system selection project, which comprises a detailed documentation of "to-be" business processes and a system requirements definition. This project step enables tight scope management and clearly articulates benefit targets from the subsequent implementation project.

1.3 Scope

The scope of this "to-be" business processes and system requirements design and documentation phase includes essentially all business processes core to the American Meter companies:

Area of Manufacturing and Logistics

- Manufacturing
  - Sales & Operations Planning
  - Production Planning
  - Master Production Scheduling
  - MRP
  - Capacity Management
  - Production Order Processing
  - Shop Floor Control
- Engineering
- Procurement
- Inventory Management
- Sales Order Entry
- Distribution

Area of Accounting and Cost Control

- General Ledger
- Accounts Receivable
- Accounts Payable

- Cash Management
- Cost Control

Non-core processes (e.g., payroll, treasury, etc.) are out of scope to this project.

All major sites are involved in documenting and approving the "to-be" business processes. The method used to capture this "to-be" requirements definition is a series of workshops with the process owners at each major site, scheduled in a cascading manner which builds on the preceding documentation and discussion. A cross-functional management oversight committee meets regularly to review results and recommendations and incorporate changes to the baseline requirements. The deliverable documentation from this project will be of sufficient quality and fidelity not only to select an ERP system but also to immediately begin system design and configuration on the selected ERP system.

2. Objectives

In order to provide value, any type of project needs to be designed to help the company achieve it's objectives. As a prerequisite to ensure success on a microlevel the project objectives need to be achieved. The following corporate objectives and project objectives were identified:

2.1 Corporate Objectives

- Sustain market leadership in residential gas meters
- Continue producing top of the line quality products
- Enhance profitability
- Improve operational excellence, increasing organizational effectiveness and process efficiency
- Increase business activities in the more profitable/growth market segments

2.2 Project Objectives

- Optimize internal processes – Continuous improvement in overhead efficiencies
- Harmonize, where possible, business processes across product lines (including best practices)

- Prepare and "set the table" for eBusiness – Anticipate changing buying behaviors
- KISS – Simplify and streamline current business practices
- Capture "tribal knowledge" in a defined, documented, sustainable set of system supported business processes
- Develop requirements document for ERP selection process
- Build momentum for ERP implementation by securing buy-in from users and local management
- Stay within given timeline and budget

3. Project Structure

3.1 Project Approach

The approach of this project followed a defined methodology, comprised of the following steps:

3.1.1 Project Preparation and Development of Time and Activity Plan

The project has a planned time line of approximately four months. Project start was February 2002. Anticipated project end and start of the following standard software vendor selection is July 2002. The major project phases cover the on-site business process analysis and design activities in the:

- Residential business unit in Nebraska City, NE
- Perfection business unit in Madison, OH
- Industrial business unit in Erie, PA
- Canadian business unit in Toronto, Canada
- Automated systems business unit in Scott Depot, VW

and the harmonization of to-be business processes and requirements across all business units (see figure 1).

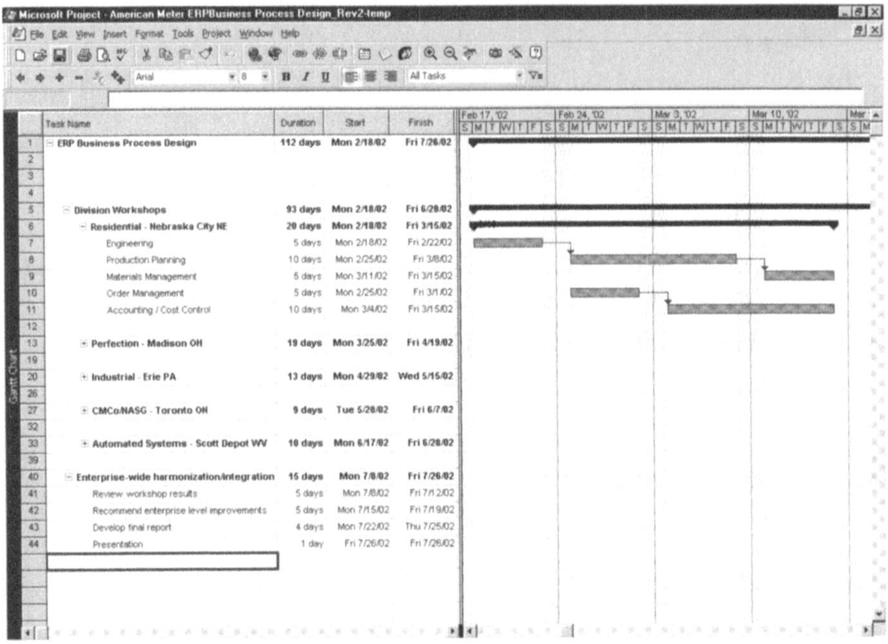

Figure 1: Project master schedule

For each business unit, the workshop participants were selected based on an appropriate mix of expertise in:

- Engineering
- Production Planning
- Materials Management
- Order Management
- Accounting / Cost Control

Some workshops are executed concurrently. However, there are never more than two parallel tracks in place to allow AMCO's project management to participate at as many sessions as possible. In order to utilize the workshop attendees' time in an efficient and effective way each workshop was scheduled in advance on a daily basis. These daily schedules were coordinated with the business units prior to workshop start. The following example (figure 2) shows the first week of the production planning workshop of the residential product line.

	Mon 2/25	Tue 2/26	Wed 2/27	Thu 2/28	Fri 3/01
8:30	Travel	Recap	Recap	Recap	Recap
		Meters			
		Production Planning - Demand Mgt - RCCP - Forecast of Consumption Items - Planning Strategies	**MPS**	**Planned Order Mgt** - Order Conversion - Order Processing	**Production Order Processing/SFC** - Order Creation - Order Release - Availability Check - Missing Parts - Print Production Papers
12:00	Lunchbreak	Lunchbreak	Lunchbreak	Lunchbreak	Lunchbreak
01:00 02:00	-Expectations -Scope/Schedule Review -Product Model and -Level I PR Review	**Production Planning**	**MRP**	**Capacity Mgt** - Loading - Evaluation - Leveling - Scheduling	- Material Issuance - Order Confirmation - Close Order - Order Settlement
03:00 04:00	**SOP** -Production Class Processing -Sales Forecast -SOP Order Board	Documentation	Documentation	Documentation	Documentation
06:00					

Figure 2: Daily Workplan

3.1.2 Determination of Project Standards

The determination of project standards comprises the selection and customer specific adjustments of standard documents, which may be used during the project. Examples of these standard documents are layouts for agendas, meeting minutes, Microsoft PowerPoint presentations, open item list, etc.

The other major area is the determination of the "ARIS standards". At this point it is assumed that the reader has a base knowledge about the ARIS Toolset, its methods and functionality. It was the objective to utilize a pragmatic and simple business process architecture. The developed framework is depicted below (see figure 3).

It consists of three levels and five model types.

- On level one the product model (product/service tree) and the enterprise business processes (value-added chain diagram) are developed.
- On level 2 value-chain elements are detailed with the help of eEPCs (extended event driven process chains). The utilization of function trees on this level is optional. Function trees can be generated from the eEPCs. It is not intended to build function trees from scratch.
- On level 3 the process steps of level 2 (functions) are detailed with the help of eEPCs. Level 3 process models are optional and are only created for areas where the additional information is crucial in order to define and identify completely

AMCO's business requirements. Function allocation diagrams are optional and can be generated.

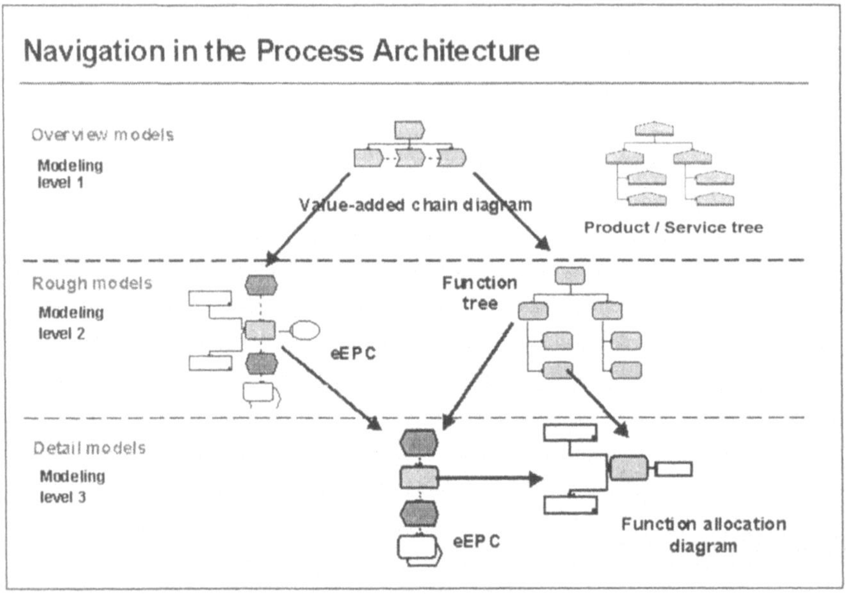

Figure 3: ARIS framework

For each of the above mentioned model types the allowed object types, attribute types and relationship types were defined. This is crucial to ensure that the required information is gathered in order to populate the final report document. From a process mapping perspective it is the intention to map all objects needed to answer the following questions: "Who executes what function with the help of which input information and what output information is created?" The function attribute "description/definition" is important from a requirements definition standpoint, because not all requirements can be depicted in a simple way, if it all, with process flows. An example is the execution of the sales forecast according to the sales organization structure (company, region, division, sales representative) per product group and/or product.

3.1.3 Executive Workshop

To gain insights about AMCO's current situation and anticipated vision for the future, an executive workshop was conducted. The purpose was to determine AMCO's opportunities, threats, imperatives, strategies, objectives, and goals. The identified objectives are mentioned above.

3.1.4 Development of Product Models

The definition of AMCO's core business processes is a critical component of this project. Products shape the business processes of a company. These business processes must be structured in such a way that they can support the tasks resulting from the existing or planned product mix of AMCO. Below is depicted as an example the existing AMCO product model (see figure 4).

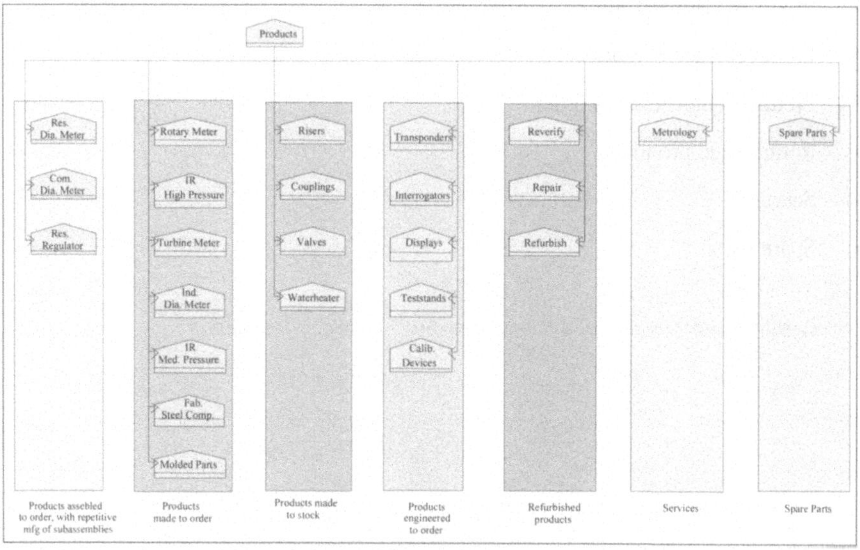

Figure 4: Product model

The used ARIS model type is the "product/service tree". This model comprises the current products and services, which are grouped in business process categories. A product family oriented product model was developed first in order to facilitate the development of this model. The initial product models were developed with input from AMCO's project management.

Adding anticipated new products to the business process category oriented product model created the to-be product model. However, in this case this did not lead to necessary adjustments of the business process categories.

A prerequisite for such a product-oriented design of business processes is a product mix based on customer needs or market needs. At the current stage of the project it is concluded that future anticipated customer segments will not add an additional dimension to the definition of AMCO's core processes.

The resulting process models, the level I enterprise-wide business processes, reflect the core business processes of AMCO.

3.1.5 Development of Level I Enterprise-Wide Business Processes

The enterprise wide business processes are developed based on the identified business process categories. The identified business process categories are:

- Products assembled to order, with repetitive manufacturing of subassemblies
- Products made to order
- Products made to stock
- Products engineered to order
- Refurbished products
- Services
- Spare parts

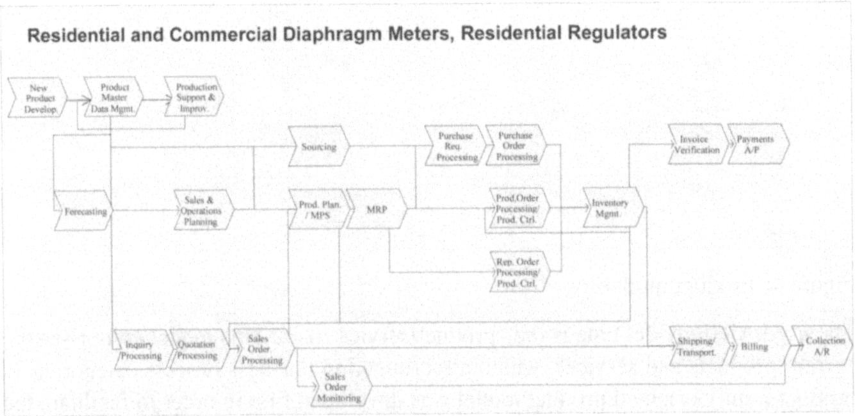

Figure 5: Level 1 Process Model

Each of these business process categories reflects distinct end to end processes. The used ARIS model type is the "value added chain diagram". Above is the example of the to-be level I enterprise wide process for residential diaphragm meters, commercial diaphragm meters, and residential regulators depicted (see figure 5) process with repetitive manufacturing of subassemblies" process category.

These level I enterprise wide business processes are the roadmap for the development of the more detailed level II business processes and ensure that those models integrate with each other.

Supporting processes such as accounting and cost control are added to the level I enterprise wide business processes in order to ensure coverage for functional areas not depicted in the high-level business processes.

The level I as-is enterprise-wide business processes are derived from the as-is business process category oriented product model. The level I to-be enterprise-wide business processes are derived from the level I as-is enterprise –wide processes and are adjusted based on gained insights through the progression of the project and based on conceptual ideas. The initial enterprise-wide business process models were developed with input from AMCO's project management.

3.1.6 Project Kick-Off

The attendees of the project kick-off included the CEO, the CFO as the executive project sponsor, and all steering committee members. The kick-off meeting served the following main purposes:

- Motivational positioning of the project within AMCO by the CEO
- Update of the management concerning all project related topics
- Finalization of the product model and enterprise wide process model as the starting points for the local business units activities
- Visible demonstration of project buy-in by the management in order to move forward

Local on-site kick-off meetings are also conducted for each business unit in order to prepare the local management and project team for the upcoming activities.

3.1.7 Development of Level II Business Processes for the Residential Business Unit

According to the above mentioned project plan, the level II business process mapping started in the residential business unit in Nebraska City, NE. The objective was to detail each of the relevant level I enterprise wide business process elements with a business process model.

Below are depicted as examples excerpts of the as-is and the to-be sales order entry processes (see figure 6 and figure 7). The used ARIS model type is the extended event driven process chain. The to-be process shows the new business requirement of supporting product configuration in the sales order process. Obviously the to be selected standard software package need to be able to provide such functionality.

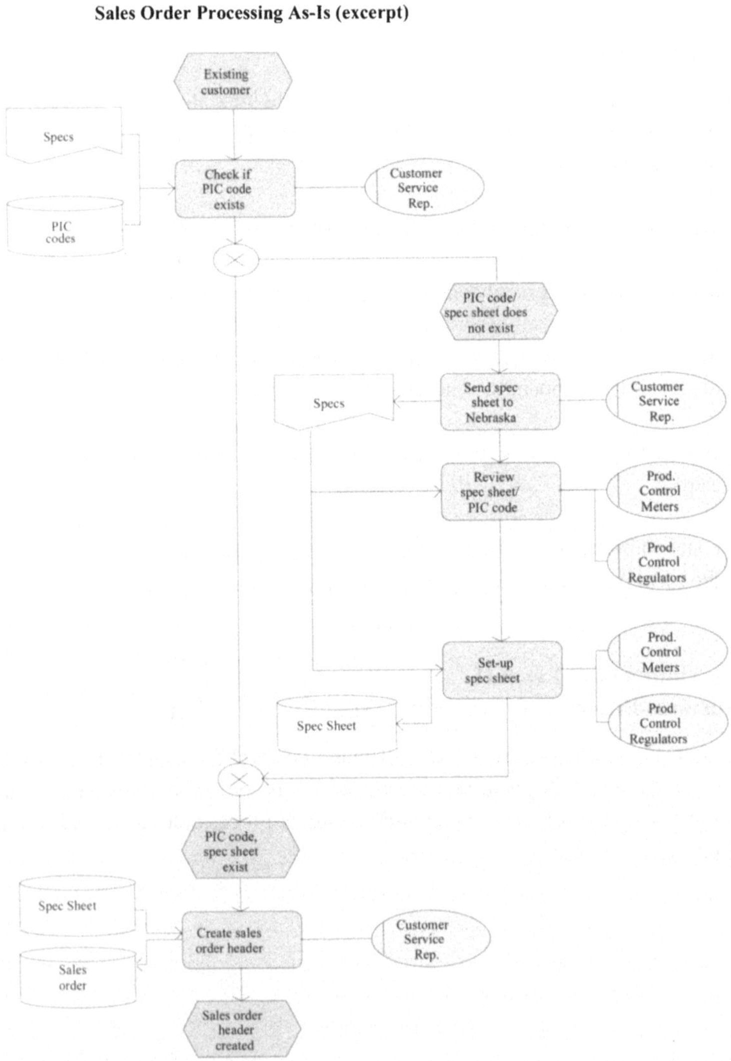

Figure 6: Example 1 eEPC model

Sales Order Processing To-Be (excerpt)

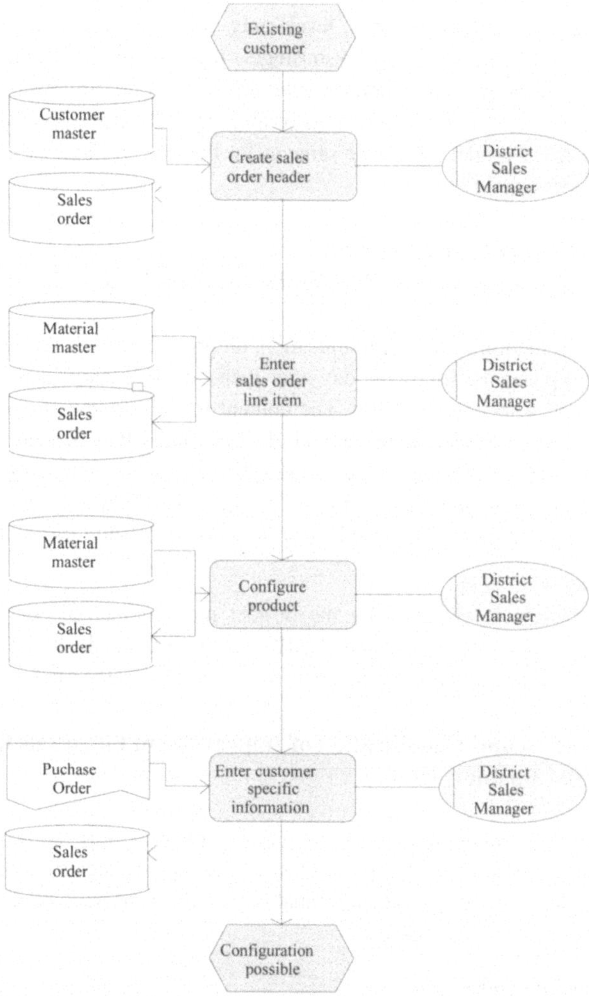

Figure 7: Example 2 eEPC model

At this level also additional sub-processes are mapped, which are not covered by the core business process elements of level one. Examples are returns, intercompany sales, free of charge deliveries, drop shipments, etc..

3.1.7 Development of Level III Business Processes for the Residential Business Unit

Process models are created on this level only in order either to facilitate the understanding of a complex current business process or to capture important requirements of a to-be process. Therefore, the objective is not to create detailed level III process models for all mapped functions of all level II business processes, as-is and to-be. The used ARIS model type is the same as for the level II processes, the extended event driven process chain.

3.1.8 Review of Level II and Level III Business Processes for the Residential Business Unit

To ensure the elimination of miscommunication, all process models are made available for reviewing purposes the following day after their development. There are a content related review and a technical review. The content related review is executed by the process owners and the project management of AMCO and IDS Scheer. As-is process models are reviewed concerning the accurate reflection of the actual situation. To-be process models are reviewed concerning the accurate description of conceptual ideas. To enable the content related review it was decided to provide plots of the process models.

The technical review is executed by the project management of IDS Scheer. The compliance with the above-presented "ARIS standards" needs to be assessed. In addition, it has to be ensured that the models are methodologically correct.

3.1.9 Identification and Classification of Improvement Potentials for the Residential Business Unit

Immediately after the mapping of as-is processes, improvement potentials are gathered in a brainstorming session. At this point most of the input relates to a wish list of the workshop attendees and to an ad hock analysis of the process model. The process models provide insights concerning:

- Organizational breaks
- Non value added functions
- Redundant execution of functions
- Redundant maintenance of data sources
- Utilization of information carriers (e.g., paper documents, databases)

Additional improvement potentials are identified and added at a later point in case the discussion about new conceptual ideas is more time consuming, e.g. discussions about a potential standard software support of configurable products or the utilization of remote sales functionality.

Improvement potentials are phrased in a way that they express the potential benefit. An example is the "reduction of data maintenance through the utilization of integrated, enterprise-wide customer master data". These improvement potentials are grouped per process area and classified. In order to keep the complexity low only three classes are permitted:

- High impact
- Normal
- Low hanging fruit

The high impact improvement potentials are the ones, which will contribute the most concerning dollar value related savings or earnings. It is anticipated that there will be no more than a 3-6 of these. The "normal" improvement potentials will be the largest group. This group comprises also the nice-to-have items. The low hanging fruits do not need for their realization the implementation of a new standard software system. Most of these items are organizationally related. These items also show the immediate benefit of this project.

3.1.10 Development of Level II and Level III Business Processes and Identification of Improvement Potentials for the Remaining Business Units

- Perfection business unit (Madison, OH)
- Industrial business unit (Erie, PA)
- Canada business unit (Toronto, ON)
- Automated Systems business unit (Scott Depot, WV)

3.1.11 Review and Harmonizing of the To-Be Processes Across Business Units

Since the project is still ongoing this step has not been executed yet. The objective is to harmonize as many processes as possible across the different business units and process categories in order to reduce complexity, to enhance clarification and responsiveness, and to lay the groundwork for a successful implementation. This harmonization process includes a content related component as well as a nomenclature related component. However, this harmonization process will be applied only as long as it is reasonable from a business perspective. For example, a best practice such as "vendor managed inventory" is not per se beneficial for all process categories, whereas the value of utilizing an enterprise-wide chart of accounts transcends all process categories .

3.1.12 Development of Final Document and Presentation of the Results of this Project Phase

The final document of this project will also include the requirements sections for potential standard software vendors. These sections will be generated out of ARIS including the to-be business processes as well as the description attribute outlining the requirements.

3.2 Project Organization

The Project Was Organized with 4 Main Objectives

1) An integrated core team of AMCO and IDS Scheer process experts, who could provide insight to best practices & continuity between locations for harmonization potential,
2) Active senior management involvement via regular steering committee and ad-hoc meetings,
3) Engage local mid-level management in decision-making,
4) Involve as many "practitioners" as possible in short bursts of time.

The project organization strucuture is illustrated in figure 8.

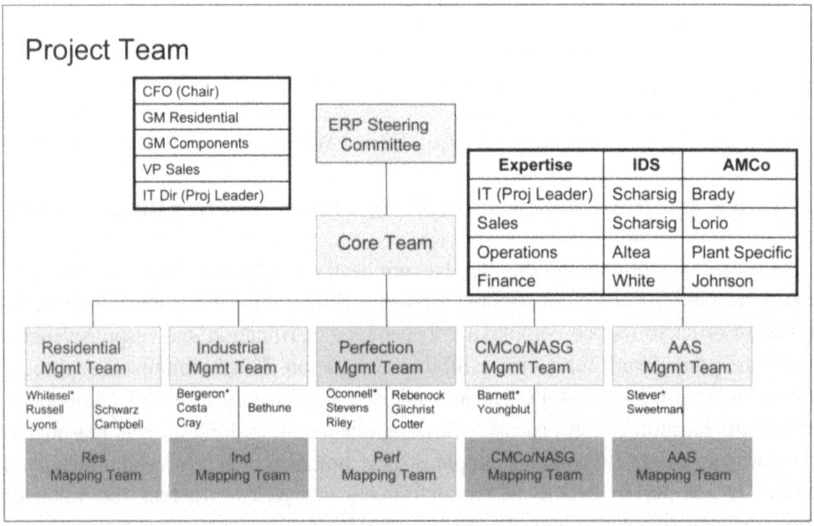

Figure 8: Project organization structure

4. Results

4.1 Results Achieved

4.1.1 ARIS Methodology Dramitacally Increases Efficiency of Process Modeling

The combination of the ARIS workshop methodology, and the ARIS toolset, enabled the effort of business process design, documentation, reengineering and system requirements gathering to be accomplished more efficiently than typical industry experience. As illustrated in Figure 9, a typical series of plant level workshops spanned 20 days, covering all major functions and process areas, as well as integration points with corporate and central functions. These workshops generated 125 ARIS process models (as-is and to-be), 363 improvement ideas, 3 major reengineered processes, a dozen "quick hits" resulting in immediate action; involving 60 process experts/practitioners and management, facilitated by 2 consultants using the ARIS tools.

3-15-02 Neb City Exit Briefing

- Accomplishment Statistics
  - ~60 Process Owners/Experts Engaged
  - 125+ Processes Mapped
  - 350+ Improvement Ideas Identified
  - 2+ Reengineered Process Candidates
  - 12 "Quick Hits" Isolated for Near Term Action

Goal	Status
Broad Buy-in • Practitioners • Management	High User Involvement (60p)
Thorough Requirement Analysis	Running List (363)
Identify ROI Areas	Preliminary Reengineering Items

Figure 9: Nebraska City workshop statistic

ARIS enforces a consistent organization of the data gathered (Functions, Organizational responsibilities, Data and system input/output dependancies, deliverables/metrics) from each process stream. This ensures "1st pass" capture of all relevent information, virtually eliminating the need to revisit processes when reviewing a subsequent or related process. In addition, it greatly enhances the downstream reengineering efforts to rationalize and streamline related processes.

Finally, the modular nature of the ARIS architecture allows the utilization of "nested" models, functions, and data sources; which can quickly be reorganized and modified to evaluate alternative scenarios and/or analyze integration points of related processes.

4.1.2 The Organization of ARIS Aids in Quickly Identifying the "80/20" Areas of Highest Return

One of the deficiencies in traditional reengineering methodologies, is the tendancy to lose context in the realm of data collected. The manner in which we gathered and organized process metrics through ARIS allowed the team to, in a matter of hours, identify the areas where a concentrated effort would yield the greatest impact. These areas were then continually refined through interactive feedback with the process owners and practitioners, to produce a short list of reengineered processes which could be baselined into the ERP system design and software selection criteria.

4.2 Results Consistent with Defined Project Goals

4.2.1 All Major Project Objectives Are Being Satisfied

The objectives identified at the onset of the project, and defined in section 2.2 above, are being exceeded to this point. In addition to the tangible objectives of simplifying and streamlining internal processes, a major objective was to build support and buy-in from the user, mid-level manangement, and corporate shareholders, by identifying obvious value in addressing each of their "pain points". This was thought to be a necessary step in building momentum for a major ERP implementation project. By that measure, the project has been very successful to date.

4.2.2 The ARIS Methodolgy and Project Organization Enabled Incremental Returns

Partially to address the inertia of a risk averse corporate culture, we hoped during this project to identify some improvement areas that were not dependant on new software, and could therefore be implemented early; yielding incremental tangible value to the company from this "business process design & system selection" phase of the ERP initiatiative. Using the ARIS methodology, and project approach adapted by IDS Scheer, we were able to isolate from our list of improvements a short list of "quick hit" actions that could immediately be adopted (unconstrained by new system capabilities), as well as the "critical few", high impact, major reengineering opportunities (dependent on new system capabilities) that would provide the incentive to sustain momuntum in following through with system implementation.

5. Lessons Learned

5.1 Change Management

5.1.1 Involvement of Local Decisionmakers is Paramount

Much is written about the importance of top down commitment in major systems projects. In theory, inevitable obstacles that arise during the course of a project of this nature can be overcome with direction from above. Equally important, is the buy-in and enthusiasm of local decisionmakers; especially in a decentralized multiplant environment. As we engaged this group of stakeholders more deeply, and enrolled them as part of the solution, the need to utilize senior management as arbitrators evaporated. Their role became steering & mentoring, which was more palatable to all.

5.1.2 Overcommunicate

As with any change, and especially an ERP system change which threatens to change how a large and cross-sectional portion of the employee population works day to day, we found communication is key to melting resistence to the initiative. "Every action has an equal & opposite reaction" is as true in human behavior as it is in physics. There is a very powerful inertial force to overcome when pushing an initiative such as this into an existing organization. However, by over-communicating our goals, methodology, and dependance on the process experts and practitioners as the key differentiators of a successful or failed project; we have thus far been able to position local management and process experts as part of the solution vs. part of the problem. In effect, we are enlisting the existing organization to pull the ERP change in. The more we have involved these critical people, the easier the project has become, and the better the improvement ideas we eventually incoporated into our system design. This is a consideration that is always discussed as a critical success factor, commonly understood at an intillectual level, but requires hard work and focus to stay on the front burner.

5.1.3 Maintain Flexible Project Manangement

The importance of monitoring "public opinion" cannot be underestimated, coupled with a willingness to institute course corrections where required to ensure project objectives are met. We laid out a daily workplan of workshops and associated exit criteria at the outset of each business unit site visit. It was important, however, to continually readjust that plan to:

- Accommodate schedules of the right personnel
- Incorporate intelligence gathered during associated process workshops that indicated more or less content was appropriate
- Allocate timeboxes for communication and feedback to local management & process owners regarding context and impact of findings to date
- Conduct senior level brainstorming discussions

In this way, our external team was perceived as part of the site team in helping them reduce day to day pain and increase efficiencies.

5.2 Project Mechanics

In an attempt to keep the intrusiveness of our project team to a minimum, we elected to faciliatate workshop discussions using digital whiteboard and flip charts for 4-6 hours per day, then build ARIS models using our core team for the ramainder of the day; freeing up time for our workshop participants to do their regular job for ½ day. In the end, we experimented with, and were more efficient, when we shifted to building the ARIS models on-line using an LCD projector. The visual dipiction of the process unfolding before the participants, coupled with the immediate feedback and adjustment as a function of the workshop discussions, proved to be much more effective; along the lines of Steven Covey's "go slow to go fast" mantra.

Business Process Management: Combining Quality and Performance Improvement

Andrzej Pluciński
ZE PAK S.A.

Grzegorz B. Gruchman
IDS Scheer Polska

Summary

ZE PAK S.A. is one of the largest power generating companies in Poland. Due to market pressures, the company had to restructure and streamline its operations. To that end, a business process optimization project was started in 1999, using ARIS software as a process mapping tool. It was followed by an ISO certification project, started in 2000. As a result of both efforts, a very effective Quality Management System was introduced. Its main impact is the cultural change within the company, providing a platform for true business process management.

Key Words

ISO 9000:2000, Business Process Management, Business Process Optimization

1. Introduction

The ISO 9000:2000 standards promote the adoption of process orientation when developing, implementing and improving a Quality Management System.[1] The standards are based on eight quality management principles. Two of those principles deal with:

- The process approach (it is assumed that a desired result is achieved more efficiently, when activities and related resources are managed as a process)
- The system approach (it is assumed that identifying, understanding and managing of inter-related processes as a system contribute to the effectiveness and efficiency of the organization as a whole)

In general, the process approach aims at achieving a dynamic cycle of continuous improvement and allows significant gains to the organization, typically in terms of product and business performance, effectiveness, efficiency and costs. The process approach also facilitates true customer focus and increased customer satisfaction through the identification of key processes within an organization, their subsequent development, and continuous improvement. The process approach encourages the organization to develop a clear understanding of all its processes; not only those that are needed for its quality management system, but other key processes as well. Last but not least, a measurement system should be used in order to gather information for process performance analysis, as well as input and output characteristics.

Within the context of ISO 9001:2000, the process approach requires an organization to identify, implement, manage and continually improve the effectiveness of all processes that are necessary for the Quality Management System. In particular, the approach emphasizes the importance of:

- The understanding and fulfilment of requirements
- The need to consider processes in terms of added value
- Obtaining results of process performance and effectiveness
- Continual improvement of processes based on objective measurement

In line with the system approach, ISO 9001:2000 requires an organization to also manage the interactions of its processes in order to achieve its objectives. The interdependencies of an organization's activities can sometimes be very complex, resulting in a network of various processes and sub-processes. Therefore, the

[1] *Guidance on the Process Approach to quality management systems*, International Organization for Standardization, ISO/TC 176/SC 2/N544, December 2000

system approach aims at coordination of key processes and a clear definition of their interfaces.

As mentioned, ISO 9001:2000 standards require an organization to manage all processes within the framework of a Quality Management System (QMS). However, a standard set or list of processes that must be documented and managed in every organization does not exist. It is assumed that each organization should determine which processes are to be documented, on the basis of its customer and applicable regulatory or statutory requirements, the nature of its activities, and its overall corporate strategy.

The new ISO standards do not describe any methodology to implement process-oriented QMS. However, the ISO organization provides general guidance on this topic, summarized below. A company that aims at the implementation of such a system should:

1. Identify the processes needed for its QMS and their application throughout the organization.
2. Determine the sequence and interaction of these processes.
3. Determine criteria and methods required to ensure that both the operation and control of these processes are effective.
4. Ensure the availability of resources and information necessary to support the operation and monitoring of these processes.
5. Measure, monitor and analyze these processes.
6. Implement action necessary to achieve planned results and continuous improvement of these processes.

The recommendations listed above were used to full extent in a project described within this case study.

2. Project Background and Scope

2.1 The Company

Zespół Elektrowni Pątnów-Adamów-Konin S.A. (ZE PAK) is a multi-plant power generating company in Poland: one of the largest in the country. It produces approximately 8% of the electricity generated in Poland and has a combined power of 2,233 megawatts. The number of employees is around 2,000, while its subsidiaries employ an additional 2,100.

Until 1994, the company was fully state-owned. At the end of this year, the privatization process was started. Five years later, the first batch of company shares was sold to an institutional owner. In the same year, a decision was made to transform the company via radical organizational restructuring and the introduction of business process management. The decision was made on the basis of:

- Increasing momentum of privatization in the Polish energy sector.
- Liberalization of the energy market
- Increasing importance of competitiveness and client orientation
- A need to increase effectiveness and reduce costs
- A need to utilize modern management practices and solutions
- Increasing importance of business process management

The need to radically restructure the company was justified by its outmoded organizational structure. For historical reasons, it encompassed too many secondary support areas. There was a pressing need to discard or outsource activities in those areas that were not cost-efficient, or not in line with company strategy.

The need to introduce business process management was justified in turn by a need to integrate activities in various organizational units. The ZE PAK structure was a classic case of functionally oriented arrangement. Activities in various units were not well connected to each other, with long cycle times, excessive costs and many other inefficiencies. Typically, those problems were directly implied by lack of communication across boundaries of organizational units. In short, ZE PAK processes were difficult to manage, or in some cases not managed at all.

2.2 Project Goals

The Quality Management System at ZE PAK was implemented as a result of two interrelated projects, namely a business process optimization project and an ISO project. The optimization project had two general goals. The first one was to create a set of process maps, to be used for various purposes. The second goal was to standardize processes and to gather information about their costs and cycle times, in order to perform internal benchmarking. In particular, the detailed objectives of the project included:

- Improvement of ZE PAK business processes
- Implementation of business process management principles
- Support of Quality Management System implementation

- Support of selection and implementation of an integrated ERP system
- Support of operational controlling and management of activity costs

The core business process optimization project was followed by several other efforts, some of them on-going. One of the follow-up projects dealt directly with implementation of the QMS and ended with ISO 9000:2000 certification. It used results of the first project heavily. In turn, the first project took QMS requirements into account and was guided by quality management principles to a large extent. Moreover, the two projects overlapped to a certain extent. The follow-up ISO project had the following objectives and expectations:

- Introduction of management via documented goals and tasks
- Defining, documenting and communicating responsibilities in the company
- Introduction of continuous improvement of the management system
- Introduction of non-conformance prevention
- Participation of all employees in the improvement of the whole company
- Identification and analysis of quality costs
- Identification of client expectations and requirements
- Creation of a platform for an Integrated Quality Management System

It was decided that as a backbone of the Quality Management System, the company's intranet would be used. Specifically, the so-called Central Improvement System (CIS) was to be created using ARIS and Internet technology. The decision was made due to a belief that there was no other effective way to involve all employees in continuous improvement of business processes and the management system.

3. Business Process Optimization Project

3.1 Project Structure

The process optimization project consisted of the following stages:

- Project Definition
- Mapping Tool Selection
- Project Organization
- Modeling of As-is processes

- As-is Process Analysis
- To-be Process Design
- Process Implementation

3.2 Initial Stages

After the top-management decision to go-ahead with the project, preparatory activites were performed during the first stage. Project goals, objectives and scope were defined, using analysis of ZE PAK strategic direction as a basis. Business problems to be solved were defined as well. Subsequently, key strategic areas within the company were defined for the project. Concentration on analysis and design of those areas was assumed, since they were the key to increased effectiveness of the company.

Following project definition, requirements for a business process modeling tool were formulated at the outset of the second stage. The requirements covered not only capabilities to model and analyze dynamic aspects of business processes, but the ability to model complex organizational structures as well. After many presentations by various vendors, ARIS software of IDS Scheer AG was selected due to its flexibility, support for organizational restructuring, many areas of applicability and considerable process optimization functionality. In particular, the reasons for ARIS selection included its abilities to:

- Create and process complex descriptions of company's operations
- Generate any report required by users
- Create process documentation automatically
- Perform automatic analysis and comparison of processes
- Test and evaluate improved processes, using animation and simulation
- Support development and implementation of quality procedures
- Generate Quality Manual automatically
- Improve quality and transparency of the Quality System
- Electronically distribute Quality System documentation
- Involve employees in continuous process improvement

An additional factor in favour of ARIS tools was that a framework process optimization methodology and modeling techniques were already embedded within them. It was felt that this would ease and speed-up front-end stages of the project, not to mention reduction of effort and costs. Last but not least, ARIS was also selected due to its support for:

- Measurement of process effectiveness
- Conceptual redesign of business processes
- Publication of process models for the intranet

The decision to purchase ARIS software was coupled with a decision to use the consulting services of SOFTLAN S.A. company, a partner of IDS Scheer AG, which was later transformed into IDS Scheer Polska.

The stages described above were completed in the first half of 1999. The third stage was started in October 1999. Within its scope, organizational infrastructure was created for the project and subsequent business process management practices, as well as for the ISO project. The infrastructure included:

- The Steering Committee
- Process Owners
- Functional specialists
- People responsible for the implementation of the Quality System

Of particular importance were the Process Owners. These were the roles with a mission to institutionalize business process management and continuous improvement principles. To set proper expectations, their responsibilities and rights were initially defined at this stage, although there were no processes to own and manage yet. The following general responsibilities were assumed for the Process Owner:

- To continuously improve his/her process
- To develop new concepts, to be used for optimization purposes
- To search the environment and to look for new solutions used by other companies that could be used internally
- To cooperate in development and improvement of process management principles and practices

Responsibilities of Process Owners were accompanied by a certain amount of organizational power. As far as rights of the Process Owner were concerned, they were allowed to:

- Issue directives to those employees that participate in owned processes
- Supervise execution of their directives, with support and assistance of employees' direct managers
- Apply for resources, required for execution of owned processes

- Review proposals for changes in owned processes
- Create inter-functional teams to analyze and optimize owned processes

3.3 As-is Process Modeling

In the fourth stage of the project, As-is processes were identified and mapped. The aim was to gain detailed knowledge of selected current processes, i.e. the ones which were to be redesigned. As a result, a model of the As-is state was created. The model described crucial relationships between the company's functional areas prior to restructuring efforts. Key processes were classified either as basic or support processes, depending on their role within the company.

The basic operating processes were defined as the ones which produce a product or service related directly or indirectly to the company's mission. Such processes usually create added value within value chains. At ZE PAK, the following processes were defined as basic processes:

- Acquisition of energy markets
- Production planning
- Production of electricity and heat
- Sales of energy
- Sales accounting

The support processes are defined as those that are required for the company to operate efficiently and to enable basic processes. However, they do not create any added value for the client. The following sample processes were classified as support processes:

- Strategic planning
- Systems management
- Management of human resources
- Mamagement of financial resources
- Asset management

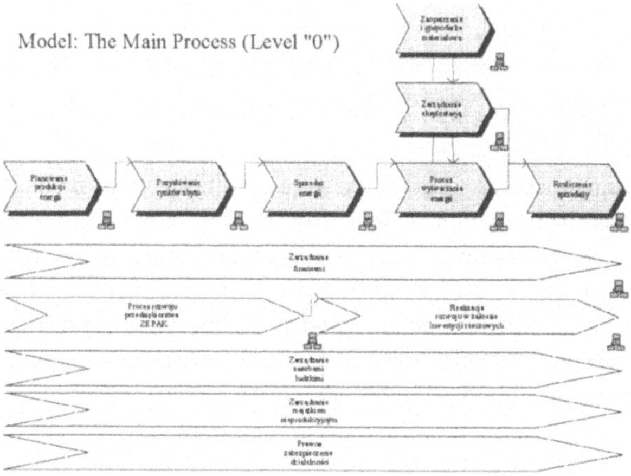

Figure 1: Basic and support processes at ZE PAK

The top-level process map for ZE PAK is depicted in figure 1. In the upper part, basic operating processes are portrayed. There are also two crucial support processes added, namely materials management and operations management. The lower part contains remaining support processes. Although it is not shown on the diagram, each process has its Owner defined, regardless whether it is a basic or a support process. Figure 2 portrays lower-level processes for the basic process of energy sales. Both pictures were created using ARIS software as Value Added Chain Diagrams (VACDs).

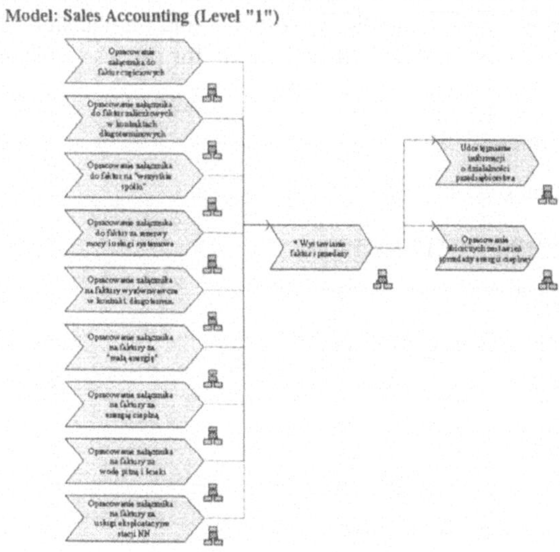

Figure 2: Subprocesses of the energy sales process

It must be emphasized that identification of key business processes within a company also constitutes a first step towards process-oriented quality management. It is the identification step that creates a basis for the development of the architecture of processes falling within the scope of the Quality System. The architecture is developed later via decomposition of each key business process down to the elementary level.

To model all relevant processes, interviews were conducted with managers from top and middle levels of management hierarchy, as well as with key employees. There were about 150 interviews, each lasting 1.25 hours on average. The resulting model consisted of almost 200 process maps, interrelated with the company's organizational structure chart. Apart from interviews, information was gathered from other sources, such as procedures and instructions, document flow descriptions, document forms and accounting records.

3.4 Process Analysis

In the fifth stage, all processes within their architecture were parametrized. For the purposes of quality management, relevant objectives, measures and target values were defined on the level of basic operating processes and allocated to Process Owners. Subsequently, the same elements were defined for support processes and all elementary processes. Elementary processes were also characterized with time and cost parameters, defined during interviews and consultations with employees and managers.

Analysis of processes covered execution effectiveness, their weak points and improvement potential. In particular, information on process paths, responsibilities, document flows, technology, software and on decision milestones was used as input to the analysis. As the main criteria for process evaluations, the following were used:

- Activity execution times
- Process execution times
- Coordination of activities and processes
- Communication aspects
- Organizational roadblocks in worklows
- Critical activities
- Activities without added value
- Task standardization
- Process outputs

- The length of control and decision cycles
- Automation of information transfer and processing
- Key competencies
- Requirements of the ISO 9000:2000 standards

The criteria above were used to identify sources of operating problems and errors, discontinuities and gaps in information flows, as well as other disfunctionalities. During the analysis of As-is process maps, attention was also paid to cases of extreme activity decomposition, redundancy of activities and implied data redundancy, the number of organizational units engaged in execution of the process and the number of applications used within the process. Process quality was also evaluated on the basis of comparisons between results of process execution and expectations of internal and external clients. The ISO 9000:2000 standards were of course also used as a process evaluation basis.

Apart from qualitative methods used during process analysis, ARIS tools were also applied to perform some fairly sophisticated quantitative analysis. ARIS simulation was used to calculate execution times and costs of key processes. Simulation functionality was also very useful in determining under-utilized resources and process bottlenecks, i.e. those resources which were over-utilized. Simulation results were presented as tables, reports and easy-to-understand graphical charts. Moreover, simulation coupled with process animation enabled participants to fully comprehend process dynamics. Additional conclusions were very useful during the conceptual design activities.

At the end of the stage, analysis results were used as the main input for development of improvement recommendations. The biggest improvement potential was seen in the reduction of process cycle times. In particular, activity wait times and information transfer times were seen as the primary reduction targets. In other words, recommendations concentrated on elimination of activities with little or no value added, as well as on the automation of many routine information-related tasks.

3.5 Process Visioning and Design

The sixth stage was devoted to the development of process visions and detailed To-be blueprints. As-is process maps, measurement system and improvement recommendations were used as input.

New process designs were created from two points of view, namely from a technological and a social one. From the technology point of view, IT and automation resources played a major role. For each process and task, technological resources were defined to support their efficient realization. Information flows, critical for the company, were also defined. This was followed by detailed rules for related document routing across the company. Part of a new process blueprint is shown in figure 3. The diagram was created as a classic extended Event-driven Process Chain (eEPC).

From the social point of view, a list of job positions was defined for all tasks within optimized processes. Using classical organizational design principles, job positions were grouped in a bottom-up manner into larger units. Using ARIS reports, responsibilities were defined for each job position automatically. Process Owners were also formally nominated at this stage. This completed development of the organizational infrastructure for business process management.

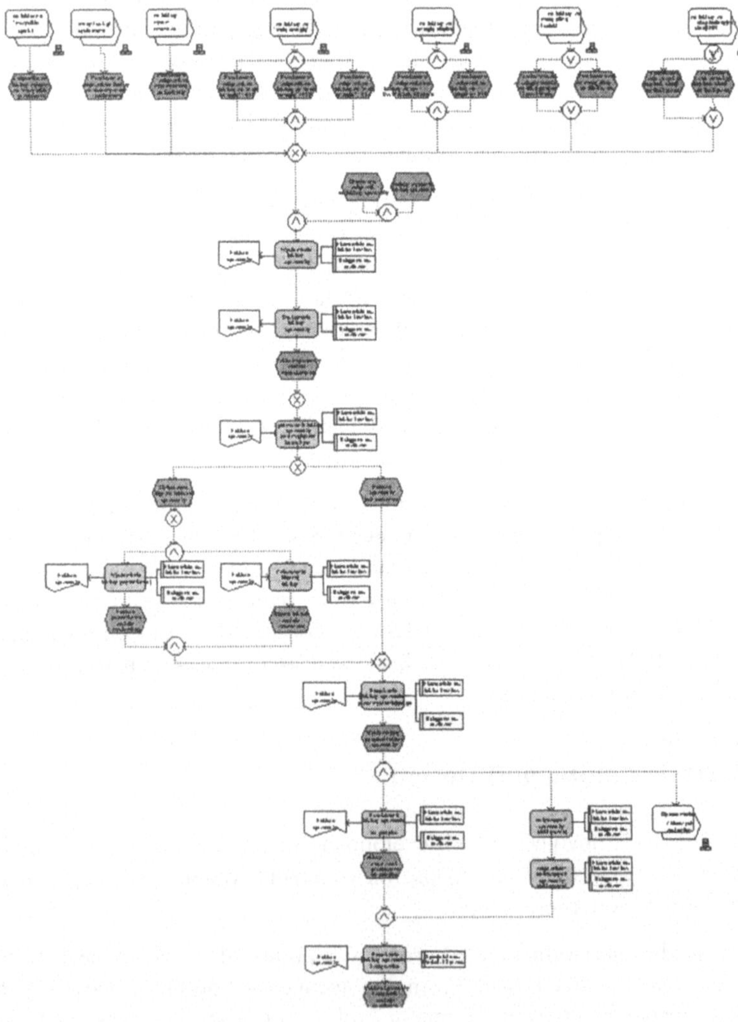

Figure 3: Part of a blueprint for an optimized invoicing process

3.6 Process Implementation

The final stage of the business process optimization project aimed at implementing To-be process blueprints. It must be emphasized that implementation efforts were of an organizational nature, since IT support was to be created in separate projects. Therefore, the implementation stage concentrated on new formal arrangements within ZE PAK. This covered changes in the organizational structure, as well as the development of new policies, regulations and descriptions of document flows.

Employees were trained on the new formal arrangements using To-be process maps, distributed via intranet. As it turned out, the decision to use this medium was fully justified. Employees were quick to comprehend new workflows and their role within the whole company. They were also able to appreciate relationships between the company's strategy and tasks performed. They were also able to see horizontal relationships between preceding and succeeding tasks, performed elswhere by other employees. As a result, employees at ZE PAK identified more with their tasks and performed them with a greater degree of responsibility.

4. ISO Project

4.1 Project Timetable

The final decision to start QMS development was made in May 1999. The subsequent milestones were as follows:

- In March 2000 implementation activities were started on the Quality Management System
- In January 2001 the Central Improvement System (CIS) was installed and started for company-wide use
- In March 2001 the first internal quality audit was performed
- In July 2001 the Certification Audit was performed by Bureau Veritas Quality International (BVQI), a certificate was granted as a result
- In September 2001 the certificate was handed over to ZE PAK during a formal ceremony

As already mentioned, the ISO project was correlated with the previous one. In particular, the CIS was used to distribute process knowledge throughout the company. At the same time, process maps within CIS were results of the Process

Visioning and Design stage, performed in the second half of 2000. The CIS was also vital in the Process Implementation stage. This is how consistency and continuity between those two projects was assured.

It must be noted that the role of the IDS Scheer Polska predecessor changed during the ISO project. During the optimization project, process analysts played a major role, along with participants from the company. In particular, between 4 and 6 consultants were involved in the project's activities at the company's site. During the ISO project, the number of consultants was decreased to two. Apart from this, the basic tasks of QMS implementation were performed by a specialized company, contracted separately by ZE PAK.

4.2 Major Project Activities

At the outset of the ISO project, a Director of Quality Systems was nominated and supporting job positions were filled. The Director of Quality Systems played a crucial role during the analysis of the existing system in terms of practices and procedures. It was found out that only 32.8% of the existing system fulfilled the requirements of the ISO/CD2 9001:2000 norm proposal.

Results of the analysis set the direction of implementation efforts. Internal auditors were selected and formally nominated. Design teams were created and trained. There was further training on quality topics, performed for the whole company. In particular:

- Basic training was performed for managers
- Specialized training was performed for internal auditors
- General training was performed for all employees

The training prepared the company for QMS design and internal audits. To ensure consistency with the process architecture, particular attention was paid to relationships between process maps and quality procedures during QMS design. The final Quality System documentation was created by applying the following steps:

- Development of the Quality Manual (description of the company and QMS as a whole, description of the Quality Policy and its objectives)
- Development of 31 Quality System procedures (describing who does what, when and why)
- Verification of all work instructions (what operations must be performed, in which situation, by whom and who is responsible for their result)

- Development of quality improvement programs (plans for achieving QMS objectives)
- Development of attachments and forms for quality records (what is recorded and where, also where are the records stored)

Prior to the Certification Audit, there were 38 internal quality audits performed. During those activities, 245 non-conformities with QMS were discovered, including:

- 52 critical non-conformities
- 103 major non-conformities
- 90 minor ones

4.3 The Central Improvement System

The most crucial result of the ISO project, apart from the certificate, is the improvement system. It is built around the Quality Manual published in the company's intranet. The electronic Quality Manual was created using ARIS repository, ARIS Web Publisher and customized scripts to enhance its layout and contents. All employees have access to CIS, regardless of what tasks they actually perform. There are many benefits of this kind of approach:

- Employees are actively involved in the company's development
- Employees are able to show their committment to change
- All crucial information is shared across the whole company
- Improvements are based on ideas of people who know process details, as well as what should and can be modified
- CIS promotes principles of Total Quality Management (TQM)

The structure and contents of CIS are shown on figures 4-7. Figure 4 portrays the main entry screen to the system while Figure 5 shows one of the lower-level menus. The main screen allows every ZE PAK employee to enter a description of the company's Quality System, a description of process architecture components, information on ISO standards and other quality issues, as well as on-line help. The sample menu screen shows all procedures within the product realization sector of ISO standards. Figure 6 shows the header of Vendor Evaluation procedure. It was generated via ARIS script using eEPC diagram attributes. The header contains such items as the procedure's objective, subject, scope, definitions and others. Finally, Figure 7 shows the graphical part of the procedure.

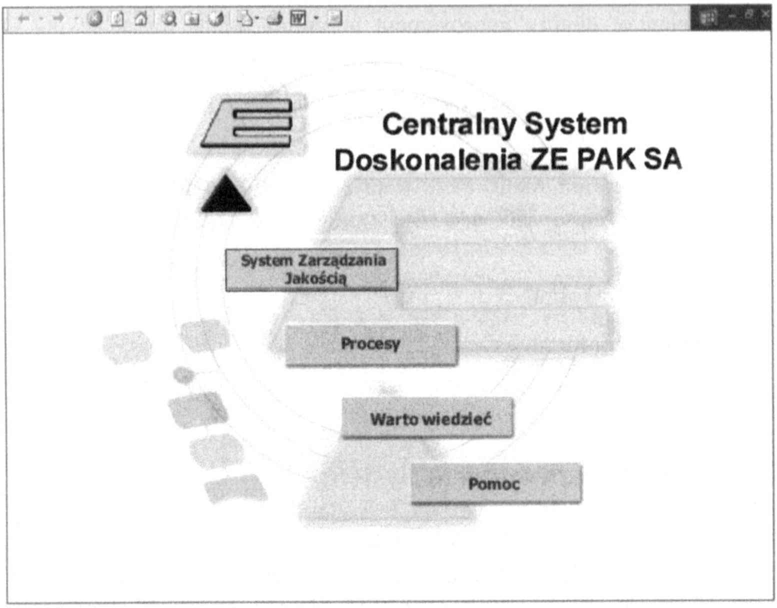

Figure 4: Top level menu of the Central Improvement System

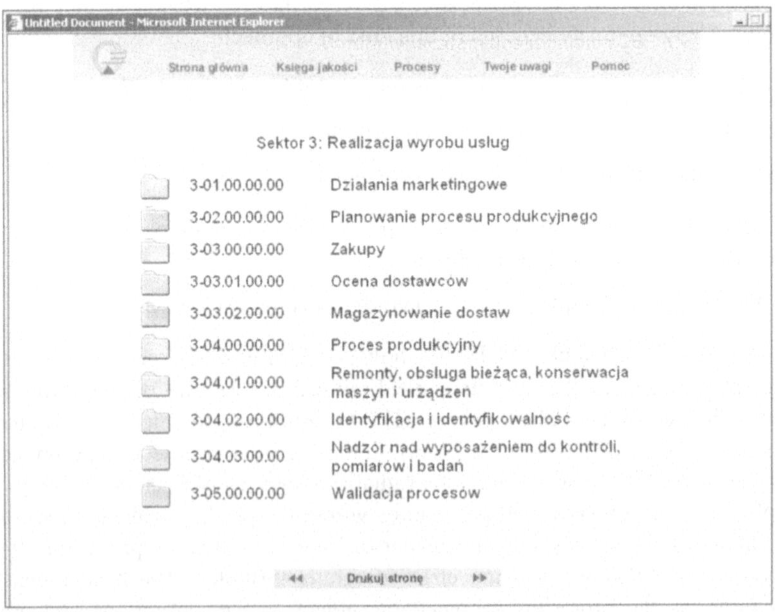

Figure 5: Lower level menu of the Central Improvement System

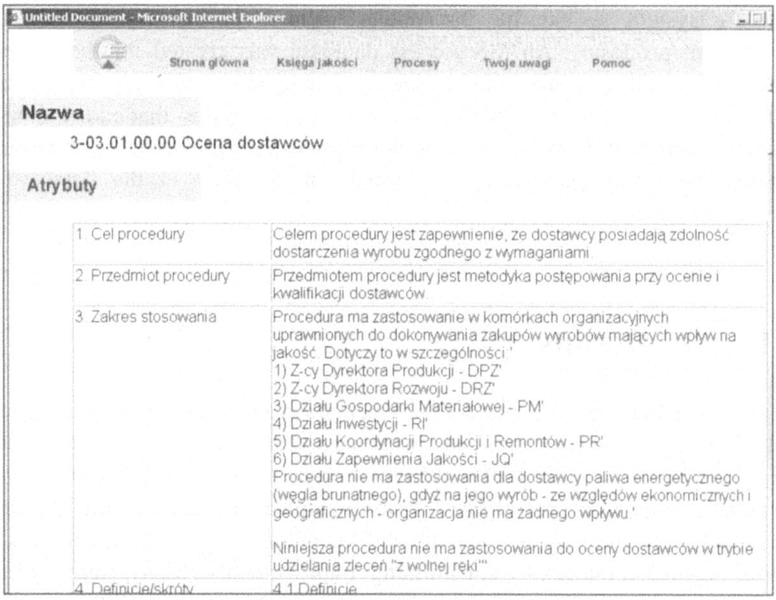
Untitled Document - Microsoft Internet Explorer

Strona główna | Księga jakości | Procesy | Twoje uwagi | Pomoc

Nazwa

3-03.01.00.00 Ocena dostawców

Atrybuty

1. Cel procedury	Celem procedury jest zapewnienie, że dostawcy posiadają zdolność dostarczenia wyrobu zgodnego z wymaganiami.
2. Przedmiot procedury	Przedmiotem procedury jest metodyka postępowania przy ocenie i kwalifikacji dostawców.
3. Zakres stosowania	Procedura ma zastosowanie w komórkach organizacyjnych uprawnionych do dokonywania zakupów wyrobów mających wpływ na jakość. Dotyczy to w szczególności:' 1) Z-cy Dyrektora Produkcji - DPZ' 2) Z-cy Dyrektora Rozwoju - DRZ' 3) Działu Gospodarki Materiałowej - PM' 4) Działu Inwestycji - RI' 5) Działu Koordynacji Produkcji i Remontów - PR' 6) Działu Zapewnienia Jakości - JQ' Procedura nie ma zastosowania dla dostawcy paliwa energetycznego (węgla brunatnego), gdyż na jego wyrób - ze względów ekonomicznych i geograficznych - organizacja nie ma żadnego wpływu.' Niniejsza procedura nie ma zastosowania do oceny dostawców w trybie udzielania zleceń "z wolnej ręki"'
4. Definicje/skróty	4.1 Definicje

Figure 6: Sample procedure header

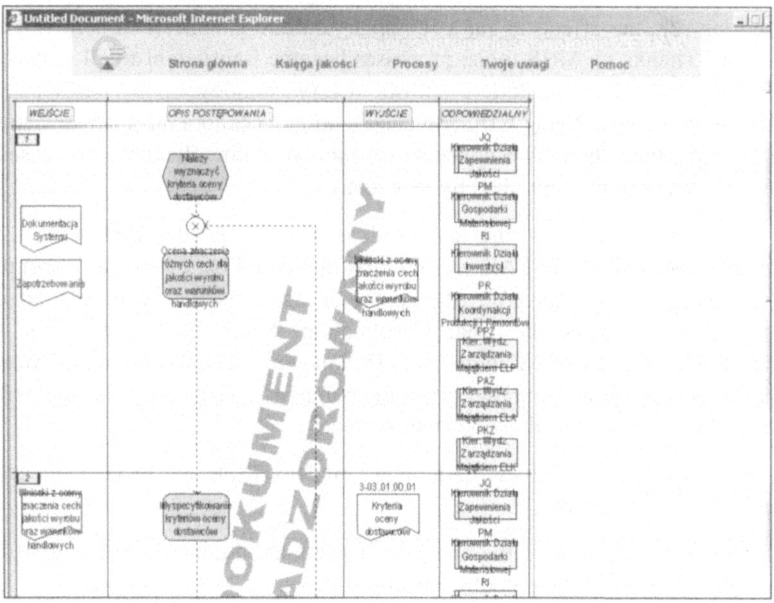

Figure 7: Sample procedure graphics

The CIS system would be incomplete without a mechanism to record improvement proposals. An MS Access database was created for that purpose. Within CIS, employees are able to enter and send via e-mail any improvement input to the system administrator. An Internet form is used to that end. It contains a process identification field, problem description and description of a proposed solution. Data from the form is recorded automatically in the database for querying and review.

5. Project Results

The results of both projects were a convincing success. The optimization project resulted in significant savings. In particular, yearly savings achieved due to implemented changes were higher than total project costs by a factor of over 2.5. The process maps also proved their value in another dimension, namely in cycle time reductions. For example, cycle time of the maintenance planning process was reduced by 40%, thanks to streamlining improvements. Many improvements, especially cost-related ones, were also introduced as a result of internal benchmarking.

In the long run, the effects as far as company culture is concerned are even more important. Thanks to ARIS tools, processes became transparent to all employees. Electronic ISO documentation allows every employee to participate in improvement efforts. Using CIS, company's employees look at processes and are able to implement their own concepts to improve them. Business processes are alive and are constantly enriched by new ideas.

The long-term effect was also achieved as a result of the ISO project. The certificate obtained by ZE PAK was the first one based on a new ISO norm in the Polish energy sector. Moreover, the approach taken resulted in a very effective Quality System. After the final Certification Audit, only one minor non-conformity was discovered in the whole company. The BVQI audit manager described this result as stunning, given the company's size and the complexity of QMS. Other results were also obtained, such as:

- An enhanced image of ZE PAK as a company using advanced management concepts and practices
- Better understanding of the company's goals among employees and stronger commitment toward their achievement
- Increased participation of employees in improvement efforts
- Better competitive position of the company
- Increased client orientation

- Better understanding of the customer's requirements
- Better risk management capabilities

6. Conclusions

It is generally accepted that classic re-engineering efforts sometimes produce significant results. However, the effects of such one-time projects usually disappear after 6-24 months or so, unless all management structures and systems are aligned to support business process performance.[2] In other words, cycle time and cost reductions will not last if processes are not managed and improved continuously afterwards. This in turn requires proper structures, roles, objectives, measures and incentives. However, effective business process management also requires changes in the company's values and beliefs. This last factor is perhaps the most important in the long term.

The business process optimization project at ZE PAK was a case of a classical re-engineering effort. It was based on process improvements - sometimes very radical - supported by a restructurization framework. During the project, formal elements required by business process management were created and institutionalized. However, they would not be effective without the follow-up ISO project. The second effort reinforced results of the first one and created a permanent process-oriented organizational culture of continuous improvement.

To summarize, the ZE PAK case shows that:

- Business process re-engineering concepts can be used successfully to reshape the company's operations and structures
- Another approach, rooted in quality movement, is needed to make permanent changes, especially cultural ones, required for effective business process management
- Without a sophisticated process modeling tool, development of a Quality Management System in larger companies is very difficult, if not impossible

The final remark deals with the relationship between the degree of formal change and top-management committment to implement it. All process-related projects in ZE PAK enjoyed a strong management support. Top-management backing is cited always as perhaps the most important success factor of any innovation project. However, this support cannot be taken for granted. Sometimes it can be traced to management beliefs and values. To a certain extent, that was also the case in ZE

[2]Paul King, "The Four Waves of Process Management", Orion Development Group, www.bettermanagement.com/library

PAK projects. However, the main reasons justifying radical changes lie usually outside the company. They belong to the competitive landscape and take the form of market pressures. The ZE PAK case illustrates this perfectly. Without outside factors, the need to radically restructure the company would not be felt. Without imperative restructurization, new process blueprints would not differ much from the pre-optimization situation. Without far-reaching changes in processes, optimization project results would be insignificant.

Process Design and Implementation with ARIS

Antonela Divić Mihaljević
Slovenica Insurance Company LTD

Summary

*The intention of this contribution is to present the business process modeling effort that was instituted in order to implement integrated information systems at SLOVENICA LTD Insurance Company (with and without ARIS e-business suite). The reasons for choosing the ARIS method, ARIS Toolset and ARIS Web Publisher are discussed, and are followed by an endorsement of ARIS business process excellence, which: *encourages standardization, *improves quality and rigor of process design, *encourages the use of a common process vocabulary, *allows multiple viewpoints, *provides analysis tools, *supports re-use, *aids validation, walk-through and testing, *is the starting point for the development of software systems, *provides ubiquitous access to all process users, *allows publishing via www, *facilitates feedback from end users and *gives us the opportunity to share knowledge. The ARIS method and modeling combined with the BPR technique is described briefly and illustrated with concrete practical examples of model structure, model types and hints, which have been used in AS-IS and TO-BE modeling of the reference model. The most important results achieved with ARIS are presented at the end of contribution together with lessons learned.*

Key Words

Slovenica's process modelling history, Why ARIS, SKOK project,Implementation of the Integrated Information System, Customer satisfaction, ARIS management, ARIS method, ARIS modelling, BPR & Top – down technical methodology, Document standardization, ARIS html models, Knowledge Management

1. Project Background

1.1 AS-IS Situation before the Project Started

1.1.1 General Information about Slovenica Ltd

SLOVENICA Insurance Company Ltd. [1] Ljubljana, is a modern, medium-sized general insurance company with its headquarters in Ljubljana and with a sales network all over Slovenia. Slovenica is the only general insurance company in Slovenia that is completely owned by Slovenian shareholders.

Names of SLOVENICA's shareholders	**%Share**
KD Holding d.d., Celovška cesta 206, Ljubljana	79.69%
ID KD d.d., Celovška cesta 206	14.95 %
KD Investments d.d., Celovška cesta 206,Ljubljana	2.10%
Zadružna banka, d.d., Miklošičeva 4, Ljubljana	1.77%
Other shareholders	1.50%
Together	**100%**

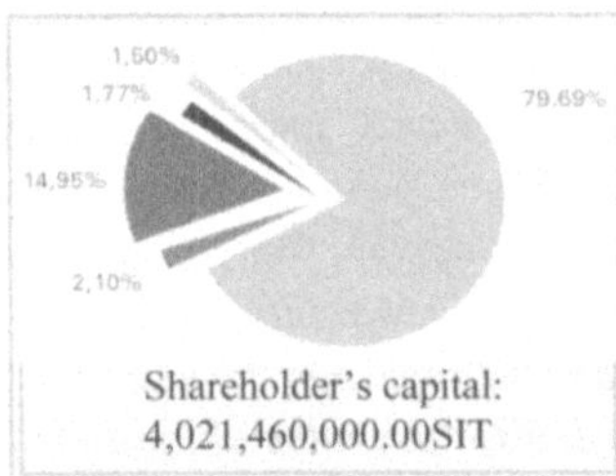

Figure 1: Names and participation of Slovenica's shareholders

The date of Slovenica's registration was 24th December 1992, immediately after Slovenia's independence. But the beginnings of SLOVENICA are connected with the biggest Croatian insurance company CROATIA Ltd[2], founded in 1884. Last year was the 100th anniversary of Slovenian insurance and on that occasion, Slovenica was proud of the original insurance policy from 1907. Slovenica's share capital is SIT 4,021,460 thousand (€18,021,140). The number of shareholders was 143 on 31st December 2001. Organizational units include: head office in Ljubljana with the Board of Management (president plus 2 members), the Supervisory Board (president plus 9 members), 4 representative offices, 4 regional offices and 15 local offices with a total of 370 employees. In fiscal year 2000, Slovenica's gross written premium climbed to SIT 8,844,000 thousand (€39,641,416). Compared to 1999, this was an 18.8% nominal growth in gross written premium.

---

[1]www.slovenica.si
[2]www.crosig.hr

1.1.2 Process Modeling History at Slovenica Ltd before ARIS[3]

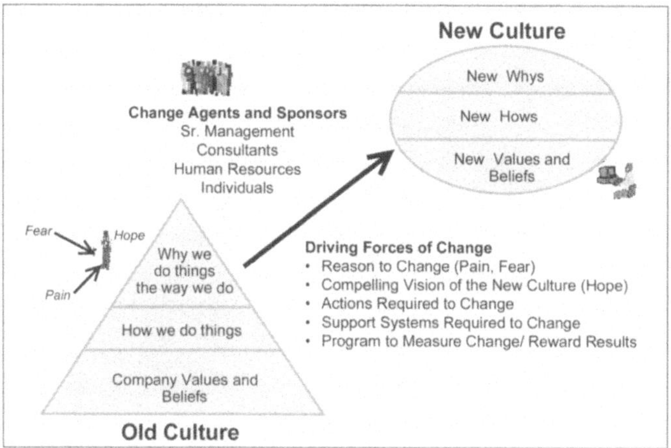

Figure 2: Managing change. Source: Gartner Group

Change is the only constant in our dynamic world and it produced pressure on the business processes. Therefore Slovenica had a strong need for managing change. The aim was not only to graphically present business processes, but also to support them thoroughly with an appropriate IT[4] solution. BPR[5] was the right way to achieve Slovenica's goals.

Since its foundation in 1992 Slovenica's IT experts have been looking for the right tool. In the past Slovenica looked at various BPR and CASE[6] tools thought to be compatible with its requirements.

From the beginning of the 1990s until 1999, Slovenica had experience with:

- ABC Flow charts (1992),
- Visio Business Modeler (1993),
- BP win and ER win[7] (1995).

In 1995 Slovenica's expert team started the Business Process Design project.

---

[3]**ARIS** – Architecture of Integrated Information Systems, the name ARIS is a registered trademark of IDS Scheer AG
[4]**IT** – Information Technology
[5]**BPR** – Business Process Reengineering
[6]**CASE** – Computer Aided Software Engineering
[7]**BP win (Case tool)** delivers new methods and diagrams, freeform graphics, a customizable dictionary, and new reporting and document generation. **ER win (Case Tool)** provides the ability to model data in the organization in relationship to other layers of design, such as exists between applications and data warehouses. Source: Slovenica's MV Project Documentation, Ljubljana, Pris Counsulting, 1995, www.pris.si

The result of that project was the MV-program application on the Oracle platform ,for supporting the insurance of motor vehicles. This partial application has been produced since 1996.

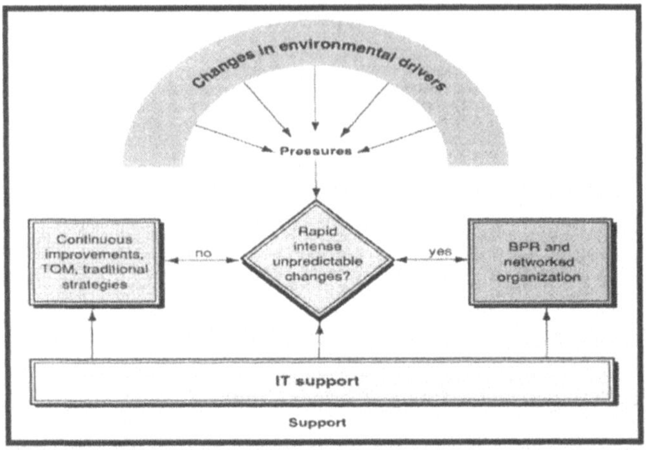

Figure 3: The IT support process

The MV Project was based on the IDEF[8] method combined with BP win and ER win. IDEF methodology provides a way to manage and communicate during every design and implementation step.

IDEF methodology improves the business process:

- Models the current process ("As Is"),
- Models the future process ("To Be""),
- Plans migration from current to future
- Investigates feasibility of process changes,
- Re-engineers the process (if necessary).

[8]**IDEF**-Integrated Computer Aided Manufacturing Definition, the IDEF method is developed in the USA with the purpose of documentation for the Ministry of Defense. Its predecessor SADT has been in use in the U.S., Europe, Australia and Japan for over twenty years. It is the most complete and fully tested system of methods for the design and description of complex systems, projects or enterprises available today. ISBN: 0- 9638750-0-0 Publisher: Eclectic Solutions; References: Jayachandra, Y., Re-Engineering the Networked Enterprise, McGraw-Hill; 1994

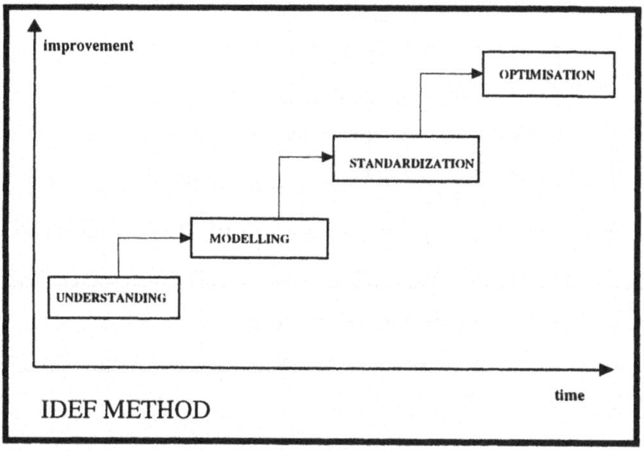

Figure 4: The IDEF method phase diagram

IDEF methodology enables:

- Understanding
- Modeling
- Standardization
- Optimization

Tools and methods that had been in use before ARIS produced only partial solutions which did not provide the expected level of satisfaction. So Slovenica continued its search for the 'right' tool.

1.1.3 Why and How ARIS 'Happened' to Slovenica Ltd.

In fiscal 1999, Slovenica's gross written premium climbed to SIT 7,442,774 thousands (€33,360,708). Compared to 1998, this represented a 22.4 % nominal growth in gross written premium. No other big general insurance company in the Slovenian insurance market achieved this growth during that fiscal year. The nominal growth of gross written premium in the field of non-life insurance was 23.4% and 16.4% in the field of life assurance.

1999 was a significant year not only from the financial point of view. This was the year when Slovenica's Board of Management decided to build an integrated **Information System**. The main document of the future 'SKOK' program (engl. 'JUMP') was established.

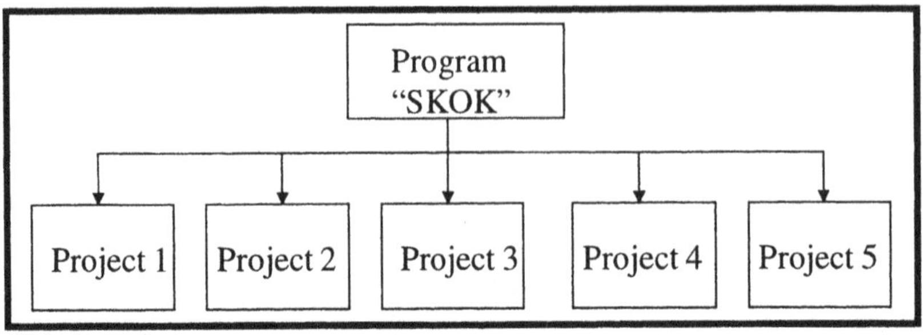

Figure 5: Project structure in the SKOK program

As a result of several years of analysis, research and planning, Slovenica's expert team presented the program's frame with:

- Strategy
- Objectives
- Organizational structure
- A network diagram of the products
- Presentation
- Deadlines
- Supervision
- Responsibilities
- Human and tool resources
- Potential of external partners
- Financial plans
- Risk measurement
- Conclusions
- Appendix.

The 'SKOK' program with its several sub-projects is still on-going. Various IT tools and programs were/are needed for the realization of that program. It was not always easy to make the right decision. It seemed to be easy to select a proper database platform and programming language, CASE tools, BPR tools, project management tools, etc.

Considering the fact that Slovenica's existing database was originally based on Oracle[9] it was logical to choose Oracle products for supporting the core business

[9]ORACLE www.oracle.com

processes. This is why Oracle products were chosen for the implementation phase. Decision making in support of subsidiary processes was a little bit harder. At the beginning it was decided to support them with SAP (SAP/R3[10]). This solution is still active or rather it has not been completely abandoned.

The possibility of the SAP option for supporting subsidiary processes was the main reason for choosing the ARIS Toolset for the BPR phase. On the other hand there was an ARIS competitor for the BPR phase. It was a BPR tool by PROMATIS Informatik named INCOME 3.3[11].

INCOME has offered Process Modeler, Simulator and Discoverer. It was supporting a way to design, analyze, and optimize processes on the Oracle database platform. Because of the BPR characteristics mentioned and a close connection with Oracle, INCOME became a very interesting tool from Slovenica's point of view. From the financial point of view it would have been more reasonable to accept Promatis' offer. Today we are all very happy that ARIS 'happened' to Slovenica. ARIS' quality is confirmed worldwide. The list of BPR tools and methods that are available on the IT market is becoming longer and longer every day. This is why thousands of organizations are looking for confirmation of the selected solution by using the service of independent market research companies. Analysts from the American market research company Gartner Group[12] have confirmed the leading international role of IDS Scheer[13] products for the year 2001. According to their analysis, IDS Scheer is the international market leader and visionary in the area of software for business process management for the fourth consecutive time. It is true that Slovenica comes from Slovenia, which is a small European country in transition, but it has the ability to follow world trends and quality standards of information technology.

Slovenica chose the ARIS method, ARIS Toolset and ARIS Web Publisher.

Therefore we are proud to present Aris Business process excellence because in our experience it:

- Encourages standardization
- Improves the quality and rigor of process design
- Encourages the use of a common process vocabulary

---

[10]SAP/R3 Enterprise Resource Planning (ERP) Systems

[11]INCOME BPR Tool by PROMATIS Informatik GMBh&Co, Desco Str.10, Karlsbad, Germany, www.promatis.de; Promatis Solution Provider and Partner in Slovenia: www.maop.si ;

[12]Gartner Group was founded in 1979. With more than 20 years' experience in identifying and analyzing the trends and technologies that have shaped the course of business, Gartner, Inc. (NYSE: IT and ITB) provides unrivaled thought leadership and strategic consulting services to more than 11,000 organizations world-wide. www.gartner.com.

[13]www.ids-scheer.de

- Allows multiple viewpoints
- Provides analysis tools
- Supports re-use
- Aids validation, walk-through and testing
- Is the starting point for the development of software systems
- Provides ubiquitous access to all process users
- Allows publishing via www
- Facilitates feedback from end users and
- Gives us the opportunity to share knowledge

1.2 Motivation for the Project

The 'SKOK' program was divided into several phases. All phases did not start at the same time and the motivation for the project varied.

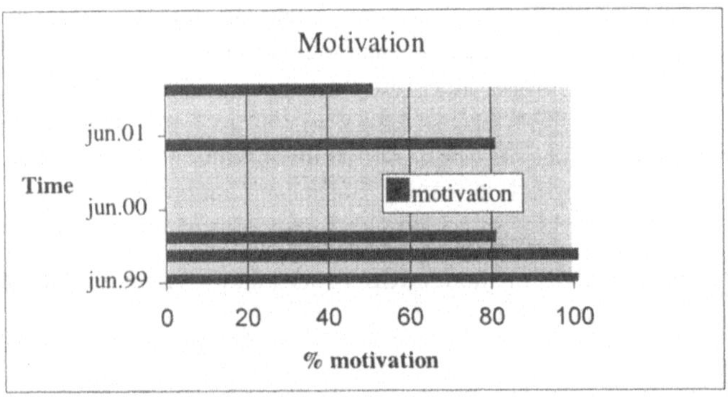

Figure 6: Motivation for the project

One of the most important aspects of the projects was that the 'SKOK' program was completely supported by the Board of Management. All members of the ARIS team had full management support to take part in a project. Team members were/are Slovenica's full time employees. Time was divided into 50% of regular working time and 50% extra time on the project with a motivational bonus. That was the first of three main prerequisite conditions for the project's success:

- Company support
- ARIS knowledge
- Teamwork

The working atmosphere was/is positive and productive. Program management was/is provided by MS Project and MS Project Central.

One of the negative facts was a Slovenica business merger process with another insurance company (Adriatic Insurance Company Ltd[14]) which was intended to be executed in all segments of operations. Unfortunately, the merger is at a standstill. The final result is not yet known. Slovenica is continuing the program, but enthusiasm for the on-going project has been waning. The main objectives are not questioned.

2. Goals - Major Business Goals

2.1 Mission and Vision of Slovenica

The mission of Slovenica is to provide the customer with insured safety. For the realization of that mission, Slovenica still supports the 'SKOK' program with a major goal which is: **Implementation of the Integrated Information System**. 'SKOK' is still an on-going project and it should result in better security, better services and a more competitive position.

DATA +	MEDIA =	MARKET PROCESS ⇨	CRM
*database *data warehouse *data mining *neural networking *scorecards	*internet *voice response *call center *intranet *extranet *interactive TV	*1-to-1 marketing, *micro marketing *database marketing *e-commerce *interactive marketing	*customer satisfaction *customer share *customer loyalty *customer retention *customer value *customer profitability

Figure 7: CRM – The result of the new market era

The vision of Slovenica:

- Customer satisfaction
- Owners'/shareholders' satisfaction
- Employees' satisfaction.

---

[14]ADRIATIC Insurance Company Ltd; www.adriatic.si

Slovenica has a clear mission and vision which is defined by a system of values of the new market era. The result of the new market era[15] is CRM.

Slovenica's plan is to improve business operations even further to increase its presence in the market, to rationalize processes within the company and above all, to continue to offer reliable insurance services of good quality.

2.2 Fundamental and Main Goals Documented with ARIS

For the documentation of business goals, ARIS Objective Diagrams were used. The main Objective Diagram consists of four sub-models defined with objectives, basic functions, and critical factors of success. Slovenica's main goals:

- Improved market position and acquisition of a larger market share
- Improved portfolio quality
- Improved financial strength and increased profit
- Realization of the 'SKOK' program

2.2 Example of the ARIS Objective Diagram

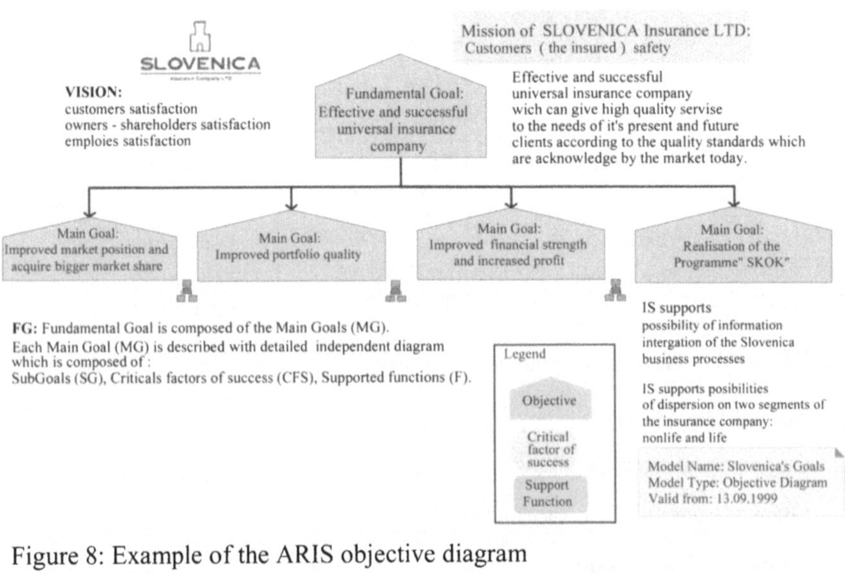

Figure 8: Example of the ARIS objective diagram

[15]Paul Postma: The New Marketing Era , Cap Gemini Ernst&Young Nederland B.V.

3. Procedure

3.1 ARIS Project Management and Responsibilities

ARIS Project Management was/is under the manager of the 'SKOK' program. Business process analyst and organizational expert were/are in charge of ARIS from the practical, technical and organizational point of view during AS-IS and TO-BE modeling. The team of ARIS users was/is made up of the technical experts who were responsible for the different business groups.

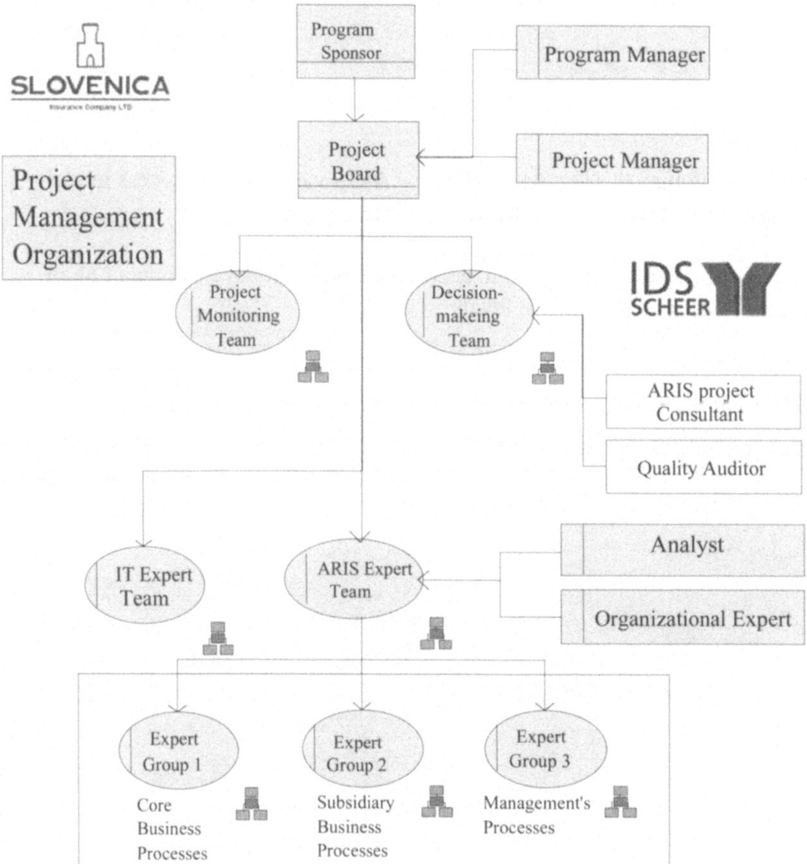

Figure 9: ARIS Project Management organization chart

3.2 Usage of ARIS Method

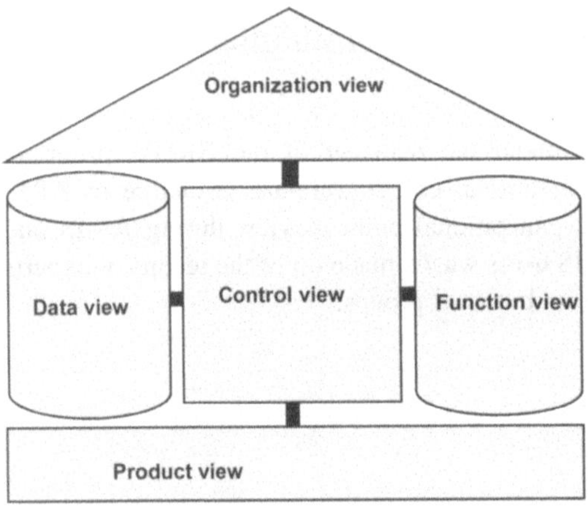

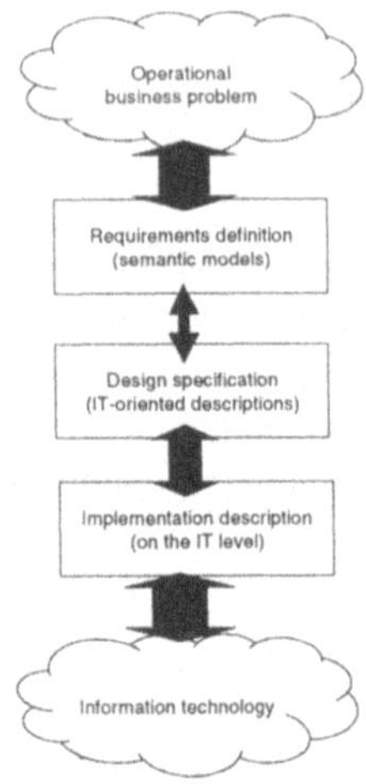

Figure 10 and Figure 11: The ARIS House – ARIS views of the process model (left); Descriptive levels of an information system (right)

ARIS resources view is structured in accordance with a lifecycle concept of an information system's descriptive levels.

The ARIS method defines three main levels:

- The requirements definition level
- The design specification level
- The implementation description level

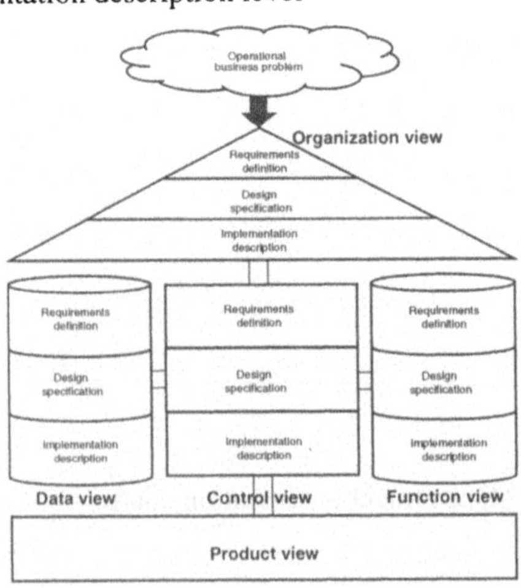

Figure 12: ARIS architecture

When designing of the AS-IS reference business process model, Slovenica used **the requirements definition level**. The organizational view gave Slovenica's organizational structure AS-IS today. In the TO-BE reference model, a generic organizational structure was produced.

The TO-BE reference model used all three levels. During the modeling of the business processes a frontal approach (which included in the process all Company activities on all levels of functionality) was used. A snapshot of the AS-IS processes was made in 4 months (June to October 1999). This focused on all business processes and not only on the processes chosen for IT support/implementation.

The team of experts was divided into three groups:

- First for modeling Core Business processes
- Second for modeling Subsidiary Business processes
- Third for modeling Management Business processes

On 13th October 1999 a presentation was made of the final version of the AS-IS reference model. The analyzing phase started immediately after the presentation but was interrupted because of the business merger with another insurance Company (Adriatic Ltd[16]). The initial plan was changed. The analysis phase of the AS-IS models was stopped because Adriatic had its own AS-IS model - also made with ARIS - and it was impossible to have two reference points for the one model. The project plan was revised during November and December 1999. Finally, TO-BE modeling together with Adriatic's expert team started in January 2000 and the first edition of the TO-BE reference model for the newly- merged insurance company was issued and presented on 13th April 2000.

Several basic and more technical conditions had to be fulfilled before the process modeling with ARIS could be started:

- Administration and set-up
- Training of users (ARIS Training 1st - 3rd June 1999)
- Processing of the conventions manual (June-October 1999)
- Definition of the database structure and permissions (June 1999)
- Processing of the timetable for the usage of the three hard keys shared inside the group of 12 team members (June 1999)

The conventions manual was processed for setting standards and the vocabulary.

HR and tools limitation:

- 12 ARIS users (team members-HR)

---

[16]Adriatic Insurance Company Ltd, www.adriatic.si

- 3 hard keys (software/hardware limitation)
- one ARIS room (working space limitation)
- 50% usage of working time for work on the project

Practical hints:

- Regular 'brainstorming' in the ARIS project room
- Direct modeling with ARIS
- On-line writing of the process technology description in the WORD template
- Regular record keeping of the meeting and the attendance list
- Technical support by LCD OHP presentation

Templates for the written technology description were specially formulated for that occasion and look like the following example.

Process		A.1.
Sub process/ function	Processing Cargo contract	A.1.1.
Position	Claims referent	
Organisational unit	Claims Department	

Input

Document	Document source	Document mark	Actual mark
Claims form	Claims Department	A.1.1.-I.1.0.	P-SDO-SXX-00 P-SDO-SS1-00

Target objective

Fulfilling the claim form.

Defining players

1. Sales Department
2. Claims Department
3. Archivist
4. Claims referent

Process description

Claims referent fulfilled the Claims form considering a given data. Program gives him opportunity to archive the fulfilled Claim form and allows him to forward a document to the Archivist who has a permission to archive the documentation with change of it's status from N-not completed to C-Completed.

Notes

Archivist is the only person with a permission to operate with archive.

Business Rules

Documents in the archive have a special mark on the form to indicate their status...

Output

Document	Receiver of the document	Document mark	Actual mark
Delivery Confirmation form	Claims Department Archivist	A.1.1-O.1.0.	P-SDO-014-00

Evaluation

Number of the operations per hour/day/week/month	1/10/55/220
Duration of the function	10 minutes
Waiting time:	1 month
Other costs	

Organisational unite:	Author:	Date:
Regional office Kranj	Janez Janez	2001-07-12

Figure 13: Example of the template created for the written technology process description

Comment on the template:

Business process written description was done in parallel with ARIS modeling and was linked to the basic functions such as external documents. Other external documents that have been linked as input/output on the object within the ARIS models are:

- MS Word
- MS Excel documents and
- Scanned images in bmp format

ARIS model types used in AS-IS and TO-BE modeling are:

- VACD-value added chain diagram
- FT-function tree
- eEPC- event-driven process chain diagram
- Organizational charts
- FAD-Function allocation diagrams
- Objectives diagram
- Office processes
- eERM diagram
- Class diagram

The most frequently used type of ARIS model was the event-driven process chain diagram – eEPC. During modeling, the main focus was on processes and not on data models, and this is why the number of eERM diagrams in our example is rather small. The following examples illustrate Slovenica's goals with the use of eERM diagrams:

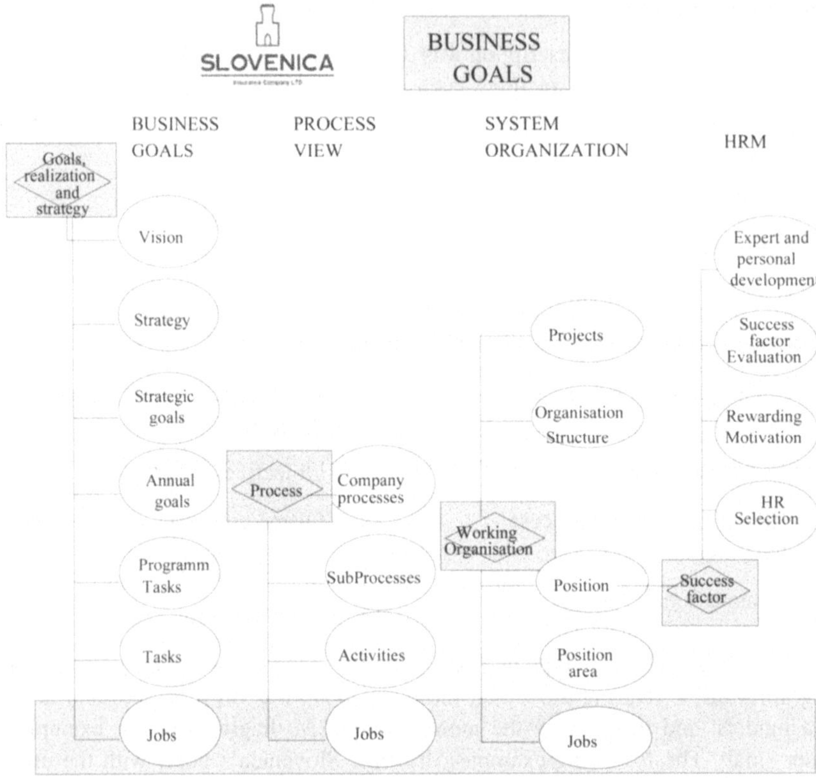

Figure 14: Business goals presented with the eERM diagram

The importance of Integrated Company Factors was illustrated by the eERM diagram.

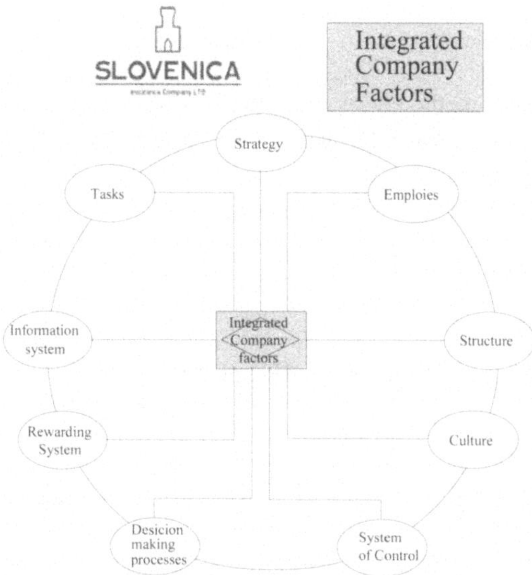

Figure 15: Integrated company factors presented with the eERM diagram

Thinking and acting during the program is defined in the **Deming Cycle.**

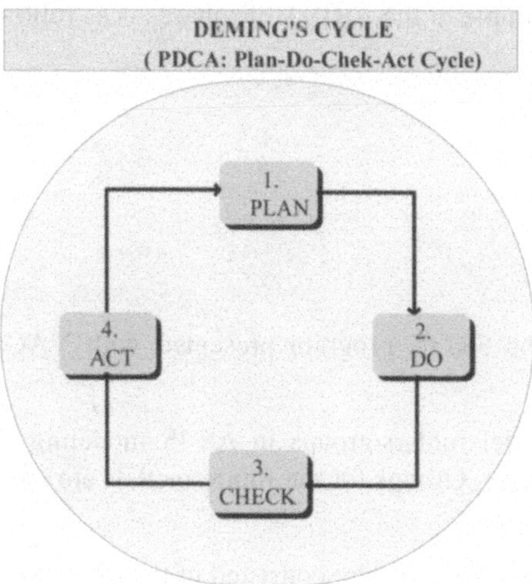

Figure 16: Deming Cycle presented with the function tree diagram

3.3 Use of Procedural Models

3.3.1 AS-IS Modeling

Top – down technical methodology was performed during business process modeling and it produced the expected results. Three basic steps were done chronologically:

- AS-IS modeling
- Analysis phase and
- TO-BE modeling

This is a theoretical example of the ARIS BPR phases.

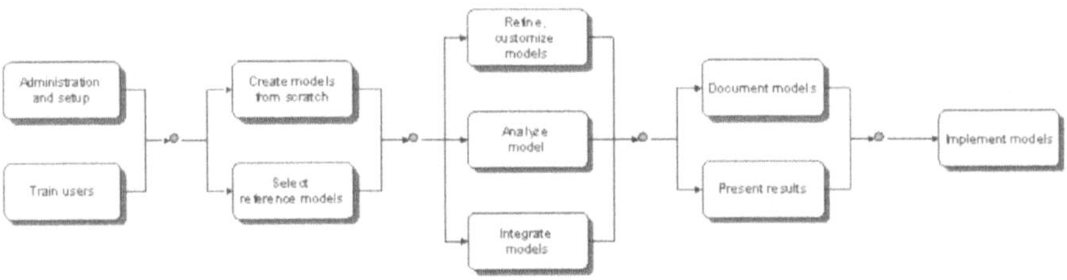

Figure 17: Theoretical example of the ARIS BPR phases

Slovenica's practical example of the ARIS BPR phases is as follows:

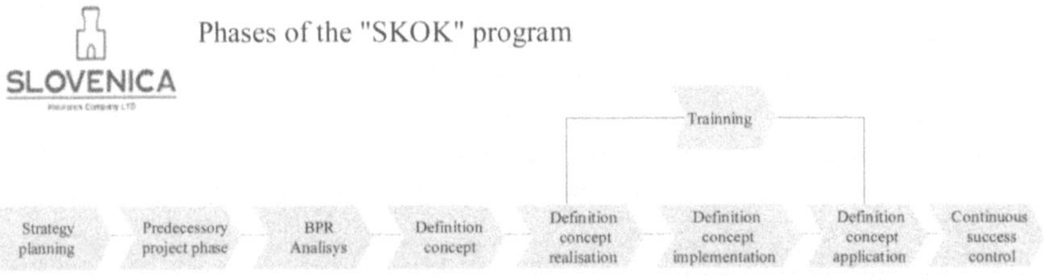

Figure 18: Phases of the SKOK program presented with VACD (value added chain diagram)

The structure of the model folders/groups in AS-IS modeling was done before modeling in the setup phase. Groups for the future models are named according to the contents.

A general reference model AS-IS folder consisted of the overview models valid for all kinds of insurance products.

Aberrations of the reference model for individual insurance products were processed as variants of the general reference model and saved in separate groups (folders) with the name of the target insurance product.

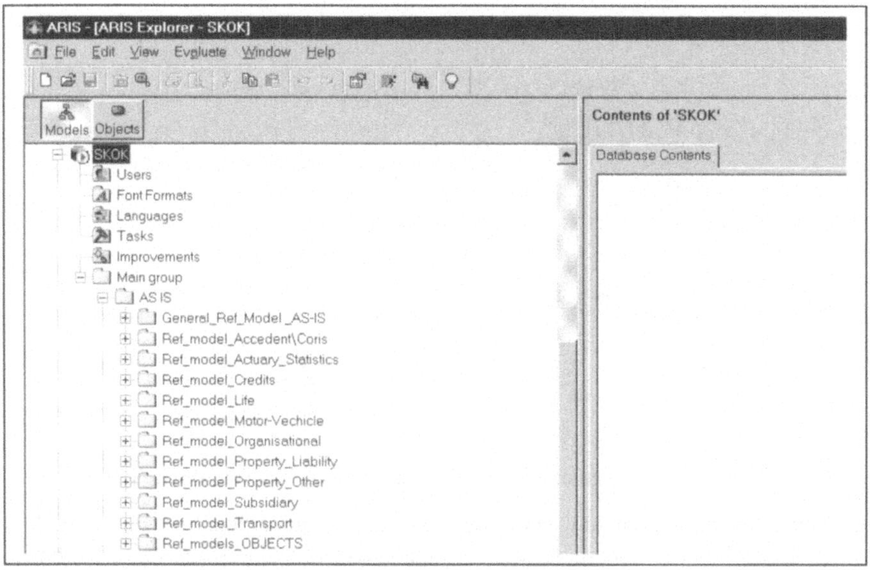

Figure 19: Example of the model organization structure in the AS-IS model

TOP model of the AS-IS reference model is the company overview model:

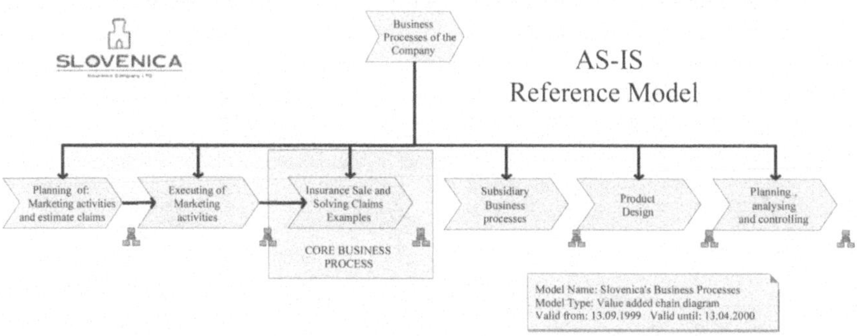

Figure 20: Company overview (AS-IS reference model)

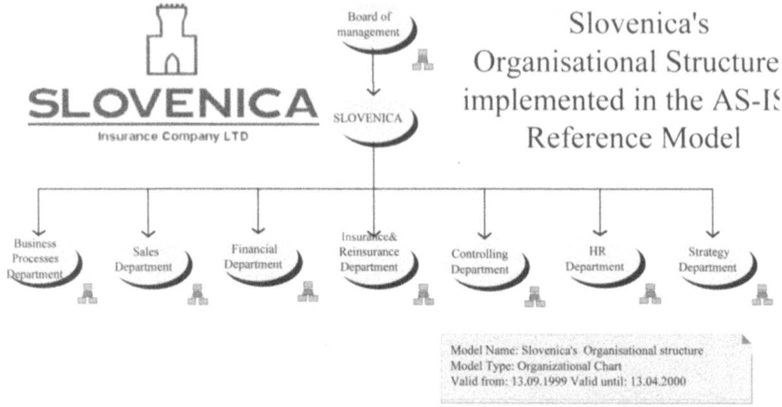

Figure 21: Slovenica's organizational structure overview (organizational chart)

The core business company was illustrated by the main function tree with the external MS WORD document which contains a technical description of the basic functions and input/output documents saved as images in bmp format. The number of collected and linked external documents was 1670. All input/output documents were saved in bmp format and linked to the basic functions. Documents were linked to the following objects: cluster, entity type and information carrier. The number of processed models is 188.

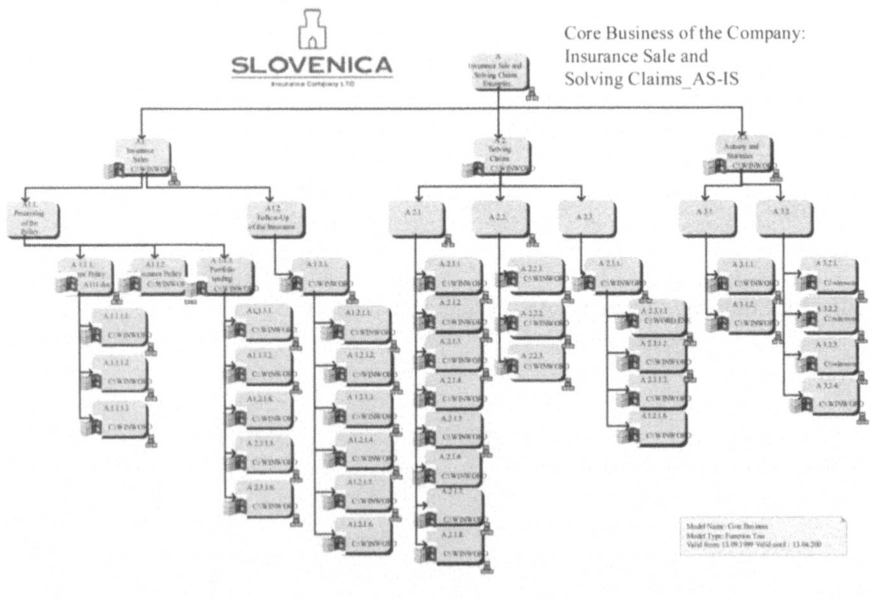

Figure 22: Core business company function diagram (function tree)

The core business company was illustrated by the main function tree with the technical description of the basic functions in MS WORD external documents in scanned input/output documents.

3.3.2 TO-BE Modeling

The structure of the model folders/groups in TO-BE modeling was set up before modeling. Groups for the future models are named according to contents.

For example, all Core Business models are in the same group. This was done to provide a better overview.

Each group has three main subgroups in the following order:

- Overview models
- Detail models and
- Fine models

An example is shown in the illustration below.

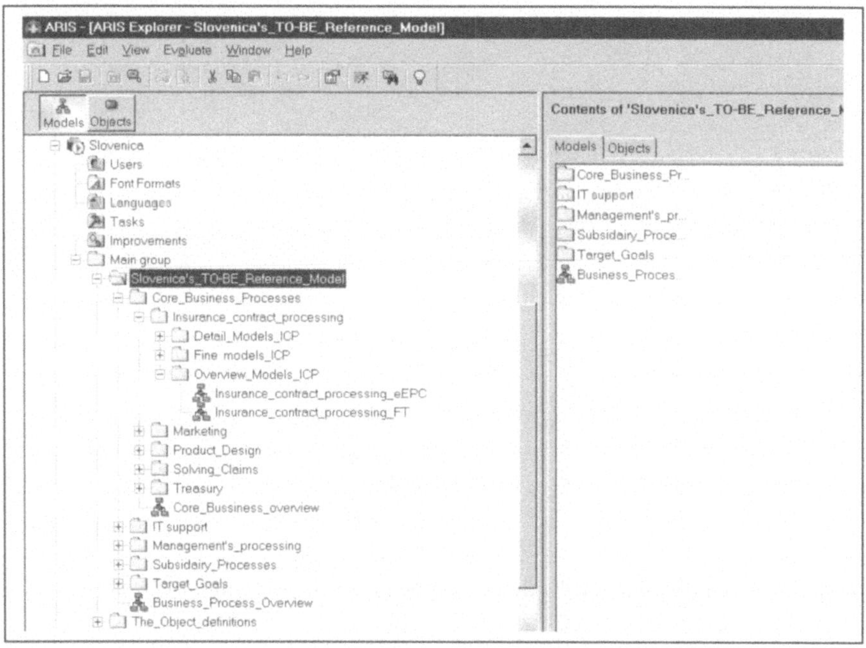

Figure 23: Structure of the model folders / groups in TO-BE modeling

External documents linked to objects of TO-BE models are all in Word or Excel format because we did the standardization of all documents needed for the core business processes. The number of linked external documents is about 200. The number of Word and Excel description documents is 154.

Standard ARIS model types were also used in TO-BE modeling. This means that the most numerous ones were also eEPC models, as they were in AS-IS modeling. Each new version of the ARIS Toolset offered something new. So while carrying out TO-BE modeling, we were using ARIS Toolset 4.11, which offered models of the office process type. Results of the office process usage were very satisfactory. This is a very good way to present business processes to a wider public (external partners, non-ARIS users, etc.). A parallel example of the eEPC and office process model:

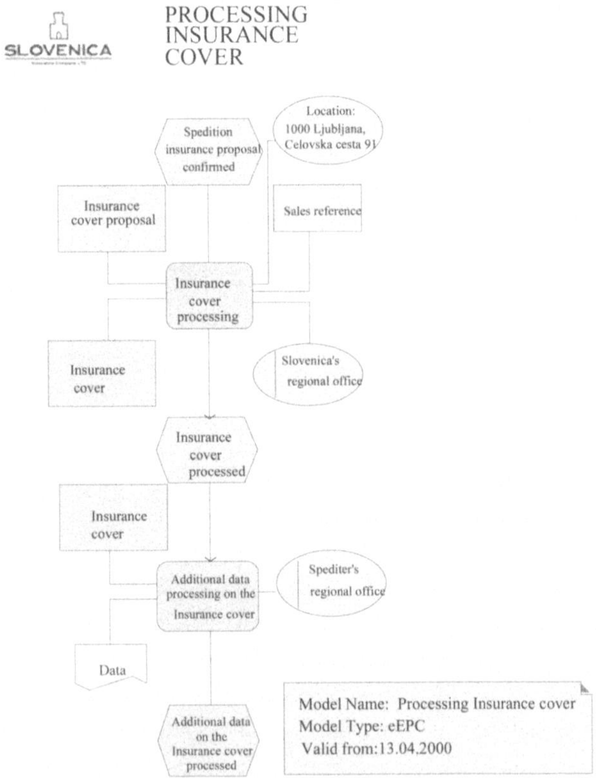

Figure 24: Example of an eEPC diagram type for the processing insurance cover

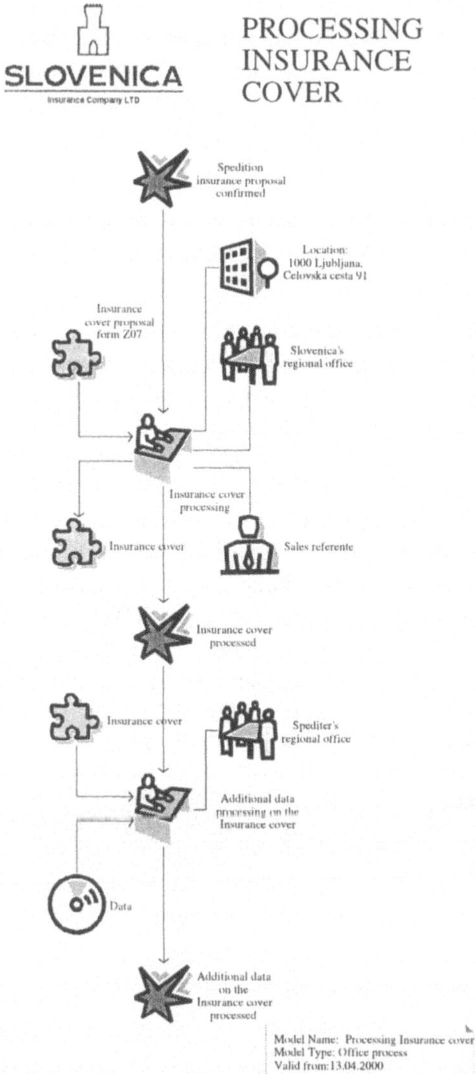

Figure 25: Example of the office process diagram type for the processing insurance cover

3.3.3 Specific Use of ARIS

With ARIS 4.11, Slovenica's models gained another new functionality. The new ARIS product Web Publisher as an add-on to ARIS Toolset offers the oportunity to generate html export of ARIS models. This enables efficient distribution of information and knowledge management.

ARIS Web Publisher supports efforts to communicate Slovenica's process models quickly and globally via the Internet. Its Web-based interface leads to a quick understanding and acceptance of basic information and is extremely cost-effective. Temporal and spatial constraints regarding the distribution of information are eliminated.

Exported models of the business processes are published on Slovenica's local network. In this way we are able to get a direct response from all team members working on the 'SKOK' program.

As a result of its program activities Slovenica is issuing versions of the information technology description for the project's external partners archived on CD-ROM. Functions chosen for IT support (information) are marked in Aris models of the function-tree type. Each function of the function-tree is described in detail with linked and customized Word and Excel templates and also catalogs of the input/output data sorted into Excel worksheets. The information (IT supporting/IT implementation) project is still an ongoing process. Fourteen revisions were made from a first version of the TO-BE reference model between April 2000 and February 2002. While issuing a version of the technology documentation, each version is saved on a CD-ROM or DVD and printed on paper. Archives are kept separately in secure storage. Revisions of the technology descriptions are done periodically. To date, we have issued numerous versions of the information technology description. The information technology description also contains a version of ARIS models in HTML format.

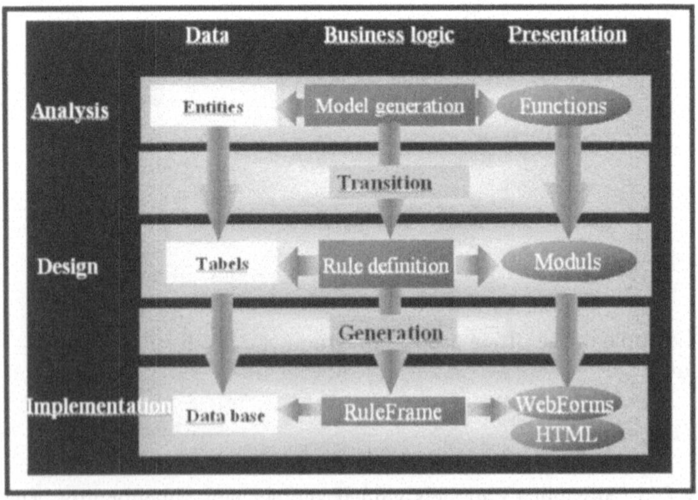

Figure 26: Business process modeling with CASE tools

3.3.4 Use of Consultants

Since the start of the program in 1999, Slovenica has been supported by IDS Slovenia[1] consultants who have provided:

- Training
- Consulting
- Technical support

Slovenica's group of ARIS users was/is small and has not exceeded 12 members. IDS's support and service was/is reliable, qualified and on time.

4. Results

4.1 Results Achieved

- For the first time in history, Slovenica has all business processes centralized and integrated in a single ARIS database
- All input and output documents of the functions in the reference models have been collected and linked as external documents
- Slovenica's business process model is a good starting point for eventual quality certification
- Export of Slovenica's html models is set and available on the internal network for all team members for the purpose of knowledge management
- Export of Slovenica's html models is used for several presentations to external partners. The last of these resulted in Slovenica's new Website. All the calculations for insurance proposals are done with the help of ARIS models exported into html format that have been handed over on DVD-ROM. This is the best example of the way ARIS works in practice
- Export of Slovenica's html models is used for internal training, introducing new employees to the company and sharing knowledge
- Html usage is also valuable during product design

---

[1]IDS Slovenia, www.ids-scheer.si; www.ids-scheer.de

4.2 Are the Results Consistent with the Defined Goals?

Slovenica's program is an on-going process. The result of a review of the defined goals is that the main objective - building the Integrated Information System has not yet been realized. This phase is now in the hands of Slovenica's external partners and the ARIS project team is less involved in that phase. We did not perform the optimization of processes but prepared them for IT implementation. All other phases that were predicted by the ARIS project have been successfully performed.

5. Lessons Learned

Naming all the lessons is almost impossible. Only the most important ones are named, such as:

- Process-oriented thinking
- Process-oriented organizational structure
- Teamwork
- Process documenting and archiving
- Document standardization (inputs/outputs)
- Knowledge Management
- Product Design

Using BPR Tools in Business Process Education

Alexander Hars
University of Southern California

Summary

Software plays an increasingly important role in education. It not only provides the student with the mastery of a tool that he may use in his work life. It also immerses the student very effectively in complex business settings. Therefore, at the Marshall School of Business we are striving to integrate leading-edge technology into high curriculum. In 1994 we selected the ARIS toolset as the main software engineering and business process analysis tool for our information systems analysis classes both on the graduate level and on the undergraduate level. In this article, we will first describe the background of our decision to adopt the ARIS toolset. We will then describe the integration into the curriculum. Finally, we will focus lessons learned and future steps to be taken with ARIS.

Key Words

Business Process Education, ARIS Toolset, Market leading analysis tool, Diagramming, Refinement capabilities, Holistic enterprise view, Reference model, Integration of leading-edge technology into high curriculum

1. Role of Software Tools in Business Process Education

The use of software is increasingly recognized as a key element of education. In the past, software was primarily used in a training mode: students needed to learn how to work with certain software, the primary goal being to master certain tasks with the software and to be able to utilize this software effectively in the business world. In this mode, students learned to work with desktop and Internet applications. This mode of learning may have been useful in the early times of computing. Today, however, familiarity with many software tools is expected when entering the university. Most schools no longer teach such basic skills. The goals have also shifted for more complex software tools such as development environments, project management tools etc. The goal is not to produce students that are masters in using a specific software tool. Rather the goal is to teach students how to think on their own and how to solve problems.

Software is an excellent tool for achieving this goal. Software is dynamic. It can capture and reflect complex relationships. It is an excellent thinking tool. The student can experiment with different configurations and patterns. His actions are immediately reflected within the tool. He can see the consequences of his thoughts very quickly. Thus a lack of understanding becomes obvious very quickly.

Software are thinking tools which are superior to books in many ways. They are active and can be adapted to the needs of the student. They allow the students to engage in a dialog and provide feedback. Furthermore, they can tie together real life scenarios and relationships rather than toy problems.

Software tools are particularly helpful in information systems classes where students have to deal with the complexity of business processes combined with the complexity of technology. Utilizing BPR software has many advantages. It enables students to think through real business processes and to discover how many issues may arise in even seemingly simple processes. Furthermore, a tool such as ARIS visualizes the connections between different aspects of a business. Students do not just draw and link diagrams. A business process reengineering tool forces students to think of a company as an integrated entity and understand much better how the different parts link together. This is very important for business students: most management schools are still organized functionally: Students take marketing, accounting, and finance classes. They always see a slice of a company but they rarely see a business as an integrated whole. With modeling tools such as ARIS, students receive a unique opportunity to reason about management from wholistic company-wide perspective.

This was the background against which the ARIS Toolset has been adopted in our curriculum. In the following we will outline our curriculum in further detail and describe how the ARIS toolset fits in. We will then describe lessons learned from our work with ARIS.

2. Curriculum

2.1 University of Southern California

USC is one of the leading research universities in the U.S. It was founded in 1880 as the first University in Southern California and today ranks as one of the top 10 private research universities in the U.S. based upon federal research and development support. It is located in downtown Los Angeles and has about 28,000 students from a very diverse background. Both the graduate and undergraduate programs are ranked among the top U.S. management programs.

2.2 Information Systems Analysis and Design Courses

ARIS is used in information systems analysis and design courses on the graduate and undergraduate levels. The courses combine the analysis and design components of information systems development within one semester. The focus of the courses is more strongly oriented towards the analysis part which matches better with the skill requirements of business students as they will not become developers. Howerver, the course also includes a development component and culminates in a project that currently combines an internet-based application using Java Servlet technology and an Oracle database. The Systems Analysis and Design course is part of a much larger offering in Information Systems provided by the Marshall School. Students typically take database management courses, courses in electronic commerce and information systems strategy as a complement to the systems analysis and design course. The University was als one of the first schools in the US to offer a course on enterprise resource planning based on SAP.

Overall, the systems analysis and design course provides methods to plan, organize and execute information systems development projects. It focuses on the detailed, systematic analysis of a business with its processes, information needs and interdependencies, a skill which is needed by systems analysts, consultants in IT-related and business process reengineering projects, systems integrators and managers of information technology. In addition, the course emphasizes the use of Computer-Aided Software Engineering tools during the systems development life-cycle and introduces the student to prototyping and rapid application development using Visual Café, a Java-based development environment.

The course relies upon group discussions, lectures, readings and hands-on work with Visual Café and the ARIS Toolset as a leading software engineering tool. In every course, students work on a realistic development project. They have to find a project sponsor within industry or with an association that needs a small new database-enabled application. The students then collect the requirements for the system. Using the ARIS toolset, they create the process, function and data models which are reviewed by the sponsor, other students teams as well as by the instructor before proceeding to the implementation. In their last step, the students develop a first prototype of the system that includes database functionality. Beginning the Fall semester of 2001, the students are building servlets with Visual Café. The servlets are run on the Tomcat open source application server. Oracle 8i is used as the backend database. In prior years, the students developed database-enabled Java applets.

Over the years, the students have developed some impressive applications. While the short duration of a semester is never enough to build a sophisticated application, several prototypes were strong elaborate enough to serve as the foundation of full development. In 2000, for example, the Marshall School of Business deployed a web-based system for managing class lists that was based on the development done by a student group. In the Fall semester of 2001 another student group developed an sophisticated web-based advisement application. Projects are not limited to university topics, however. Student groups have developed prototype applications for health care (patient management in the Los Angeles Free clinic), order management, video stores and many others.

The course objectives are:

- Plan an information systems development project
- Analyze business processes
- Develop process, data, function and organization models for an information system
- Develop a prototype of an information system and design user interfaces using PowerBuilder
- Use BPR tools in a systems development project

The course is structured around the information systems devlopment life-cycle. A typical session schedule is shown in Table 1. The course begins with an overview over the problems of large scale informations ystems development. The reasons for project failures are analyzed using such prominent examples as the Denver Airport disaster.

Next different classes of information systems development approaches are discussed – from waterfall to spiral, from Foundation to Rational Unified Method. After understanding the main activities in IS development (see Figure 1), the course covers project management and project planning. Much time is then spent on systems analysis, where the students learn process, function and data/object modeling. Use cases are covered first. They are an excellent stepping stone to the more formal diagramming methods. The capstone are data and object models which have the steepest learning curve.

In parallel to these topics, the students begin to work with the ARIS Toolset and learn the basics of the Java language. While students have little difficulty in understanding ARIS, Visual Café and Java provide a much greater challenge as business students typically have no programming experience.

Table 1: Concise syllabus (1:50h per session)

1	Introduction: Success rates for IS projects; Systems Analyst
2	Systems development methodologies I: Life-cycle approaches
3	Practical work with Java: (Lab session) 🖳 VisualCafe
4	Systems development methodologies II: RAD&JAD
5	Systems architecture: IS blueprints, web-based architectures
6	Systems planning & evaluation: success criteria for IS projects; feasibility;
7	Project management & requirements specification
8	Systems analysis: interview techniques, interviewing exercise
9	Activity and process modeling: Use cases, function trees, process chains
10	Using 🖳 ARIS Toolset (Lab session)
11	Advanced process modeling
12	Data/object modeling
13	Advanced data/object modeling: Generalization relationship
14	Midterm preparation
15	Additional modeling perspectives: Organization & network
16	Midterm
17	Object-oriented analysis and design UML 🖳 Rational Rose
18	Design: Transformation of process models, transformation of data & object models
19	Advanced ARIS and Java (Lab session)
20	Implementation of Standardsoftware Guest speaker
21	User interface design I: Input and output design
22	User interface design II: Next-generation user interfaces
23	Development tools and practices: Visual Basic, Borland Delphi & JBuilder
24	Sytems testing, 🖳 SQA TestSuite, Guest speaker
25	Implementation: Training, installation & cutover
26	Maintenance: 🖳 PVCS (Version management), case: road to client-server
27	Change management: Best practices; Outsourcing
28	Enterprise-wide information systems: 🖳 SAP R/3 live demo
29	Presentation of term projects
30	Final Exam

Planning	Analysis	Design	Implementation	Maintenance
Identify need Identify alternativ. Analyze benefits & risks Define IS architecture Prepare proposal Select people, methods, tools	Collect information Develop data, process, organization models Define & prioritize user requirements	Select target system platform Acquire hardware & software Build db. schemas Create database Code applications Create documentation	Install hard- and software Configure & integrate systems Transfer data Train users & administrators Perform cutover	Correct errors Assist system users Backup, recover data & software Adapt systems to new requirements Migrate, integrate systems
QUALITY ASSURANCE, TESTING				
Define test strategy	Define test procedures, survey project feasibility	Build test cases, test modules, Alpha-testing	Test module integration Beta-testing	Extension testing
EVENTS				
Presentation of project proposal Kick-off meeting	Interviews Data conference RAD, JAD sessions	Structured walk-throughs Milestone reviews	Training sessions Cut-over Post-implementation audit	(all events that occur in the previous phases)

cross life-cycle: **PROJECT MANAGEMENT, DOCUMENTATION**

Figure 1: Breakdown of Systems Development Activities (Phases overlap)

In the later part of the semester, the focus switches toward design and implementation. First, the students learn how to translate their process, function and data/object models into logical and physical designs. In this phase, database issues receive most attention. The semester is now in an intensive phase as the students begin to develop their prototype. Some of the assignments are explicitly designed to show the conflicts arising when a larger group works in parallel on highly interdependent tasks. Toward the end of the semester additional topics are covered including enterprise resource planning systems and change management. The semester ends with a presentation of the term projects.

2.3 Using the ARIS Toolset

The ARIS Toolset is an integral part of the entire course on systems analysis and design. The students use the tool to understand the concept of a CASE and BPR tool in a practical setting. An important objective is to understand the difference between a diagramming tool such as Visio and PowerPoint and a CASE tool that is built around an object repository.

The students work with the tool when learning the different diagramming methods – process, data and fucntion models. They then apply these models during the systems development process and see in practice how the initial ideas represented by their diagrams are modified, refined and extended in a project.

Figure 2 shows the typical process of using a BPR/CASE tool in a project setting. In the following the experiences and aspects of using such a tool are discussed for each process element:

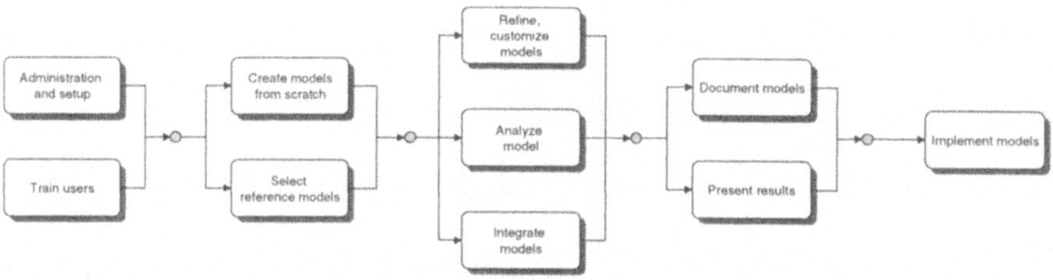

Figure 2: Process model for using CASE tools in an IS project

2.4 Administration and Setup

Before BPR/CASE tools can be used productively, they need to be acquired and setup. In the educational setting, administration presented several challenges. At the Marshall School of Business more than one hundred lab machines are equipped with the ARIS toolset. In a lab setting, the tools are used very differently than in the typical business setting that ARIS Toolset was developed for. Students only work on their diagrams for a short time – a few hourse per session at most. When they return, they usually use a different PC. In the meantime other uses may have used the initial PC. Furthermore, students often work on the same problems: For a given assignment they all create the same diagrams.

The lab settings thus introduced several complications: Students had to be able to save their work and take it with them on disk or transfer it to their FTP account. Initially we asked the studens to copy their .dat and .idx files but this meant that the student had to know about the physical location of the database, remember that he had to copy two files etc. which led to much frustration.

To solve this problem, we developed a small launcher application that provided the student with several options at startup and shutdown of ARIS (see figure 3). The launcher allowed the student to select a directory with a database file that was then copied into the right place within the ARIS Toolset directory structure. It also allowed to create an empty database – thus eliminating the problem that the next user would have to deal with the previous user's diagrams.

After importing the database or creating an empty database or doing nothing, the launcher then starts the ARIS ToolSet. It waits in the background until the ARIS Toolset is closed and then allows to copy the database the user worked with to a user directory or floppy disk. The launcher application greatly reduced student frustration that did not originate from a design problem within ARIS but from a mismatch between the intended use of ARIS and the way the tool was used in an academic lab setting.

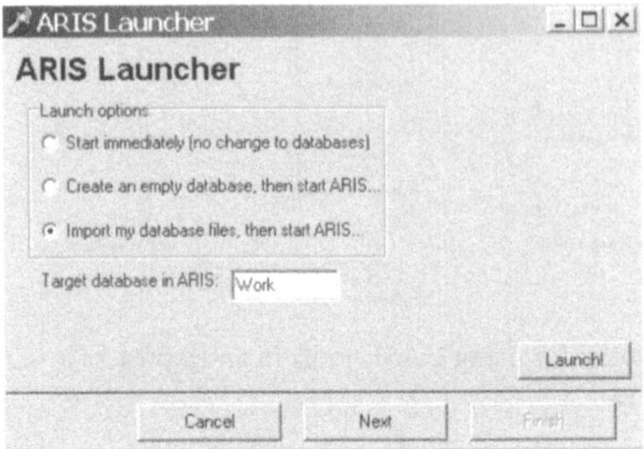

Figure 3: Screenshot of the ARIS Launcher Utility

2.5 Train Users

Training is another key activity in using software tools. Because of the limited time available, training had to be minimal. In each course, one lab session of 2 hours allowed the students to acquaint themselves with the tool. While this did not allow us to go much into the depths of the tool, we were glad to find out that it clearly was sufficient. The main goals of the lab session is to show the students how to create diagrams – which is very intuitive – , how to organize diagrams (which we could only briefly touch on) and – most importantly – what the relationships between the diagrams are.

This is the most critical part. The students need to understand, that every item shown on the screen reflects an object that is stored the tool's repository. This object may occur in many other diagrams. Much of the power of the tool arises from its ability to leverage these relationships as well as object attributes. In the lab session, we demonstrate this by creating two diagrams, copying one object from one diagram to the other and then changing the name of the object in one of the diagrams. Students then observe firsthand that – contrary to what would happen in a diagramming application –, the name of the copy also changes immediately. This clearly shows the difference between the CASE tool and a typical drawing applicatin.

After this brief introduction, the students were able to work productively with the tool on their own. Our experience also shows that it is not necessary to provide much user support for the toolset. While we use a teaching assistant to answer ARIS-related questions, most of the support needs concern methodological issues rather than issues of how to work with the toolset.

2.6 Create Models From Scratch

Most of the activity in our systems analysis and design class is focused on this step. The students learn the different types of diagrams. We begin with use-case diagrams (which we have based on the eEPC diagram type) and then refine the use-case diagrams by adding larger event-oriented process chain diagrams. Subsequently, function trees and data models are created. Finally, we add organization charts. Process chain diagrams and functions trees provide few problems for teaching. They are quite intuitive, once students understand the differences between the operators. The major difficulty, however, is to understand on what level of detail one needs to model a given process. Here, experience is key. The students have more difficulties understanding the concepts behind data models. We need to spend considerably more time on data models than on process models. Besides learning the specific diagramming techniques, the students also need to understand that a large number of diagramming technologies exist on the market and that there is no single set of diagramming methodologies that is perfect.

2.7 Select Reference Models

Most systems analysis classes are taught from the perspective of developing an entirely new system from scratch. This ignores the large percentage of systems development projects that modify an existing system are that are built on standard software. In the latter cases, the analytic problem changes from translating ones' domain knowledge into an adequate system representation to identifying and adapting the representations already available. In our class, therefore, we incorporate references models from an SAP ERP system which is available at USC. The students are often surprised to see the size and complexity of these models which greatly differs from the toy problems and examples typically used in education. In addition, we use the ERP models to explain the customization process to the students.

2.8 Refine and Customize Models

In this step, students learn how to refine and revise a model by adding submodels to it and how to change the properties of model elements. In classroom practice, we spend little time on these issues as students do not build large models. In addition, the time that students spend on working with each model is short compared to real-world development projects. In their final project, however, the students work in a group of five on developing a larger set of models describing their application. At that time, they perform some of the refinement tasks.

2.9 Analyze Model

BPR/CASE tools differ greatly in their ability to analyze the models. ARIS has great features in visualizing and simulating business processes which the students learn about when they develop their process chain diagrams. The ability to check the consistency of a model is also useful for students when they work on their first assignments and don't yet fully understand the structure of the diagrams. Once they have passed the initial stages, however, consistency checks are used less frequently. A key element of model analysis is the detection of overlap and relationships with other models. ARIS greatly simplifies making changes to a set of models by showing in which models certain objects are appear and which relationships these objects have to other objects. In our course, we make sure that students understand querying the relationships. A typical example is when we decide to change or split the responsibilities of a specific person (position). This requires for the students to identify all processes in which the person is active. Then the responsibilities in these processes need to be regrouped and finally reassigned to the redefined positions. This clearly shows the analysis needs of such a tool.

2.10 Document Models

Documentation is an essential part of any development project. Students incorporated their diagrams into their project book – a document that described their project prototype. In addition, many students used the ability of ARIS to publish the model on the internet for online documentation.

2.11 Present Results

At the end of the semester, the students present their prototypes to the class. An integral part of this event is the discussion of the process chains. While the students were not required to show the process models as a diagram, many groups do. In addition, we encourage the students to use a screen capture utility to link the key functions in their process model directly to the graphical user interface. As ARIS allows to attach a file to any diagram element and subsequently launch it, it is straightforward to attach a screenshot to each function. An example is shown in figure 4.

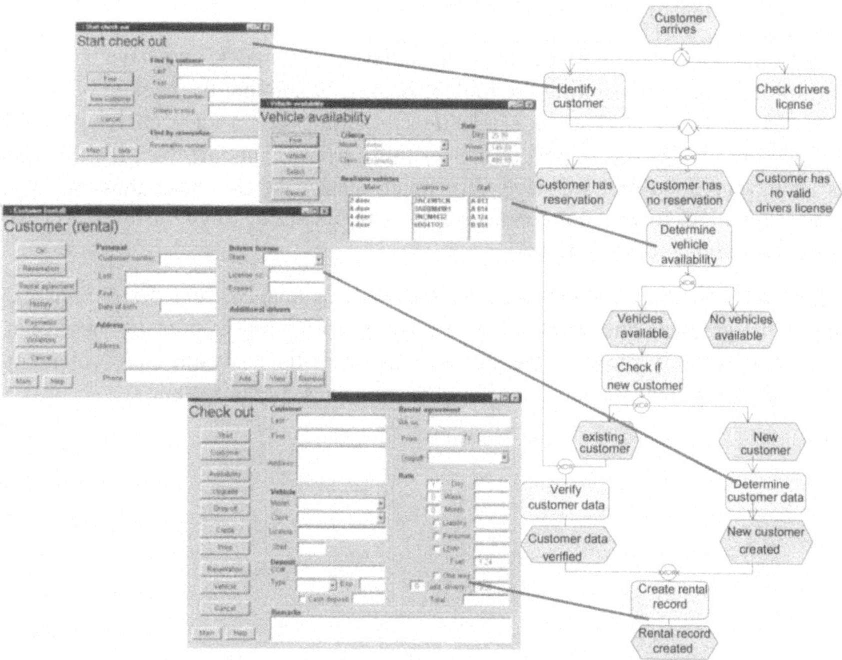

Figure 4: Linking ARIS process chain with user interface screens

2.12 Implement Models

The last stage in systems development is to implement the models. Unfortunately, ARIS provides little direct support for this phase. Therefore the students manually convert their designs into database and application code. We experimented with documenting the implementation structures within ARIS but have mostly refrained from doing so.

3. Lessons Learned

ARIS has been extremely useful for our systems analysis and design class. We have compared it to other tools – including Rational Rose – and see many advantages, particularly the ability to support the organizational view that is so important for a business student. Furthermore, the diagramming and refinement capabilities are much more powerfull within ARIS. Besides the benefit that the students learn to work with a market leading analysis tool, the tool has the benefit of clearly showing the complexity of business processes. It helps students to see the company as a whole and better understand the informational, organizational and process-oriented relationships.

Supporting a tool such as ARIS can be a challenge. With ARIS, we have had very few problems in administering the tool. However, organizing the backup of ARIS databases for every student in a volatile lab setting has been a challenge. We provided our own export/import utility for this purpose. Support from IDS Scheer has been very good and we have very much appreciate the willingness of IDS Scheer executives to visit our classes and present on cutting-edge business process engineering and consulting issues.

In summary, ARIS is a great asset for our systems analysis and design classes, both on the graduate and undergraduate level. By providing systematic view on a business, it not only provides the student with skills for analysing IT problems it changes the way that students conceptualize a business organization.

Process Modelling and Simulation in the Media Industry: The Television New Zealand Example

Michael Rosemann
Queensland University of Technology

Steve Browning
Television New Zealand

Summary

This chapter describes the experiences of Television New Zealand (TVNZ) with business process engineering and the use of ARIS. It is explained how a new internal Business Process Improvement team approached the analysis and redesign of key business processes in an increasingly competitive industry. The key business processes are outlined and summarized in a business process framework. The application of ARIS in different projects is discussed and the server-based newsroom project is described more comprehensively. This chapter ends with a brief discussion of lessons learned.

Key Words

Media Industry, Television, Broadcasting, Change Management

1. Project Background

1.1 As-is Situation

TVNZ is the state owned broadcaster in New Zealand with two network channels – TV ONE and TV2, plus the internet portal nzoom.com. TVNZ's subsidiary company Broadcast Communications Limited (BCL) provides the distribution infrastructure for all terrestrial channels in NZ, while TVNZ (Australia) conducts operation and maintenance services for a number of Australian Broadcasters. TVNZ Satellite Services provides satellite linking and infrastructure development services focused on the Asia-Pacific region, and TVNZ International provides a range of global consulting services in all aspects of broadcasting.

TV ONE broadcasts over five hours of Live News coverage daily to one of the world's most news hungry populations. TVNZ News and Current Affairs employs over two hundred and fifty people, located in four bureaux, spread throughout NZ, as well as overseas bureau in Sydney, Australia and London.

1.2 Project Motivation

In a time when the Free to Air Broadcast business is under increasing pressure to maintain it's financial performance with shrinking advertising revenues and digital conversion costs, cost efficiency is seen as paramount.

In late 1999 an internal Business Improvement Team was created as part of a strategy to ensure the organisation was continually improving its internal processes and working as efficiently as possible.

The main *objectives* of this Business Process Improvement initiative were:

- the top down description of the current processes on different levels of abstraction,
- the analysis and improvement of core business and support processes,
- the Intranet-based distribution of process-relevant information, and
- the simulation of selected processes.

Overall, the team aimed to increase the awareness for TVNZ's business processes.

A year earlier TVNZ's CTO had recognised the need for strong project management to successfully deliver system and process change. A Projects Office was established with the development of a project management methodology (PMM) that fitted the culture of TVNZ but incorporated best practice from the *Project Management Institute (PMI)*. The Projects Office employs professional project managers to facilitate business change, system delivery, broadcast events, and engineering projects in successfully achieving their objectives.

The third component in ensuring TVNZ would be able to achieve the efficiency gains required was change management. The recognition that staff would need to feel part of the change and not see it as a cost cutting exercise, but a journey into the future.

2. Core Business Processes

Overall, 14 business processes have been identified that capture TVNZ's core business and the required support processes.

- Sell Airtime

The process of selling airtime (Advertisements, Infomercials, Sponsorship, etc) off the back of the programme schedule, which results in advertisements going to air and customers paying for the service.

- Programming, Scheduling

The process of creating a programme schedule by evaluating programme content and allocating it to specific slots within that schedule.

- Packaging & Delivery

The process of managing the physical medium (video and audio by tape, satellite feed, live camera, etc) Supply Chain, Play Out, and Inventory Management.

In the new world of digital distribution this process must now include all forms of delivery (e.g. Analogue (Wireless, Cable), Digital - DTT, DTH, Cable, etc). It should also consider the equipment required to enable delivery (e.g. Broadcaster equipment – high sites, satellite transponders, etc and Consumer equipment – analogue TV, Digital TV, STB, PVR etc)

- Acquisition of Programmes

The process of acquiring programmes for transmission. This includes all potential sources of programmes (e.g. output deals, distributors) and the contract negotiation process, which results in the right to screen the programme.

- Commissioned Programming

The process of negotiating with external parties for local content to be produced (including rights, funding, and resource considerations), and the management of the delivery of this content.

- Internal Production

The process triggered by the decision to make a programme rather than buy (including rights and funding considerations). This covers all internal programming, therefore the News and Current Affairs, Sport, Lifestyle, Maori, Avalon, and Moving Pictures business areas are included. This could be described as the content operations of TVNZ.

- Internet Selling and Content & Delivery

The process of selling Internet related products and services. Plus the creation and publication of web site content on all TVNZ external web sites. This includes all sources of content be they external or internal.

- Teletext Selling and Content & Delivery

The process of selling Teletext related services. Plus the creation and publication of Teletext pages for all clients. This includes all sources of content be they external or internal.

- Licensing

The process of obtaining licensing rights to reproduce or use a brand, character, image or data on a product or service.

- Captioning Services (External)

The process of selling captioning services for external clients including the creation and publication of caption content.

- Sell Satellite Space

The process of selling satellite space to external and internal clients. Including the acquisition of space on global satellites and the operational requirements necessary to manage the delivery.

- Programme and Footage Sales (International and Local)

The process of selling the right to play TVNZ owned content (video and audio).

- Facilities & Production Services

The process of providing facilities (people and equipment) to support media related production (for internal and external clients), and the allocation of these resources to support the production activity. This should include the Production and Post Production business and consider TVNZ as a Broadcast facilities provider (e.g. to Maori TV service, Ministry of Education, etc).

- Sell Broadcasting Services

The process of selling covers intellectual capital (knowledge, skills and experience) for media related events (including Host Broadcast, Events coverage, etc), both to the NZ and international market.

These business processes have been depicted at the highest level in a business process framework. The idea of such a framework is to capture the main core and support processes of an organisation in one comprehensive and easy to understand level 0 process map. These frameworks are the entry point into detailed process modeling with tools like the ARIS Toolset (Davis 2001). They are supposed to form the single point of entry into all underlying process models. At the same time they can help to form a graphical logo for the entire process improvement project and facilitate the positioning of single initiatives.

It has to be stressed that business process frameworks are supposed to describe functions and not organisational units. Thus, it requires attention to chose names that do *not* correspond with parts of the organisation chart. The business process framework for TVNZ is depicted in figure 1, with the next level drilldown in figure 2.

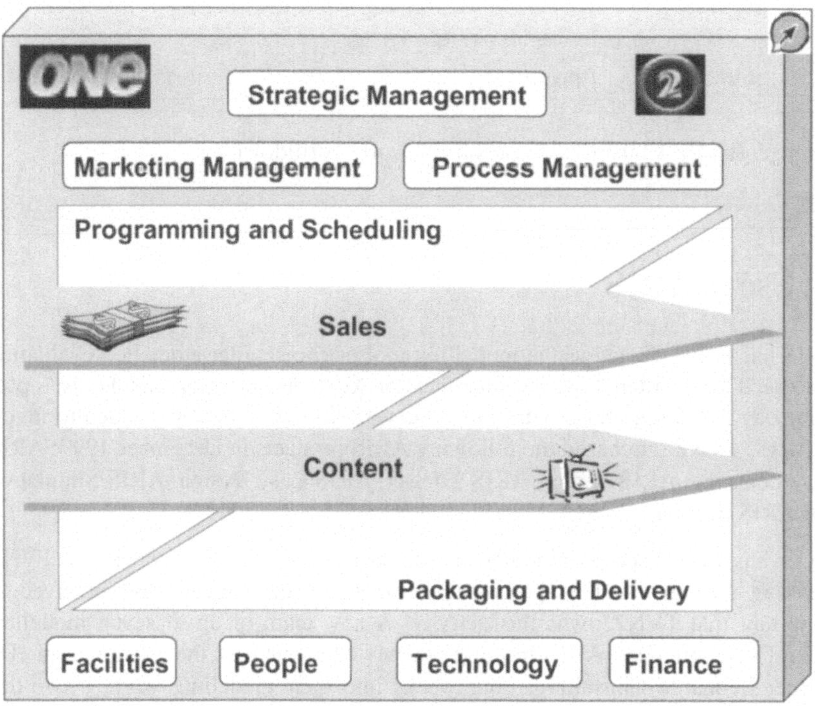

Figure 1: TVNZ's business process framework

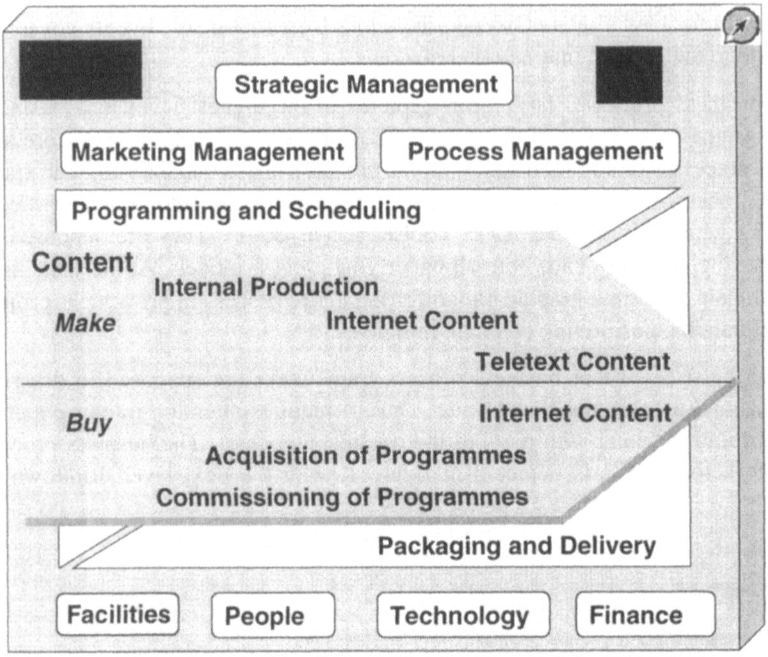

Figure 2: TVNZ's business process framework – drilldown

3. Use of ARIS

ARIS has been selected as the modelling tool of choice after a detailed evaluation process. TVNZ ordered evaluation copies of ARIS Easy Design and Toolset, plus a one day ARIS introductory training course, before they finally decided to invest in ARIS. TVNZ purchased the following ARIS products in December 1999: ARIS Easy Learning, ARIS Server, ARIS Toolset, ARIS Easy Design, ARIS Simulation and ARIS Weblink.

ARIS has been used to complete a full process modelling exercise at TVNZ covering all core business processes. From the beginning, it was perceived as important that TVNZ owns this activity. A new team of up to seven modellers from TVNZ attended ARIS training courses conducted by the Australasian IDS partner Leonardo Consulting. Four weeks into their modelling work, a two-day review workshop was conducted in order to evaluate the quality of the initial modelling work and to define the direction of future work. This time was also spent on reviewing and revising the modelling guidelines (Becker et al. 2000).

Further issues that have been discussed covered the detailed issues related to process simulation as well as the comunication strategy, i.e. the roll-out of the models to the members of the organisation.

Value Chain Diagrams and Event-driven Process Chains have been used to describe all processes underlying the business process framework. The level two Value-added Chain Diagrams were modelled with two views in mind. One described the sequence of the main activities, the second indicated which organisational units (departments) are involved at each step in the business process.

An example of a value chains at level 1 can be found in figure 3, which describes the core business process Selling Airtime in more detail.

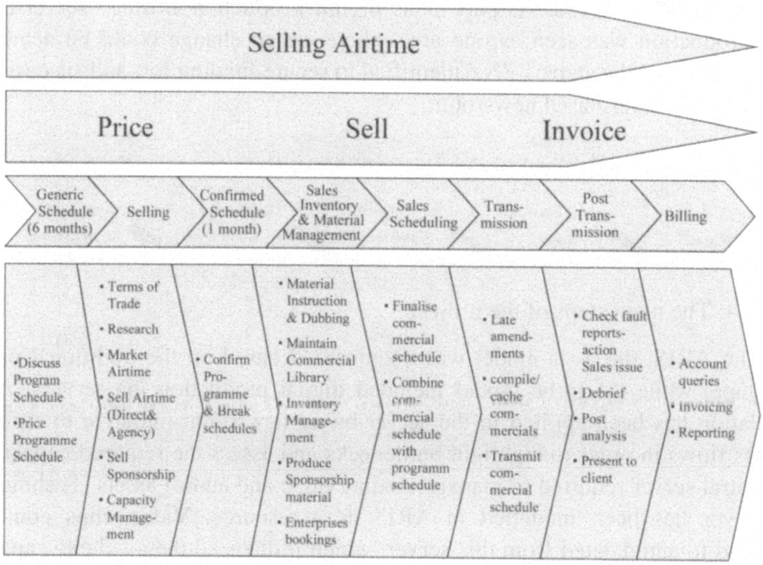

Figure 3: Value Chain – Selling Airtime

The intensive work has quickly lead to positive results like a new and more complete understanding of the business processes and the identification of weaknesses.

Furthermore, ARIS was used to document and model the descriptive and prescriptive states for the Production and Resource Management process culminating in a major SAP implementation (project, capacity planning, and human resource modules). The models were used to engage with the departments to understand their requirements, assess the cost/benefit, model the future workflow, and assess functions, workload and consequently staff positions. The new processes built by the project team, supported by SAP functionality, are documented as training and reference material in ARIS. Therefore, future process change, system upgrades, etc. have documented processes as a starting point. The use of ERP reference models is also discussed in Rosemann (2000) and Rosemann (2002).

4. One Initiative in Detail

The process review has sporned a number of initiative, one in particular is discussed here in detail.

TVNZ took a hard look at its production processes and as successful early adopters of new and innovative technologies saw the opportunity that server-based news production offered. As part of its *digital production strategy* server-based news production was seen as one area where a step change could be achieved. Figure 4 lays out the steps TVNZ identified to secure funding for, and successfully implement, a server based newsroom.

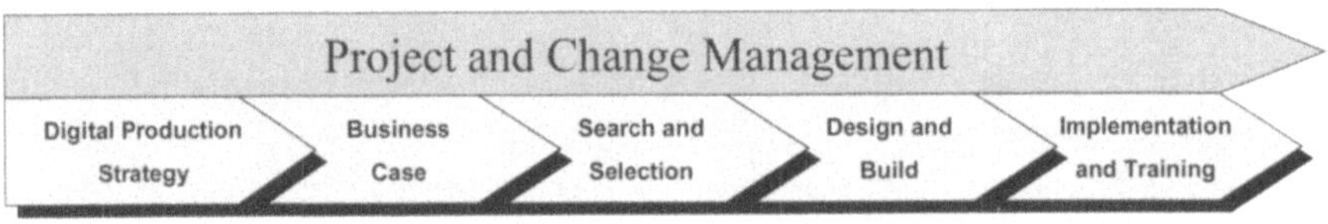

Figure 4: The main steps of the project

Utilising ARIS, the as-is model was documented based on the traditional use of videotape, while the to-be model included digital production via servers. ARIS Simulation has been applied in the server-based newsroom initiative to simulate process flows in order to highlight bottlenecks and assess the required capacity of the central server required to manage media (video and audio) assets. Technically, the server has been modelled in ARIS as a resource. Video clips could be uploaded to and deleted from this server, which influenced the available capacity. The execution of different simulation scenarios helped to identify an appropriate sizing of this resource. Different types of stories (e.g. foreign stories, sport stories) were taken into account and the effects on the server capacity carefully evaluated. Based on ARIS simulation, it was possible to ensure optimisation of the huge investment planned in the new technology

The *Business Case* development (figure 5) required analysis of the current state of the news production process to understand the true cost of the tape-based news operation. This was achieved by modelling (through ARIS Event-driven Process Chains) the current process and incorporating operational metrics and financial data in the model.

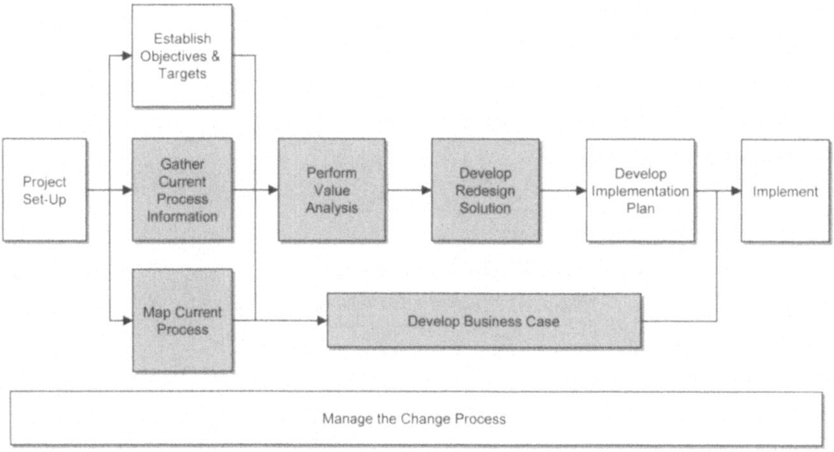

Figure 5: Business Case Development

By comparing current process flows and the associated cost, TVNZ was able to focus on the key functions in the process where the new technology would impact on cost and efficiency. This combined with a prescriptive model of the process once the technology was introduced gave a clear picture of the gains to be made by its introduction.

With Board presentation successfully completed and funding secured, the project moved to the next critical phase. It was crucial that TVNZ selected appropriate technology partners who could not only provide the required equipment but more vitally understand the TV news business, illustrate a technology development strategy in parallel with TVNZ's, have highly skilled implementation staff (who are available when required) and fit the culture of TVNZ.

TVNZ applied a best practice *Search and Selection* methodology, within the PMM, which ensures all aspects of a selection criteria are given an appropriate weighting and all potential partners are given equal opportunity to demonstrate their credentials in meeting the requirements. Figure 6 illustrates TVNZ's search and selection methodology, which places significant emphasis on involving staff who will be responsible for the system when it is in production – both operationally and technically.

Phases two, three, and four (Business Case, Search and Selection, and Design and Build) are far from linear in their execution. The cost of the technology (finalised on the search and selection phase) is critical to the business case development. The Design is born from a combination of strategy / prescriptive model of operation / preferred partners system design. This emphasises the importance of continuity in the project team. This was achieved at TVNZ through a consistent project owner (involved at every step) who had the conceptual vision. Other key personnel were the project sponsor, to ensure the initiative received high prioritisation at executive level, and a project manager who understood the vision and was able to put in place the appropriate project structure to execute the plan.

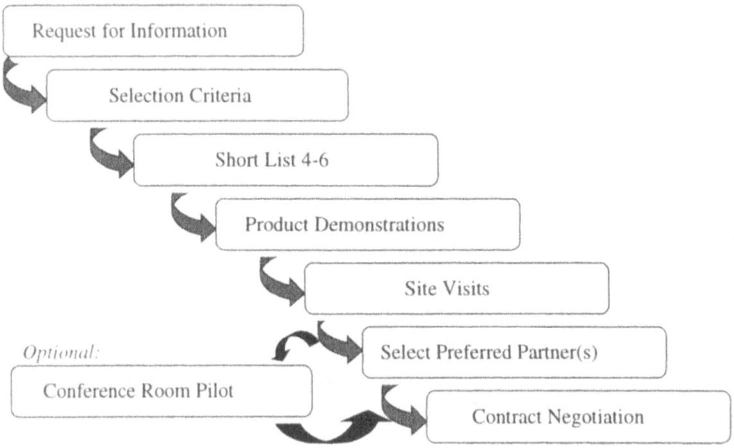

Figure 6: TVNZ's search and selection methodology

System Design was completed in partnership with the selected system and integration partners utilising the ARIS process models to support the design decisions. This was important to achieve the critical aspect of business buy-in. The best technology is no good to you unless your people feel they own it and want to make it work. TVNZ's core project team included news staff from the strategy and business case phases, through search and selection and into implementation.

Throughout the learning curve the core team was going through, all staff in the newsroom were constantly being kept up to date with progress. Newsletters, training videos, a project brief, presentations, and meetings ensured that all concerns were addressed. Communication is as critical as a quality system implementation. TVNZ placed a significant emphasis on involving as many people as possible.

This ensured that all staff were 'prepared' when they were rostered to attend training and not apprehensive about this project that was happening around them, which would change their jobs.

The project team also conducted a series of regular detailed workshops involving staff from every role in the newsroom. Utilising the process models from the business case phase they were able to ease the changeover from current processes to new processes as the staff helped design them.

This illustrates how TVNZ has combined Business Process Improvement, Project Management, and Change Management to deliver significant process and technology change.

5. Lessons Learned

TVNZ took a topdown view of their organisation and spent time upfront assessing where to apply their limited resources. Using process modelling techniques they were able to capture where the major opportunities existed to improve their processes and therefore improve their products and services for their customers.

The downside to this approach can be that processes are mapped that have little room for significant change and time could have been better spent moving straight into specific initiatives. There is not right or wrong answer here, it may well depend on the position the organisation is in and the overall objectives of the modelling exercise.

TVNZ have found that they have utilised the majority of the process models for many different purposes. From training new staff to redesigning significant parts of their core business processes.

6. References

Becker, J., Rosemann, M., von Uthmann, Chr. (2000): Guidelines of Business Process Modeling. In: Business Process Management: Models, Techniques and Empirical Studies. Eds.: W. van der Aalst, J. Desel, A. Oberweis. Springer-Verlag: Berlin, pp. 30-49.

Davis, R. (2001): Business Process Modeling with ARIS. A Practical Guide. Spinger-Verlag: Berlin et al.

Rosemann, M. (2000): Using Reference Models within the Enterprise Resource Planning Lifecycle. Australian Accounting Review, Vol. 10, No. 3, November, pp. 19-30.

Rosemann, M. (2002): Application Reference Models and Building Blocks for Management and Control (ERP Systems). In: Handbook of Enterprise Architecture. Eds.: P. Bernus, L. Nemes, G. Schmidt. Springer-Verlag: Berlin et al. (in press).

Scheer, A.-W. (2000): ARIS - Business Process Modeling. 3rd ed., Springer-Verlag: Berlin et al.

Scheer, A.-W. (2000): ARIS - Business Process Frameworks. 3rd ed., Springer-Verlag: Berlin et al.

Business Process Analysis and Design for Performance Improvement in Utilities Companies

Karel Dietrich-Nespěšný
Jihomoravská energetika, a.s.

Paul Eschbach
BASE CONSULT GmbH

Klaus Miksch
IDS Scheer AG

Karel Hrbek
IDS Scheer CR

Summary

Using the example of Jihomoravska energetika, a.s. (JME), the largest utility company in the Czech Republic, this presentation will show how the firm has repositioned itself in the light of the new market situation following the liberalization of the energy market.

Corporate strategy was used as the starting point in the creation of, among other things, a new Controlling conception and IT-strategy, and in realizing these initiatives with corresponding supporting measures.

Strategic reorganization entails a complete overhaul of the company's business process landscape with a view to creating a consistent, customer-oriented and unified system of process execution.

Modern information technology plays a decisive role in the Business Reengineering effort because it enables the firm to completely redesign its processes.

In the context of the project, the effects of individual substrategies are realized in technological, organizational and personnel actions.

With regard to the technological and organizational considerations, the new strategic alignment means increased standardization and flexibility as well as the automation of administrative- and routine tasks to increase employee productivity.

Jihomoravská energetika has decided to use ARIS for the analysis, optimization and continuous improvement of company business processes. This combination of ARIS software and strategic consulting supports a rapid, efficient and high-value project realization. In this way, an integrated project can be realized within the appointed timeframe - from strategy through conception to operational implementation - with maximum benefit to the client.

Key Words

Liberalization of the european utility market, company strategy, controlling concept, business process reengineering, continous process improvement, ARIS company process model, benefits of ARIS

1. Challenges of the Czech Energy Market

The political and economic map of Central Europe changed dramatically during the last 10 years of the 20th century. The previous division of Europe into two hostile blocks was overcome by the courageous deeds of citizens and politicians.

Political adaptation and change also presented a difficult test of the social and economic systems. Very different systems had developed on both sides of the 'curtain' as a consequence of 45 years of differing political and economic conditions, and these systems now collided with force at the former border between Central and Western Europe.

The liberalization of energy markets was prepared and implemented in most member countries of the European Union (EU) during those years.

The competition among suppliers for markets and customers replaced the formerly protected regional monopolies of energy suppliers.

Because of its borders with Germany and Austria, the Czech Republic is also directly touched by liberalizing efforts in Europe. Parts of the Czech energy market have been liberalized already (in 2002), but the biggest markets remain to be opened for competition in the coming years.

This field report describes the targeted use of ARIS-based business process management for the reorganization of the state-run company into an efficient and competitive utilities company.

1.1 JME Jihomoravská energetika, a.s. Company Description

JME Jihomoravská energetika, a.s. is a joined-stock company supplying the Southern Moravia Region with energy.

The Southern Moravia Region is located on the border with Slovakia (Bratislava) and Austria (Vienna).

The company, with its 2,000 employees (as of February 2002), generates sales of approx. 450 million € in the following value-added stages

- Energy distribution in the high voltage network
- Energy distribution in the medium and low voltage network
- Energy supply to customers

The company's own energy production capability is negligible.

The company is headquartered in Brno. There are 7 regional centers responsible for network maintenance and customer service in the region.

The company sold approx. 8 TWh to its 1 million customers in 2002 and thus has a market share of approx. 14% of the Czech energy market. The supply area constitutes 15,000 km², so that the company is geographically the largest energy supplier in the country. The company is number 2 in terms of sales (as of 2002).

The following map shows the location of the company in the Czech Republic.

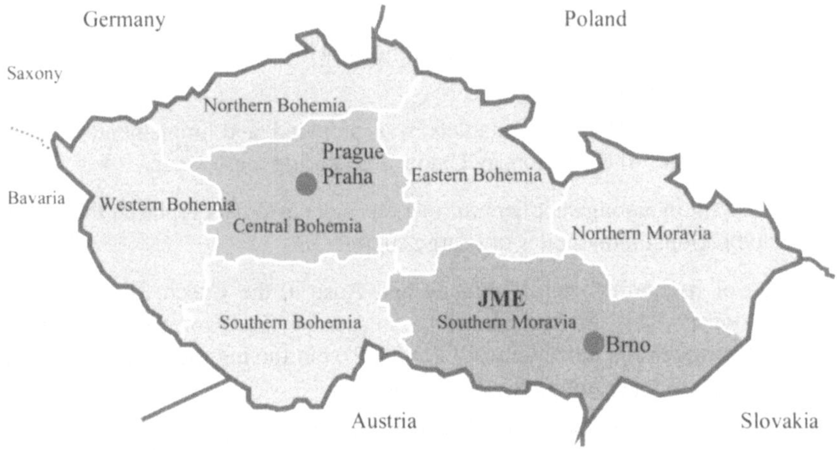

Figure 1: The Czech Republic –location of JME

1.2 Privatization of State Companies Engenders Willingness to Change

Previous state-run companies were to be transformed into industrial companies during the big privatization wave of the forthcoming market liberalization of the Czech Republic.

Shares in all Czech energy suppliers have been or will be sold to investors.

Two investors from Germany and Austria have held participationsin JME since 1999.

A company like JME must be willing to face positive changes for two reasons:

1. The challenge of liberalization

   The coming liberalization forces companies to strengthen their customer orientation substantially in all areas of business. The change from a regional monopoly to freely regulated competition entails changes whose implications cannot be overestimated. Issues such as customer satisfaction, customer orientation, product development, marketing, and sales strategy are just some of the areas that were unknown in the company before now. These tasks cannot be solved in small, evolutionary steps. It is necessary to establish a reference that will align the company correctly for all time.

2. The challenge of privatization

   Privatization brings a new dimension in company management. Because of the changes expected in revenues and costs, orientation to market shares, profits and value development represent another dimension in these market changes. The company must be active in these areas in order to be able to build a strong and lasting position for its new shareholders.

The existing management and information systems in the company are not capable of handling these new tasks. Therefore, the company management will be required to implement a profound structural change over a very few years that will prepare both company and staff for the changed market.

1.3 Process Management as the Core of the Extensive Restructuring Project

The decision to approach these new challenges actively and to define and implement a new company direction for the changed market was taken in 2000.

The objective of the O.R.I.O.N. reorganization project was defined clearly and rigorously:

... to create a competitive customer-oriented and process-managed business organization which will be capable of exploiting future opportunities in the energy market...

It was clear before the project started that this "revolution" could only be implemented if a new management culture were established and accepted within the company. The key was the process-orientation of the whole company. This strategic task had to include and integrate all levels of the company:

- Owners and supervisory board
- Board of directors and management
- Workers and employee representatives

The need for this project was recognized in the light of the anticipated development in the market and the business sector. The question was not whether to work towards this objective, but how to reach it. Process-oriented approach and behavior was one of the keys to the implementation and to the company's future.

2. Setting the Project Objectives

"When the wind of change blows, some build walls and others windmills" (Chinese proverb)

The objective of the project was defined in the clearest terms before any work was begun on the operational project.

The answers to the following questions were of paramount importance:

- What will the company gain and over what period?
- Why are the changes necessary ?
- Why is business process management a suitable course of action to secure the future of the company?
- What should business process management achieve?
- What has been achieved in the past with business process management (including by other companies)?

The following success factors in the energy sector were fundamental for JME:

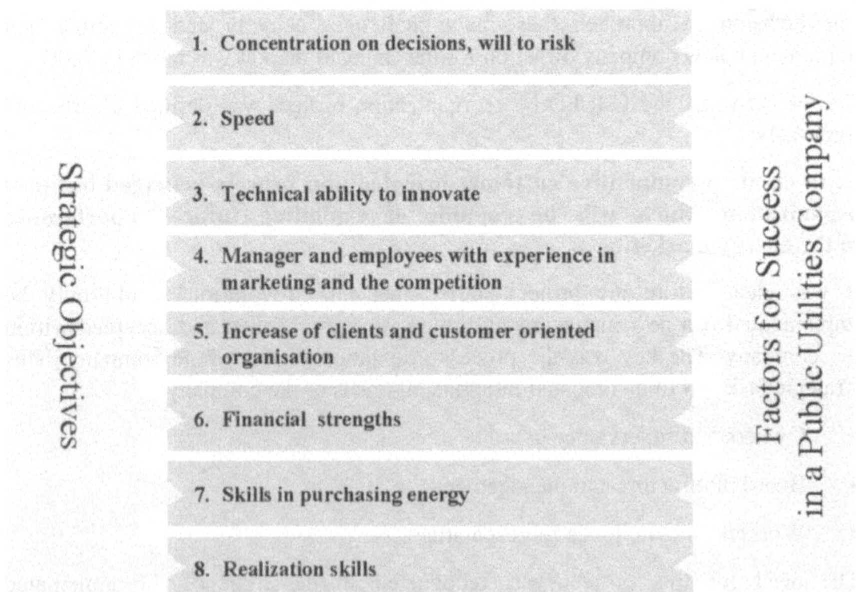

Figure 2: Eight factors for success in the energy sector

The following items are listed in order of their significance for all companies in our sector:

1. Challenging employees' business thinking and behavior
2. Competitive advantages by bringing new products and services to market faster
3. Additional innovative development of the product and service portfolio
4. Employment of competitive staff with experience in the sector and projects
5. Consistent focussing of all company departments on customers and market segments
6. Sufficient financial means for the continued and timely implementation of the company change process
7. Optimization of energy purchasing in respect of the process, price and risk aspects
8. High speed between decision and implementation of concepts based on higher level of employee responsibility

JME has to establish a basis for future development so that the company will:

- Continuously place the focus on customer requirements
- Apply a process-oriented approach without exception
- Adopt highly efficient work practices
- Be managed in a target-oriented way
- Make parallel improvements
- Position itself as the "best practice" in sector benchmarking.

The project described and the critical success factors demanded the development of a detailed view of the entire company. This was the only way to identify all the options for cutting existing operational process costs substantially and to eliminate wastage of resources. This will pave the way for vastly increased productivity in the future.

Other objectives are as follows:

- Replacement of the existing heterogeneous IT system
- Preparation for the installation of an integrated standard software solution (SAP R/3)

- Process-oriented preparation and installation of the CRM[1] and customer clearing systems (SAP CRM & IS/U[2])
- The extension of information systems for optimal support of target- oriented company management

These factors pinpoint the most important business fields in which the company must be refurbished and retooled for competition.

The challenges the company and the project team will have to face is shown clearly in the following overview of the various business areas.

Processes	• Use of ARIS Toolset for development and documentation • Structure of QM and Continuous Process Improvement systems for active management and measurement of processes
Controlling and Asset Management	• Decentralized management and planning • Controlling systems • Structure of the internal market • Concentration on value-added services
Marketing and Distribution	• Integration of new client process (CRM) • Client orientation and measurement of performance • Multifunctional teams
IT system	• Substitution of heterogeneous functional system with integrated standardized software supported in process • Definition of IT as a service centre with standards of output
Strategy	• Implementation of company strategy in profit centers with orientation for the process • General realization of company strategy with consistent process models down to the lowest planning level
Human Resources HR	• Institutionalization of process management • Process management = a new management and professional career • Transparency and information = opportunity for personal development

Figure 3: Business areas of the company

[1]CRM = Customer Relationship Management
[2]SAP IS/U = SAP industry solution utilities

3. Project Procedure

3.1 Two Implementation Steps for the Process-oriented Company

As was indicated previously, the company does not need a marginal optimization of the existing structures but a program of radical change. This ambitious composite task must be communicated and managed purposefully within the company.

The conversion of JME into a process-oriented company will be implemented in two interconnected stages.

"Each journey around the world begins with the first small step"

The reorganization project O.R.I.O.N. was the first important stage that enabled the foundation for all other changes to be laid. This project had to be implemented in a short time, to ensure that the opportunities arising from the liberalization of the market were not missed.

"Management by processes"

This stage will be used to develop the concept and implementation in the second stage and to convert the company from a functional organization to a process-oriented company. This conversion is a much more difficult task and will take several years.

“Process-managed company”

3.2 Introduction and Definition of Business Processes in the Re-engineering Project

The reorganization project O.R.I.O.N. included the following content and items:

- Definition of a strategic framework for the liberalized market
- Aims of process optimization
- Development of the process model on the basis of ARIS
- Preparation of the organizational structure proposal
- Proposal of the controlling system
- Specification of the new IT system requirements
- Development of the implementation plan and other measures

The existing business activities have been defined on the basis of ARIS in the processes of this first level of reorganization. Because of a different organizational structure and very heavy decentralization in many areas of activities, the process model had to be changed quite significantly for the new business concept.

The following issues were central to deliberations:

- The centralization of managing functions from the regional branches to headquarters and concurrently decentralization of process handling
- Reduction in the number of regional branches and thus also the concentration of activities for achieving critical mass
- Clarification of competencies and authorities
- Assimilation of the organization into the new process groups
- Conversion of process groups (gathering homogenous processes in one division/section) into the new organizational structure

This conversion of the "old" organization in the framework of the O.R.I.O.N. project did not, and does not mean the end of reorganization but rather a start of subsequent improvements in the sense of the global development.

Selected business processes have been further improved and harmonized under the auspices of the O.R.I.O.N. project. That was the basis for the process-oriented establishment of management and information systems. The specific projects have been defined for implementation in a special plan to be realized over the next 2-3 years.

This particularly included:

- Installation of the new ERP systems on the basis of SAP R/3 with a process-oriented functionality concept
- Development of the new controlling concept on the basis of the new company organization, including the following items:
  - Introduction of center-management
  - Establishment of the company internal market for settling transactions between centers
  - Establishment of the planning and budgeting system
  - Coordination of the reporting system
- Replacement of all IT systems for customer management (target systems SAP IS/U, SAP CRM)

The following illustration provides an overview of the range of projects for the implementation of process management at JME.

All these projects have been implemented in a strictly process-oriented way on the principles of business processes documented in ARIS. The information basis in the ARIS-based process model of JME has been improved and refined step-by-step.

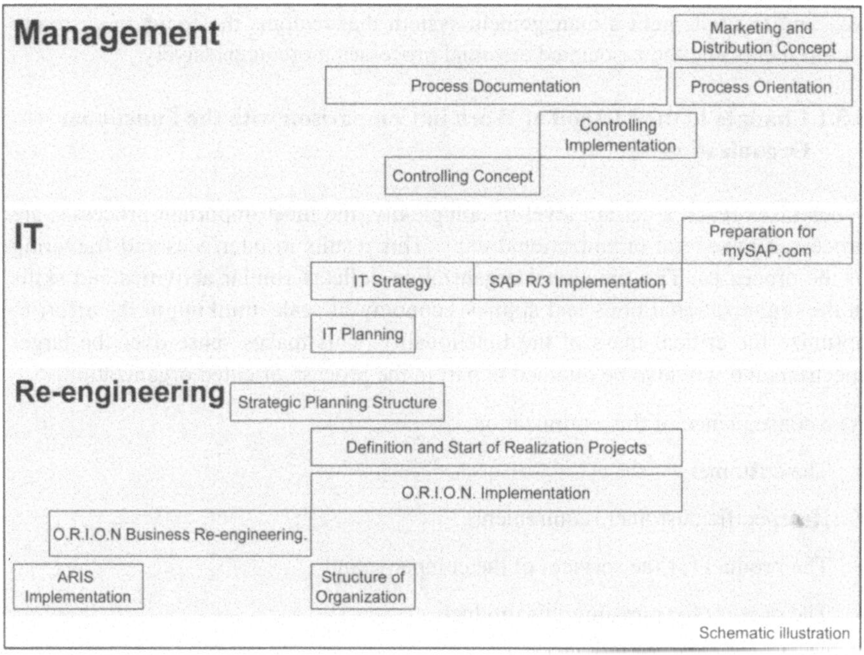

Figure 4: Strategic projects in relation to process orientation

3.3 Transformation of the Company into a Process-Oriented Company Structure

Applying the results of the O.R.I.O.N. project to the consequent implementation projects, the company was able to implement a number of the most important organization measures in a targeted way.

A comparison with the international sector reveals that other energy supply companies are several steps ahead.

"Think in advance, start small and act fast !"

In the context of strategic planning in the company, the analytical and preparatory work is being refined to enable JME's conversion to a fully process-oriented company in the next few years.

JME aims to take a leading position in the sector comparison. This seems to be necessary to allow exploitation of the potential of optimization, which cannot be developed by conventional optimization in functional organizations.

JME intends to overcome the limits of the functional hierarchy organization in this way and to implement a management system that realigns the focus to customer requirements and the associated essential processes more aggressively.

3.3.1 Changes to the Method of Work in Comparison with the Functional Organization

When tasks reach a certain level of complexity, the most important processes are processed in several organizational units. This results in interfaces and fracturing of the processes. The functional organization collects similar activities and skills in the organizational units and applies 'economy of scale' thinking in the effort to optimize the critical mass of the functionality. This makes sense over the larger spectrum and will also be retained in part in the process-oriented organization.

As a consequence of this optimization,

- The customer,
- His specific customer requirement,
- The product (or the service) of the company, and
- The process for pursuing this product

recede into the background.

Employees and their functions should be used where they can bring the highest added value. Bundling of homogenous functions as such will be suppressed to enable work to proceed in the autonomous process flows.

This method has been applied successfully in other industries for years. (A group task in the automotive industry is noteworthy here).

These principles are valid not only in the core processes of a company (production in the automotive industry) but can also be applied in support and management processes. The organization of controlling may be mentioned as an example.

The reorganization of controlling normally results in the centralization of all control functions in the company, and consequently in striving for effects in departments. At JME, controlling tasks are split into

- The controlling of the company
- Controlling of the profit centers
- Controlling of the decentralized regional managements

Company controlling operates centrally as the service provider for company management and also for the decentralized units.

All responsibility for the controlling tasks of profit centers and regional centers is decentralized. Each decentralized unit (profit center or regional management) has employees with controlling skills performing these responsibilities. The majority of controlling tasks is thus performed in the teams in a decentralized way. Only overall management remains centralized.

The connection between centralized and decentralized controlling tasks is assured by business processes. The secondary effect of this clear separation of tasks is the simplification of the defined process models, since the number of authorizations and approvals is substantially reduced.

The idea seems obvious and also successful. This form of organization has proved itself fully by the long years of experience in other companies in the energy industry.

The idea may also be applied in other areas of the company. It does not matter if these areas are

- Core processes,
- Management processes, or
- Support processes

of the company.

The teams associate all the important skills (functions) in the group, and can organize themselves optimally and concentrate on meeting process performance.

The following diagram shows some differences between functional and process-oriented organization.

How was the organization controlled <u>in the past</u>?	**How will the organization be controlled <u>in the future</u>?**
• The manager is responsible for procedures and for the business unit. • Managers check tasks performed and do not pay attention to the result of the procedure. • Managers concentrate on their own departments. • Improvements are made on the basis of the managers' feeling, connection with the result of the process is not assessed.	• We want the process owner to have full knowledge of the process that he continuously improves. • We want participating employees to understand their part in the process and to search for methods on how to achieve best results. • We want the manager to take an active part in cooperation at all levels of business. • We always want to achieve the best results in the main process (without the introduction of various initiatives and projects).
Functional management supported in process	**Management concerned primarily with process**

Figure 5: Comparison of functional and process oriented management

3.3.2 The Advantages of Process-Oriented Management

Besides the necessary changes in the form of management, the introduction of process-oriented management also brings advantages to customers and employees as well as other positive influences to the company.

Advantages for customers:

- Strengthening of the company's customer orientation, since fewer interfaces are influenced by the customer processes
- Improvement of products for customers
- Better services
- The offer of multi-utility services

Advantages for employees

- Positive change in company structure
- Setting of specific targets and orientation to them
- Delegation and assumption of responsibility
- Faster and simpler decision making
- Enrichment of work for employees (a possibility for self fulfilment)
- Involvement in CPI process[3], as a contribution to improvement in the company.

3.3.3 Elements of Process-Oriented Management

The introduction of process-oriented company management is mainly a cultural change. It affects almost all areas in the company.

It must be seen and approached from a correspondingly broad perspective and should not be mistaken for the extended use of the tools in use in the company.

The company must plan it as a strategic project lasting several years.

Process oriented management must stem from the company vision and corporate strategy. It must direct all implementation measures including processes at the level of the individual toward the same end.

---

[3]CPI = continuous process improvement

The complexity of this change in the company corresponds to a second re-engineering. The following second-level issues must be addressed:

- Early integration of process-oriented company structure into the company strategy
- Increase in consequent customer orientation by training and education of employees and managers
- Introduction of quality management ideas and methods, in order to achieve permanent process improvements in CPI
- Support for and introduction of teamwork in multifunctional units as a replacement for the functional groups in the company
- Establishment of an incentive system so that employees support this new method of working. The hierarchy will be replaced by the process performance.
- Introduce of methods for measuring process performance (Process Performance Measuring)
- Change and adoption of organizational structure into a process-oriented team structure
- Definition of processes

These activities must be accompanied by supporting measures such as:

- Active change to the company structure at all levels of the company. The thinking starts and ends with internal and external customers.
- Further development of an effective and usable process documentation for all process participants.
- Adoption of existing information systems and introduction of new information systems in support of the process-oriented workflow in an active and efficient way.

Because of the complexity of the plan, the tools used for process documentation obviously play a key role, but they must always be perceived within the overall framework of all project contents. Too strong a concentration on the 'tools' does not bring us any further in this process of change with many 'soft factors'.

3.4 Institutionalizing Process Management in JME

The process idea is institutionalized at JME by a Chief Process Officer (CPO).

As a person with overall responsibility for the process, the CPO checks all the relevant data (time, quality, costs) and paves the way for process for continuous improvement in cooperation with the people responsible for the project.

The processes implemented are thus subject to constant further development.

3.5 Use of ARIS in Business Process Modelling

JME will incorporate all aspects of company organization into business process modelling on the process basis. The description of the processes will enable a total view in a stronger way than it has previously be the case:

- Assessment of the needs of internal and external customers,
- Definition of essential products and services,
- Set-up of relevant targets,
- Showing the necessary processes in the company,
- Specification of interfaces with external partners

The following slide is a schematic diagram of the integration of many business aspects into the JME process model.

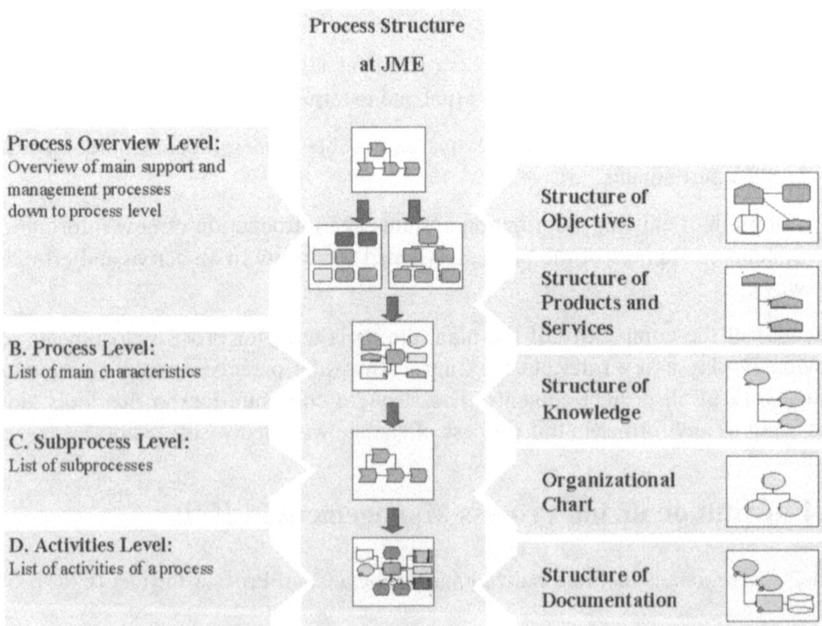

Figure 6: The structure of the JME process model

With the increasing complexity of the model and of the size of the company (approx. 2,000 employees), various levels of process modelling including

- Process
- Subprocess and
- Activity

are implemented in a broader concept of roles. This makes it possible to use the competencies and skills of the employees correctly from a subjective and professional view.

The following slide shows the JME concept of roles for senior management, process owners and process team members.

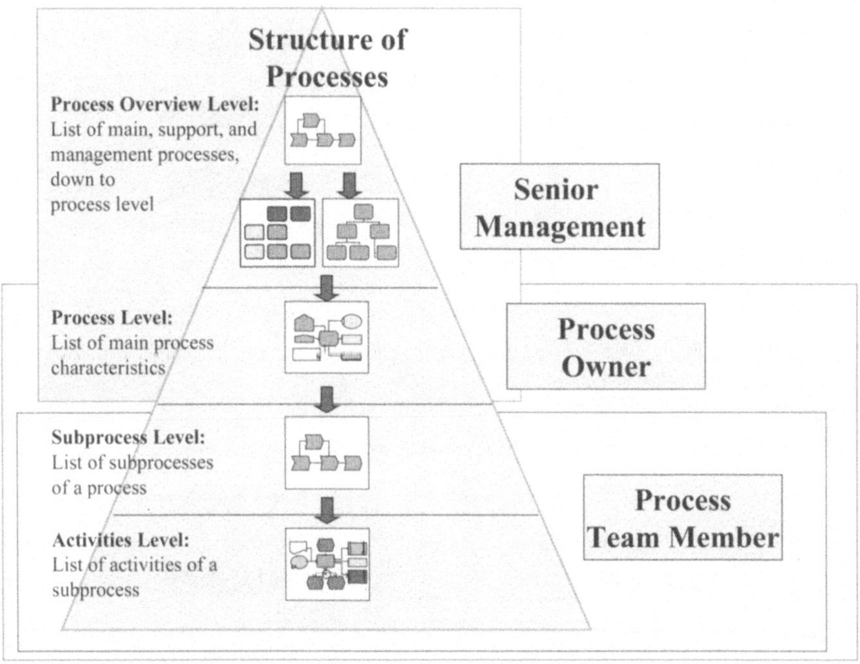

Figure 7: The concept of roles in Process Management

3.6 Process Models in Use at JME

3.6.1 General Structure of the JME Process Model

An approach has been selected during the re-engineering stage of the O.R.I.O.N. framework equating more to a bottom-up approach. The existing processes have been selected, improved and integrated into the organic structure of the company in the form of homogenous process groups.

This procedure was practical at the re-engineering stage and proved itself very well because of the speed of implementation.

The process will be inverted in the second stage of the process orientation and a top-down structure is being planned. This will establish the hierarchy structure of

- Core processes
- Management processes
- Support processes

with the relevant products. The following slide is a schematic representation of the process model:

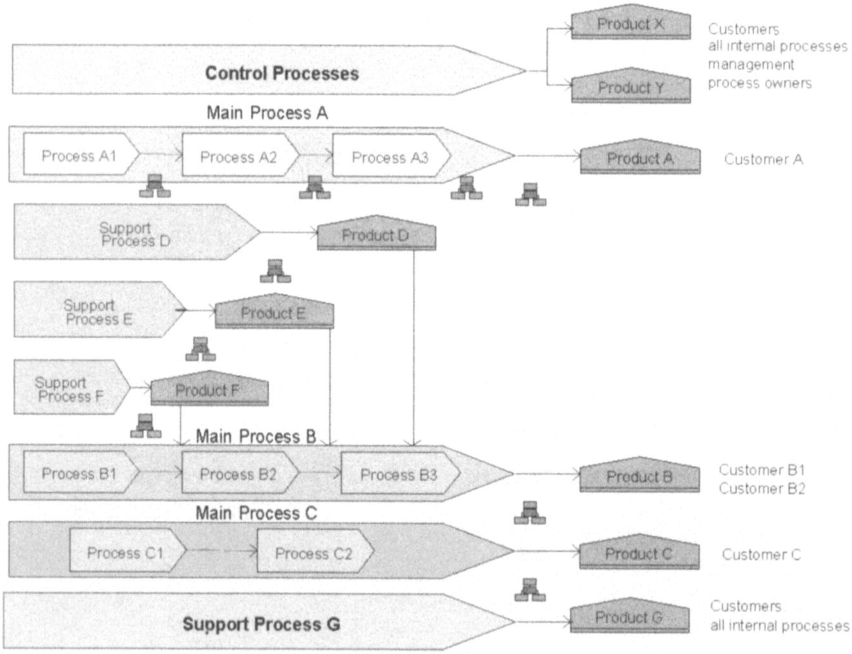

Figure 8: The structure of the business model in JME

3.6.2 Use of ARIS as a Tool for Process Modelling

In order to be able to use the ARIS tool for generating process models, an effective environment and organization of work must be established for manipulation with the tool and a relevant concept of the roles must be implemented.

The individual process teams must be able to work correctly at the processes reflecting their specific area of expertise.

In the next stage, the established and released process models must be made available to the employees of the company and the people working on the processes.

JME provides this with the Web for access to the relevant process models via the intranet.

The following slide shows the structure of ARIS tool use at JME.

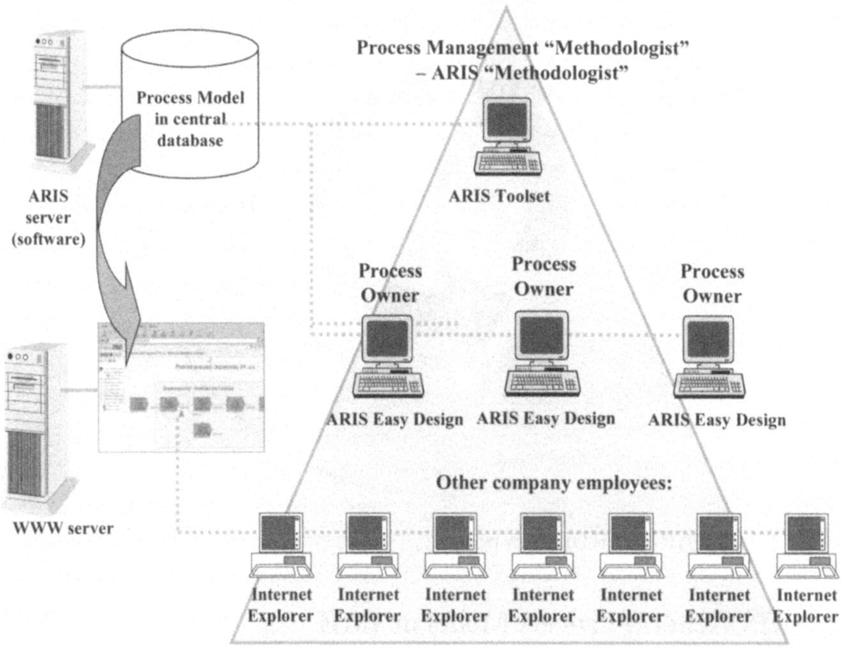

Figure 9: Use of the ARIS system

4. Results of ARIS Use

An important project result at JME is the ARIS business process model .

4.1 ARIS Database – Information Portal

The access into the implemented database enables very user-friendly and simple navigation through the whole of the JME company business process model.

Depending upon the view selected, it is possible to navigate in the simplest way from a highly compressed overview model up to the lowest model level with a high archiving depth.

The user acceptance of the process models have been maximized in this way.

Figure 10: The ARIS information portal

4.2 ARIS General Process Model at JME

The company business process model developed by ARIS is used as the basis for:

- Analyses
- Definitions of indices and measurements
- Rapid change and response to new market situations
- Reduction of failure rate during the processing of offers and complaints
- Identification of new and better working methods

4.3 Potential Benefits of ARIS

The application of ARIS and the selected procedure method offer numerous potential short, medium, and long-term benefits for JME.

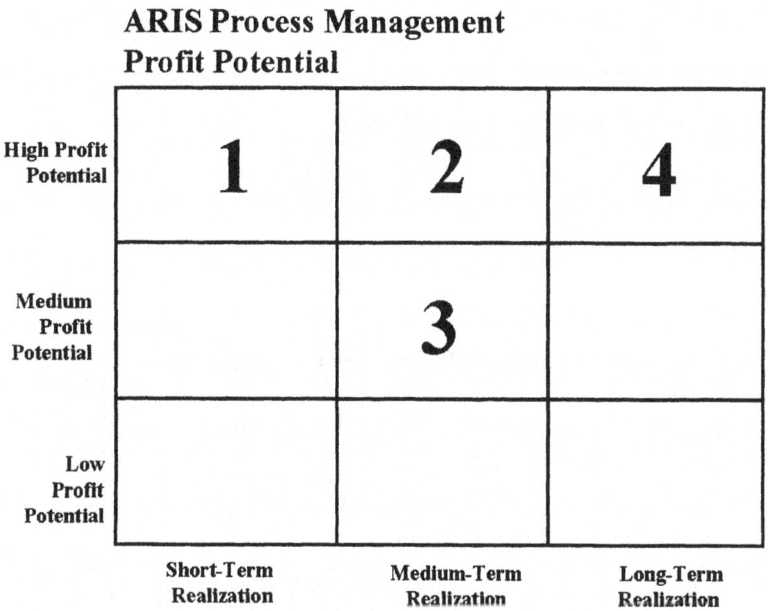

Figure 11: Potential benefits of ARIS process management

4.3.1 High Potential Benefit / Short-term Implementation

- A uniform procedure for modelling business processes
- Improved transfer of know-how for employees
- Standardization of the workflow and reduction of duplication of effort and inconsistencies.
- Homogenous and transparent representation of progress, of accountabilities and of the IT infrastructure
- Machine generation of consistent business process documentation
- Direct and flexible approach to further development within the framework of dynamic internal and external changes

4.3.2 High Potential Benefit / Medium-term Implementation

- Support for strategic decisions by a structured representation of business processes
- High project benefit due to the ability to use results repeatedly
- Transparency of information due to Web presentation of results on the intranet
- Elimination of media conflicts
- Reduction of activities that do not add value
- A well-understood, unified presentation of business processes for all participating areas after only a short introduction.
- Support for application of TQM[4] in the company

4.3.3 Medium Potential Benefit / Medium-term Implementation

- Development of the general company model showing all business processes and the organizational structure
- Export of process models via intranet or Internet enables independent study and ensures the clarity of the workflow
- Analysis of the process models according to various evaluation criteria
- Increased satisfaction of internal and external customers due to rapid and unique identification of the relevant contact person
- Appropriate documentation effort and prevention of redundancies and duplicated work

4.3.4 High Potential Benefit / Long-term Implementation

- Long term maintenance of the competitive level (benchmarks, indices etc.)
- Integration of other business areas (also internationally)

[4]TQM = Total Quality Management

5 Experience with the Project Course

5.1 Overview of Success and Failure Factors

The following table lists success factors that have been identified and confirmed repeatedly in the course of the project.

For the sake of completeness, the table also lists important failure factors that must be monitored constantly during the project work:

↑ Success Factors	↓ Failure Factors
↑ Clear commitment of the management ↑ Communication of strategy, workflow and targets ↑ Strong practice-oriented know-how of the consulting partner with respect to methods, products and industry ↑ Change from the status quo ↑ Concentration on primary business processes crucial from the competitive perspective ↑ Reorganization of secondary business processes ↑ Multidimensional management (customer satisfaction, time, quality, costs) ↑ Permanent sensitivity and integration of the relevant employees ↑ Sufficient budget for the implementation ↑ Integration of customers and customer needs ↑ Professional project management during the implementation, a constant project team ↑ A practically tested procedure model ↑ Institutionalization of the process management	↓ Management involvement lacking ↓ Management not 'visible' ↓ No definition of objectives ↓ No strategic concept ↓ Technology instead of strategic and organizational routing ↓ No overlapping process building up ↓ Unrealistic targets and expectations ↓ Objectives aimed only at cost reduction ↓ Inflexible company and employees ↓ Preference for the status quo ↓ Pessimistic approach and fear ↓ Strong resistance in the organization ↓ Disregard for employees' apprehensions ↓ Uncoordinated parallel project activities ↓ Insufficient budget for the implementation ↓ Non-existent or inadequate methodology for the procedure ↓ Permanent changes of employees ↓ Strongly theoretical project build up

Figure 12: Success factors and failure factors

5.2 Critical Review

In order to succeed in a climate of increasing international competition, the companies in the energy sector have no alternative – customers do not offer a second chance to individual companies – they change their supplier.

In summary we may say that the buildup of the strategic project, the high and permanent motivation of in-house and external project participants and the correct selection of partner companies were important factors in ensuring the success of the JME project.

The combination of ARIS software and of strategic consulting supported a fast, efficient and valuable project implementation. In this way, an integrated project, starting with strategy and flowing down through the functional design to operational implementation was completed on time and with maximum customer benefit.

5. 3 Vision – Outlook for the Future

The process-oriented company is the organizational form of the world under the conditions of a constant change.

(Michael Hammer)

Due to the positive experience and previous project successes, JME will also analyze and optimize in the medium term the relevant business processes that extend outside the company. The objective will be to accomplish new performance advantages and thus also competitive advantages.

JME will:

- Measure and analyze business processes using **P**rocess **P**erformance **M**anagement (PPM[5])
- Accelerate operational procedures and raise quality standards
- Continue to identify and implement potential cost reductions
- Continue to improve customer satisfaction and customer relations
- Integrate and optimize **E**nergy-**D**ata-**M**anagement (EDM[6])
- Optimize company management with the balanced scorecard approach

The participating external partners will support JME during all these future changes.

---

[5]PPM = ARIS Process Performance Manager
[6]EDM = the integration of power data into the system environment

Design of a Process Model with ARIS Toolset for a Telecommunication Company

Ing. Marek Mitáček
ČESKÝ TELECOM

Zdeněk Závodný
IDS Scheer ČR

Summary

In August 2001 a certification audit of the Quality Management System was successfully completed in the ČESKÝ TELECOM, a.s. units – Wholesale Services Group (WSG). Based on the audit's results, Lloyd's Register Quality Assurance (LRQA), a British certification company, granted the units a Quality Management Certificate for:

- *Design, development, and provision of wholesale telecommunication and WSG division interconnection services.*
- *Design, development and provision of IOL Fixed, IP VPN, and IOL unit SERVER HOSTING services.*

For the design and development of the Quality Management System (QMS) with a new effective management-oriented approach which is to improve processes and the entire company, ARIS methodology and tools supplied by IDS Scheer were used.

To our knowledge, ČESKÝ TELECOM, a.s. is thus the leading telecommunications operator in the country and it is also among the first telecommunication companies in the world to achieve certificate to the new ISO 9001 standard.

Key Words

ARIS, Process, Process model, ISO 9001

1. Project Background

1.1 Situation in Process Modeling before the Beginning of the Project

At the beginning of 2001, the ČESKÝ TELECOM operation committee adopted a resolution to build a Quality Management System (QMS) compliant with the ČSN EN ISO 9001:2001 standard in units that are in direct contact with customers. By building individual QMSs and subsequently obtaining their certifications, ČESKÝ TELECOM, a.s. expects, above all:

- To win marketing advantages in the liberalized telecommunications market;
- To provide a definition of quality for internal customers;
- Increased efficiency in the management of business processes;
- To be included in the ranks of certified European telecommunications operators.

The use of a range of SW tools is nowadays a commonplace necessity when building and maintaining large quality management systems. These tools are designed to ensure that the QMSs produced are flexible in the first instance, but also compatible with other tools and system elements used in a company. To build the ČESKÝ TELECOM quality management systems, the ARIS tools supplied by IDS Scheer were used. These tools had been used for some time in ČESKÝ TELECOM, but only in limited local form and mostly without any methodological support clearly defining the scope of such an advanced tool.

This was the reason why the primary need was to 'anchor' this tool in the company in terms of methodology and information technology so that it can fulfil its role as defined. Work on a solution respecting both angles began in the 'ARIS Tool Implementation' project.

2. Objectives

As has been indicated, the main objective was to create a company process model as a professional base for company management that could also be used for other system activity, adding considerable efficiency to company management. Detailed targets of the ARIS Tool Implementation project were derived from this objectives.

- Creation of a methodology clearly delineating the scope of ARIS use
- Definition of responsibility and authority of all the company employees participating in any way in generating a process model for the company.
- Definition of an ARIS database structure meeting the needs of all employees and compliant with the methodology used.
- Visualization of the process model on an intranet, that is; making the process model generated available to all employees on the intranet.
- Linking of the system to other IS's in support of company management; that is, removal of all ambiguities and ensuring information flow in such systems.

3. Processes

3.1 Project Management

Work on the ARIS Software Tool Implementation project was regulated by the current ČESKÝ TELECOM organizational rules. The project as defined by the basic documents, -the Project Charter and Project Plan - was managed by a Project Steering Committee. The project funding was backed by working out a business plan in which contributions were quantified and qualified.

The following diagram shows individual project stages and their contents.

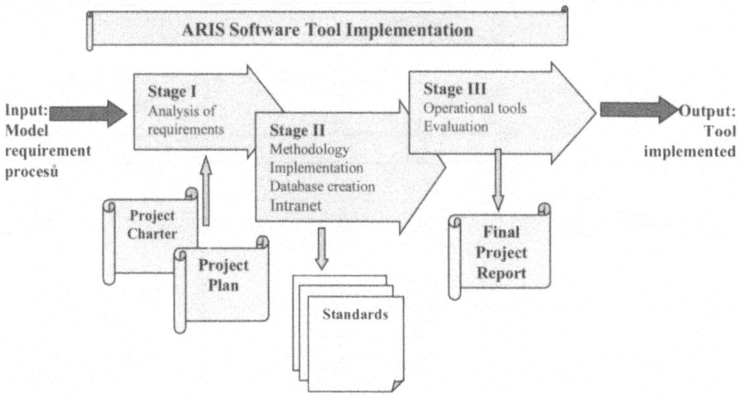

Figure 1: ARIS Software Tool: Implementation Workflow Diagram

3.2 Responsibilities and Authorities

As part of the ČESKÝ TELECOM transformation, the Quality Management department was transferred to a newly established Quality Strategy and Management division reporting to the Chief Executive Officer. This change in organization allowed the basic authorities within the created process model to be assigned. Specific authorities and responsibilities were defined within the ARIS Software Tool Implementation project described above. These involved, above all, the authorities and responsibilities of:

- Administrators
- Methodologists
- Users

3.3 Philosophy and Methodology of Process Modeling

At ČESKÝ TELECOM, the philosophy of company process modeling has been outlined in an organizational directive. The ARIS method is based on a structured approach to a company. In ČESKÝ TELECOM, this method was employed with the aim of creating a company process model that would provide a professional base for other system activities such as process cost management, process re-engineering, and others.

The structured approach of the ARIS method is clearly demonstrated in the basic concept of the method entitled ARIS Architecture.

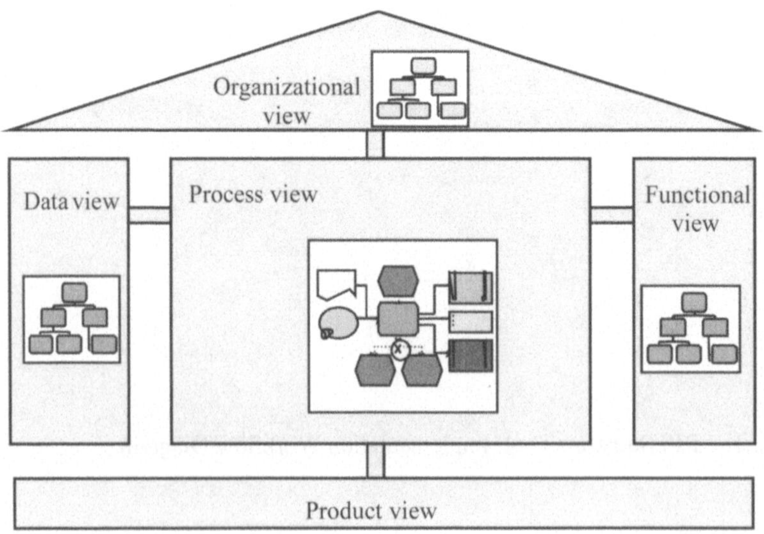

Figure 2: ARIS Architecture

This concept offers a comprehensive system view of the company process model and includes several substantial partial views.

Organizational view – comprises data on the company organizational arrangement of the company

Data view – comprises data used within the defined processes.

Functional view – comprises operations that transform the process input into output; the functional view is closely related to the goals since the set goals are supported by functions.

Product view – comprises all the input and output performances of both tangible and intangible nature.

Process view – comprises all the business processes and relationships between other views.

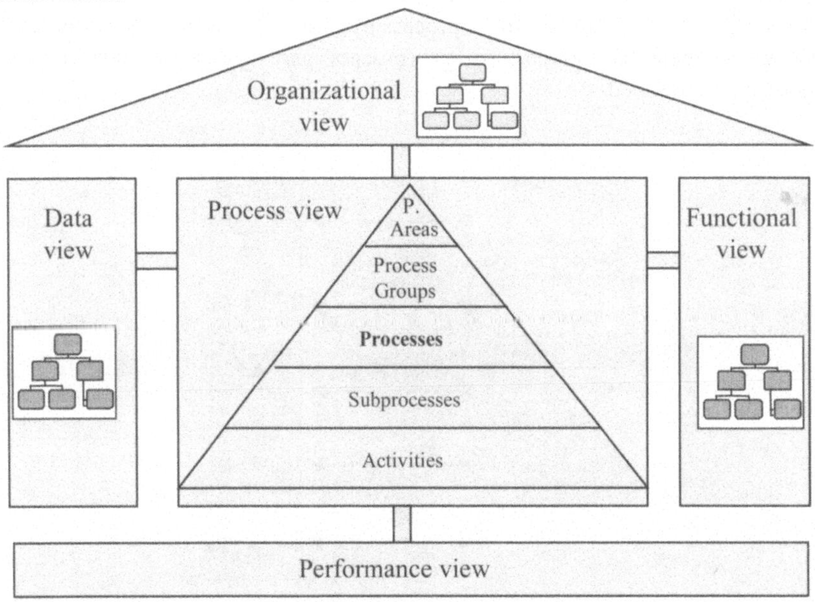

Figure 3: ČESKÝ TELECOM process model in ARIS Architecture

The theory of systems uses two different notions, that is, system structure and system behavior. System behavior denotes the static view of the system (firm) while its dynamics are described by the system behavior. In a process model, dynamics are expressed through the process view while modules and system structure are described by organizational, data, functional, and performance view models.

Thus a process model determines the way in which a process is viewed in the company, the way in which it is structured, and - above all - described.

The process model in the philosophy as applied in ČESKÝ TELECOM is characterized by a 5-tier process pyramid in which the first two tiers describe the basic structuring of processes into areas and groups.

The third tier identifies each process as a black-box focussing mostly on the definition of input and output data and the basic organizational responsibilities. It is also important to point out here that this is the level at which the basic process attributes necessary for process management are defined, that is, the process goal and a parameter that can be used to determine whether that goal is being achieved or not.

The fourth tier defines the structuring of the system into subprocesses, and the fifth describes each process element (subprocess) by listing its individual activities. Each of the five tiers of the process pyramid is assigned one model type in ARIS by which the given process (process part, group of processes or subprocess) is described.

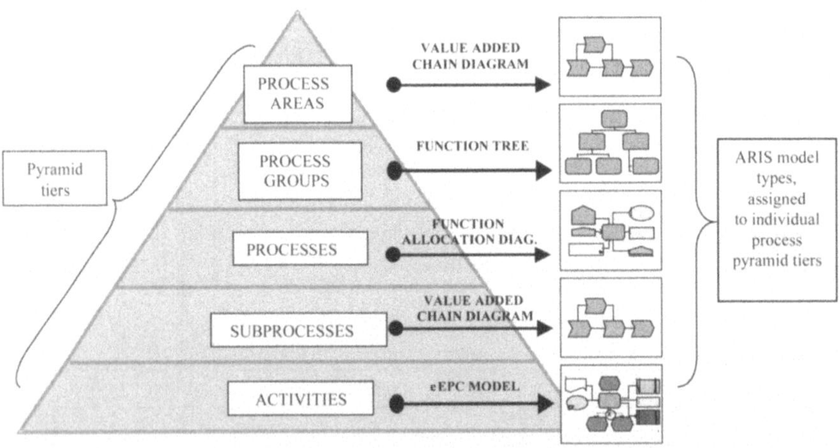

Figure 4: The process model showing the tiers and the "ARIS model types" assigned to them

Each of the five tiers of the process pyramid is substantiated within the QMS. The first two tiers (process areas and groups), designed mostly for company management, define the scope of the QMS. The third, fourth, and fifth tiers, intended for the participating employees, define precisely not only what a process should look like, but also the method used for its measurement, which parameter is measured, and what its value is. These three "participating" tiers of the process pyramid provide the basic metrics for process management, which are needed for and required by the ISO 9001 standard, and which are outlined in the following diagram:

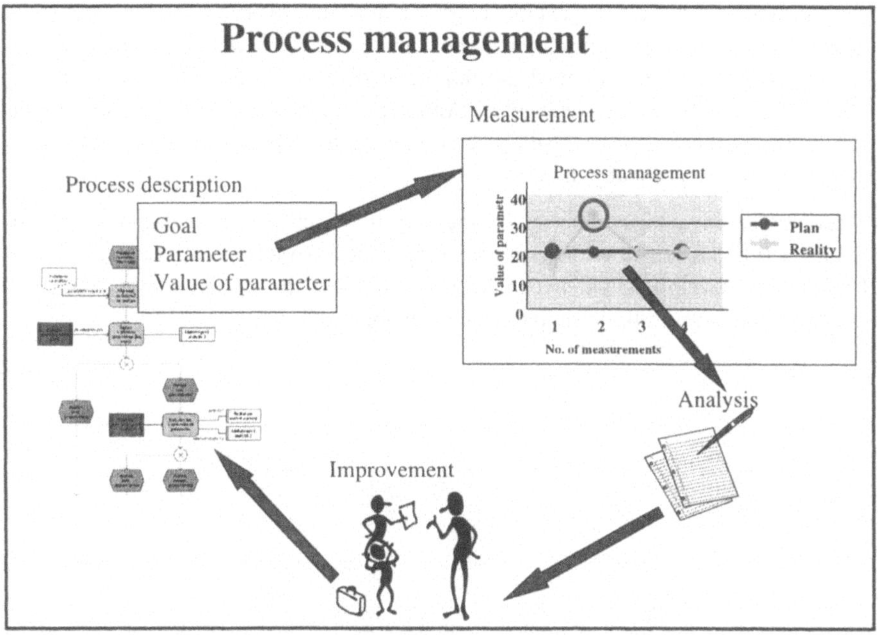

Figure 5: "Process Management" diagram

The issue of an organizational directive describing this philosophy sets the basic rules for the work of those who describe the processes and those who approve the process descriptions / models created.

The new philosophy outlined the basic framework for the using the ARIS software tool in ČESKÝ TELECOM. The exact description of the way the software tool is to be used, the definition of authorities and responsibilities, the use of each model and object, were provided in Process Model Methodology.

To create a process model using ARIS it was necessary to create a user-friendly environment for all employees who would be working on the descriptions.

3.4 ARIS in the ČESKÝ TELECOM Quality System Management

ARIS can produce various listings to be used to present the described processes also to those who cannot work directly using ARIS. One of the most suitable output forms is an intranet application using html format which enables active work with the models (such as quick search for information) instead of passively viewing static pictures.

This format can be used to establish an active hierarchical relationship between linked models; model attributes can be viewed (e.g. by whom the model was created, approved, etc.) as well as individual objects; it also enables model or object retrieval by name, type, etc. Another undisputed advantage this output format has is that it can be easily placed on certain Web servers with subsequent presentation on a company intranet.

These major advantages determined the way in which the created and approved model will be presented to the company employees. An intranet Company Process Model was developed which can be used to view the designed processes for approval and, above all, those that have been approved (valid).

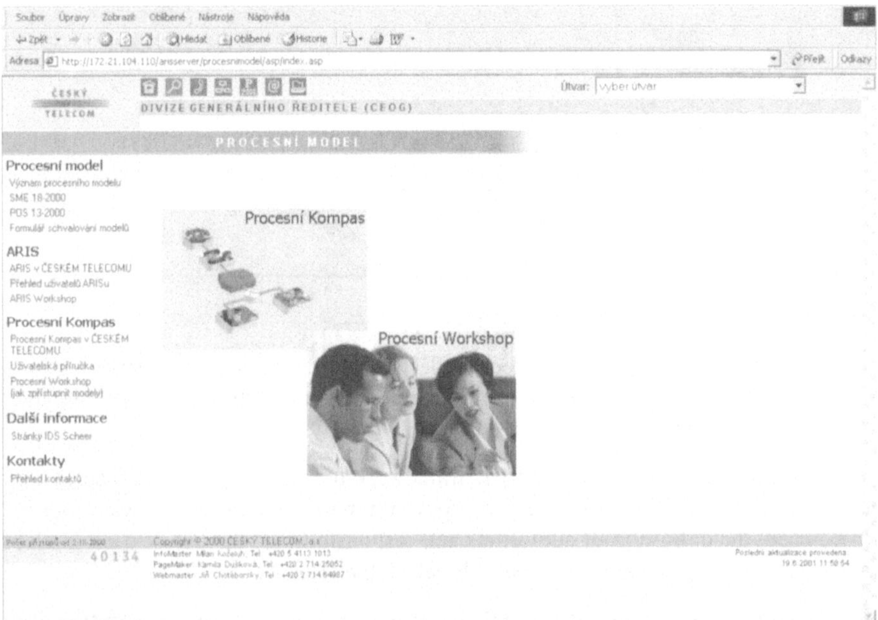

Figure 6: A sample intranet page with published ARIS models

All models (process descriptions) are available on the intranet site to receive critical comments from all the employees involved as part of the procedure for comments on the designed processes. Each employee can make a comment on each process model thus presenting his or her view of such a model. Because of its clarity and readability, this type of process model in the intranet environment is referred to as the Process Workshop.

A certain form of automation is no doubt one of the major advantages of this method of the procedure for comments. It is at the discretion of each employee who creates process model designs to decide when which model should be placed on the intranet for comments. The models marked by this employee are automatically placed on the Website at a precisely defined time. The Website also provides information about the person who created the model and when it was placed there.

Once approved, the process models are stored in the approved and valid version of the Process Model on the intranet. For its aptness and readability, this version is referred to as Process Compass. Apart from the display of relevant process models, the current state of processes documented here also includes a window in the navigation menu that can be used for better navigation in the structure of the process pyramid of the company to access a desired model more quickly. At present, the Process Compass includes all the processes of the certified organizational components, and other units and departments are adding their created, commented and approved processes at an increasing rate.

3.5 ARIS – Electronic Quality Manual of the ISO 9001 Quality Management System

According to the ISO 9001 standard, the basic document of the Quality Management System (QMS) is the quality manual. Its task is to exactly define the QMS in question and to create links between the required and applied standards. A quality manual must of course meet all the requirements of a "controlled document" and must be available to all employees involved in the QMS in question.

The quality manual of the certified systems of selected organizational units at ČESKÝ TELECOM is conceived as a group of interlinked ARIS models where each chapter of the standard is further presented as a model specifying its requirements and, above all, how these requirements are met within the quality management system created. Below is the hierarchical structure of this quality management:

a) Standard-basic-model level

b) Chapter-subchapter level

c) Subchapter-individual requirements level

d) Level referring to particular processes of a requirement

The first three model levels describe the requirements of the standard and their structure. The actual fulfilment of the requirements in a given organizational unit is only reflected at the fourth level.

Major advantages of the electronic Quality Manual include:

- ***Reference to the standard*** – each chapter, subchapter, and even requirement contains an exact html-format reference to the standard so that, for each particular requirement, it can be easily verified whether it is correctly understood and fulfilled.
- ***High flexibility*** – thanks to this approach, particular references and links to practical models can be amended, changed and deleted very quickly, which enhances and develops the QMS under construction.
- ***Clarity*** – because of the hierarchical organization of each model, any part of the process model can be easily accessed by a few clicks and a statement can be made as to how a particular standard requirement is fulfilled.
- ***Easy accessibility*** – using the html output format and the active form of this format (lower levels can be accessed by clicking on an object), every employee can view the entire process model as well as the designed QMS including all hyperlinks to the controlled documents, quality records.
- ***Easy control*** – due to the electronic format of the documents and the fact that each VOS employee has his own PC, it is possible to ensure that only the valid version of the document is displayed on the company intranet.
- ***Links to other documents*** –thanks again to the html format, hyperlinks can be used to link the entire quality manual to all the necessary controlled documents and all the company intranet pages.
- ***Links to the process model*** – as has been indicated previously, the process model may easily be accessed and particular process (subprocess) models displayed via links to specific models.

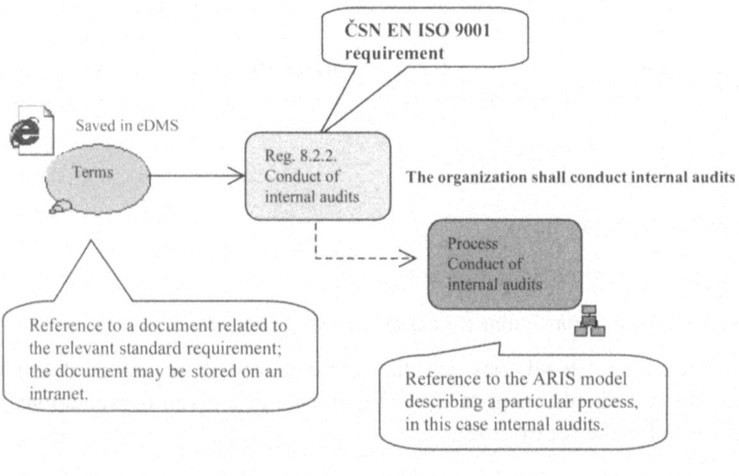

Figure 7: Sample fourth level of the Quality manual

4. Use of Consultants

As was stated earlier, ARIS has been in use at ČESKÝ TELECOM for some time, but only in some company areas and in a non-unified and non-systematic way. In 1988, a department for quality system management and support was established at ČESKÝ TELECOM. This was done at the time of the initial huge transformation measures that affected the entire company. The quality management officers at the time were ordered to identify and describe the company's major internal processes. The resulting material was intended to provide support for the majority of company employees who were gradually facing new working conditions resulting from each transformation step. However, to produce such materials a suitable tool was needed to visualize individual processes. As ARIS was already available in the company at that time without this fact being generally known, once the first processes had been identified, they began to be graphically visualized or described using various tools such as MS Office, Visio, All Clear, etc. However, when a purchase of the above tools was being considered, it was found that ČESKÝ TELECOM already had ARIS, supplied by IDS Scheer, as the standard for process modeling. Next it was ensured that this tool was available to all the employees of the Quality Management department or installed on the pertinent PC's. It soon became evident, however, that support for the use of this tool was necessary to a maximum extent to exploit the excellent qualities that ARIS was offering.

Therefore the ARIS distributor for the Czech Republic was identified. At that time, this was COMSOFT, s.r.o. in Brno (today, IDS Scheer ČR, s.r.o.). This company then trained selected Quality Management department employees in ARIS operation. The first of these training courses took place in the spring of 1999, which is also the time that may be taken for the beginning of a successful and beneficial cooperation between ČESKÝ TELECOM and IDS Scheer ČR, s.r.o from which all the ARIS licences have been bought. ČESKÝ TELECOM also started to use the consulting services offered by IDS Scheer ČR, which consisted in organizing the necessary training courses (for example: ARIS Easy Design and ARIS Tool Set control, ARIS Database Administration, etc.). It was the consultants of the IDS Scheer ČR who organized these training courses with very good results.

After the training which was so well organized and attended by ČESKÝ TELECOM employees, it was clear that a group of employees was being formed which would be able to use the ARIS modeling tool regularly. Since ČESKÝ TELECOM is a company operating throughout the territory of the Czech Republic it became necessary to set unified rules for using ARIS inside the company. It is well-known that ARIS is an open software product that can be configured to meet the requirements of specific customers. Here again, the services offered by the consultants were used. Within the above-mentioned ARIS Software Tool

Implementation project, a work team was appointed from among ČESKÝ TELECOM employees and IDS Scheer ČR, s.r.o. consultants. From this team's activity, a set of organizational rules resulted that became binding for all ČESKÝ TELECOM employees upon approval. These materials clearly define the area of ARIS application and are regularly used and updated to suit the needs of the company.

The following are examples of other activities which IDS Scheer ČR, s.r.o. consultants organized or in which they strongly participated:

- **Customer solution design** for the publication of a company process model on a company intranet. As part of this activity, IDS Scheer ČR, s.r.o created software scripts jointly with the programmers to enable automatic transfer of selected parts of a process model to a company intranet.
- Another activity was a customer solution to the problem of creating an interface for exporting organizational structures between the process model under construction and the company information system. These issues were also included, on the part of IDS Scheer ČR, s.r.o. in consultants' activities and the resulting solution became known as **HR link**.
- A significant activity of IDS Scheer ČR, s.r.o. consultants is also **servicing,** both for ARIS and for the customer solutions provided.
- At the request of ČESKÝ TELECOM, the IDS Scheer ČR, s.r.o. consultants also help in moderating negotiations and working meetings of various teams that deal with issues of ARIS use.

By way of conclusion, it is possible to say that the cooperation between the customer, in this case ČESKÝ TELECOM, and IDS Scheer ČR, s.r.o. consultants can be viewed as very successful, and it is desirable that it should be developed in the future.

5. Results Achieved

The appraisal of the results contained in this chapter refers to the period when this article was written - early 2002. These are the comments on the results achieved:

- The **ARIS standardization** at ČESKÝ TELECOM has been completed. This is also due to the issuance of organizational rules that define the platform for using ARIS in a unified manner across the entire company, including the definition of the methodology for its use.
- The responsibilities and authorities of all company employees who take any part in generating a process model have been defined.

- Within the framework of individual steps performed to standardize the tool, an **ARIS database structure** has been defined, and database maintenance and administration rules have been set.
- In the middle of 2001, the ČSN EN ISO 9001:2001 **Quality Management System** was certified by Lloyd´s Register Quality Assurance, an international certification authority.
- A customer **solution** has been created for **the presentation of a company process model in an intranet environment**. This has created conditions for use of the process model by all ČESKÝ TELECOM employees .
- By creating an HR link interface, a link has been established to all other applications of the IS that supports company management. In this connection, a requirement has been identified for creating other links between ARIS and individual software applications.

6. Conclusion

The authors are evaluating practical experience collected during the implementation of ARIS across an important company operating over the whole Czech territory, which is certainly the case with ČESKÝ TELECOM. At this stage it can also be said with some satisfaction that sound knowledge and experience clearly prevailed . during a process of the complexity described. Both participants in this process - ČESKÝ TELECOM and IDS Scheer ČR, s.r.o. - can unequivocally say that the existing model cooperation based on the high levels of professionalism of both employees and management of both companies is the best investment for the years to come.

ISO 9001 Certification of the Selection and Recruitment Department of Air France (DP.GS)

Benoît Vannier
IDS Scheer France

Laurent de Castelbajac
IDS Scheer France

Laurent Teysseyre
Air France

Summary

The aim of this project, based on an initiative to analyze processes and implement a dynamic of continuous improvement, was primarily to achieve certification in ISO 9001 v. 2000 for Air France's Selection and Recruitment Department. This was an important project for IDS Scheer France because it represented the first certification initiative in France supported by ARIS. The project, which was truly successful, also provided IDS Scheer with the opportunity to optimize the conditions under which ARIS would be used in such an initiative.

Key Words

ISO certification, Quality initiative, Process control, Web Publisher

1. Introduction

Among a number of campaigns launched by Air France, one was the initiative to obtain ISO 9001 version 2000 certification for certain of its key departments, and to establish control of processes.

In this context, it should be noted that Air France selected ARIS at the Company level, not only as a tool for analyzing business processes, but also as a support for all the activities leading to ISO certification initiated within the Company.

The new version of the ISO standard undoubtedly places processes at the heart of the certification initiative. To this end, offering as it does a system and a structure that can be used in studying processes, ARIS provides highly effective support for this type of initiative.

In January 2001, the Central Quality Directorate of Air France contacted IDS Scheer France with a view to defining the principles of expertise and assistance that IDS Scheer would be able to contribute in the certification initiative by Air France's Selection and Recruitment Department.

The initiative unfolded in a climate characterized both by rapid growth in recruitment and internal and external customers requirements.

The project is ground-breaking in the sense that, inspired by the new ISO standard requiring study and control of processes, on the one hand it is one of the first attempts in France to achieve certification with the support of the ARIS tool, and on the other that it is among very few ISO certification programs undertaken by a global recruitment department.

This project was executed over the course of 18 months, from the launch of the initiative until the certification audit in December 2001, which proved to be successful.

2. Objectives

The primary objective was of course the achievement of ISO certification, but other goals were also associated therewith:

- Consolidation and partial optimization of processes
- Ownership of processes by staff
- Publication of processes on the intranet
- Creation of a dynamic of continuous improvement based upon the processes

3. The Initiative

3.1 General Approach

Modeling in ARIS was done on the basis of results provided by working groups.

The construction of the documentation system was simplified considerably by the use of a modeling tool.

The modeling effort was "top-down" in nature, based on the general process map of Air France's Selection and Recruitment Department.

Important difference: the framework does not concern the recruitment processes of Air France as such, but rather all the processes managed by the " Selection and Recruitment " organization.

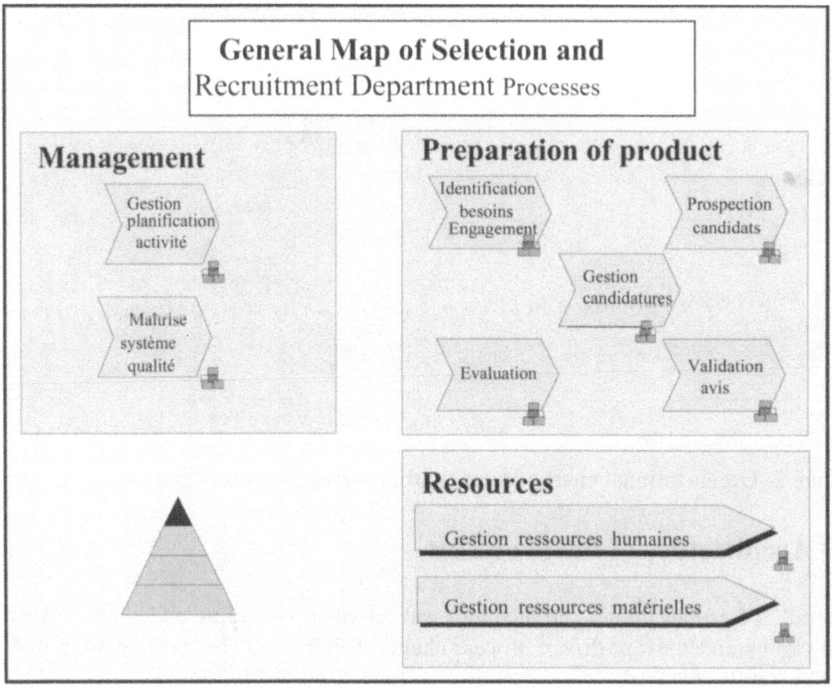

Figure 1: General view of the Selection and Recruitment Department's processes

In the modeling phase, significant attention was devoted to the interfaces between the processes, a challenge that has been recognized as a major element in studying processes, particularly from the point of view of Quality. The interface zones between processes have indeed been identified as factors in generating added value.

3.2 Resource Modeling

With respect to resources ("shared data"), only human resources and some "specific terms" have been represented. The official organizational chart was not used. Instead, an organizational chart was constructed on the basis of roles, featuring the profiles essential to the processes.

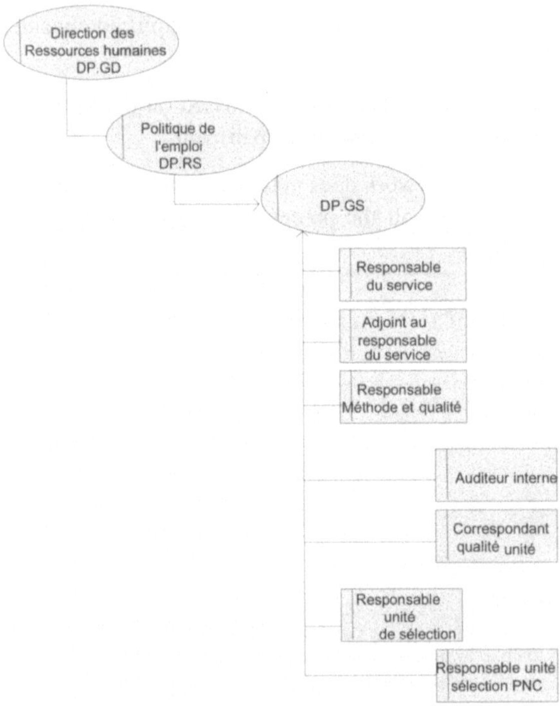

Figure 2: Organizational chart of roles (partial view)

3.3 Architecture of the Processes

Overall, a four-tier process architecture was adopted: two value added chain tiers, and two extended event-driven process chain (eEPC) tiers. The most detailed EPC level is rarely required.

In some cases, an intermediate level was used to adapt a process to different scenarios (function tree).

It is worth emphasizing here how important is for all recipients and beneficiaries of the project to be able to navigate easily through the documentation base in such an activity.

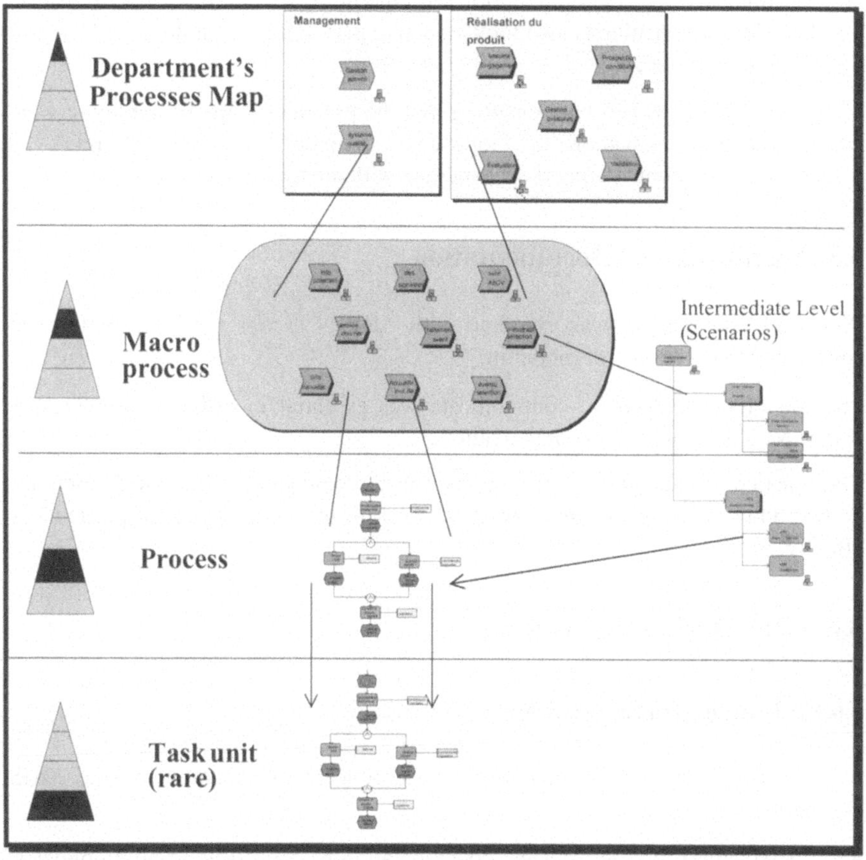

Figure 3: Architecture of models in Selection and Recruitment Department

3.4 Role of IDS Scheer Consultants

The IDS Scheer consultants were directly involved in setting up and analyzing the process models, in direct collaboration with the project coordinator at Air France. The IDS Scheer consultants also took an active part in the methodological support of the Quality approach.

They were further tasked with ensuring that the practical limits of modeling were not exceeded (observation of "top-down" boundaries, systematic reuse of resources...), and contributing their expertise with the tool in consolidating data.

3.5 Distribution of Documentation

Web Link (the project was executed with ARIS 4.1) was used successfully to communicate the results of modeling.

The use of the intranet to communicate was essential in order to promote the "process culture" within the organization.

The practice of attaching "Word" or "Acrobat" documents to the ARIS reference system and exporting the entire body of work to the intranet proved particularly effective.

3.6 ARIS During the Audit

3.6.1 Advantages to the Auditor

- The auditor was very interested by the concept of navigating in the ARIS base.
- The standard requires that the documentation be accessible to all employees. Web Publisher satisfies this requirement and has proven to provide a viable alternative to a paper-based documentation system.
- The auditor thus had evidence that, thanks to a documentation system easily accessible via the Web, the organization was entirely committed to the notion of processes which constitutes the heart of the ISO 9001 v 2000 standard.

3.6.2 The Auditees' Viewpoint

The users appreciated having a "single point of access" to the documentation leading to

- The process documentation
- The procedures for local applications
- The Quality manual

A further advantage lies in the provision of centralized system of documentation management, which guarantees that:

- Information is immediately accessible
- Information is updated on a continuous basis

This last requirement points up the need to have an administrator dedicated full-time to the documentation stored in ARIS.

4. Results Achieved

- Most importantly, the approach of modeling processes in ARIS contributed to the success of the initiative by the Selection and Recruitment Department of Air France to achieve **certification** to ISO 9001 v. 2000 a in December 2001, which certification shall remain in force for a period of 3 years.
- The chief contribution of the tool was to promote **ownership of the processes** by the staff members of the Selection and Recruitment Department involved in the project, due on the one hand to the establishment of a vital intranet, and on the other to the interdisciplinary exchanges among those involved at the working group stage on which the process analysis activities were based.
- More significantly, the **consolidation of processes** revealed opportunities for improvement which will be exploited as the initiative continues to be developed following the audit. This represents the first phase of process improvement.

5. Lessons Learned

Since the publication of the 2000 version, the ISO standard is heavily oriented towards processes. It follows that the audits themselves are conducted according to processes. Thus, in order to obtain certification, an organization must complete the step of studying the major processes for all types of component processes indicated in the map for Air France's Selection and Recruitment Department. ARIS provides optimal support for this activity by concentrating the focus on processes for purposes of study and by its use during modeling on the basis of working groups, in order to reflect real-life conditions as closely as possible. However, some points should be borne in mind for any similar projects in the future.

- The need to give due weight to the interactions (ISO term) between processes as represented by process interfaces (ARIS object) to facilitate navigation and understanding of the logic of the system, for recipients in general and the auditor in particular.
- The need to integrate the notion of documentation management under ARIS. Indeed, just as with a paper-based documentation system, it is essential to indicate clearly the existence of such a management system under ARIS, highlighting in particular the roles, the archiving rules and the updating processes associated therewith. Beyond the graphical representation of the processes, it should therefore also be demonstrated that document management has not only been addressed, but also mastered.
- The need to integrate the notion of "process review" in the ARIS system. Process reviews are triggered by the process coordinators, have a pivotal role in this initiative, and are designed to study the following points: process updating, analyses of performance indicators, establishment of a plan for improvement by process.
- In addition, in order to ensure that processes are completely under control, it is essential to assign one or more relevant key performance indicators to each macroprocess. After all, the notion of performance measurement is central to the principal of continuous improvement, as illustrated most effectively by the familiar "Deming cycle" (Plan-Do-Check-Act).
- Finally, in the same spirit as the control and coherence of the processes included in the system, it is necessary to implement a mechanism for managing archives and database version control.
- This project helped to establish the importance of assigning roles in the base, clearly and in detail, so that all responsibilities associated with a project of this magnitude are considered and assigned. By the same token, the role of "process coordinator" is absolutely critical because this personage must act as a driver for the initiative.

The comments by the auditors were also highly instructive:

- The auditor was very interested by the concept of navigation in the ARIS base, which he had not encountered before.

- Levels of detail: However, in the auditor's opinion, some EPCs were too full and too detailed. Indeed, guided by the old standard, the modelers appear to have continued down to the task level, whereas the new standard requires this level of detail for only 6 quality control procedures.
- The standard requires that the documentation be accessible to all staff. Web Publisher satisfies this requirement. Nevertheless, the practice of printing models from the intranet is not optimal. Also, the volume of information provided by the standard intranet exceeds the needs of the users.
- Since the Company filter was not originally quality oriented, certain information pertinent for ISO (name of modeler and dates of process reviews, for example) have been added "by hand" in free-form text. This observation confirms the need to re-establish conventions and a filter when new objectives are assigned to the modeling activity.

Based on the observations of the end users and the auditor, the project will be modified as follows:

- The conventions and filters must be adapted to respond to the challenge of certification as indicated in this pilot project
- With regard to document production via reports, a distinction will be made between "process records" having an average level of detail and "procedural records" having a high level of detail. These procedural records will relate only to the 6 quality assurance procedures, including the process for document control in ARIS itself.
- In order to obtain process records, it will be necessary to rework some eEPCs to provide an intermediate level between the first (and often only) eEPC level and the last level of value-added chains.
- Simplification of information provided on the intranet.

6. Review of Current Situation: Role of ARIS Today

On the basis of this first initiative for the purpose of certification, ARIS today is a key and an accepted tool for:

- Assuring that the documentation system allows full retrieval, that is to say that a permanent record is preserved of past and present tasks.
- Reviewing and updating processes, particularly at the start and end of process reviews.
- Anticipating future needs and/or simplifying current modes of operation.

- Contributing, in a supporting capacity, to the control of the department's activities in their entirety, as well as those of any sub-contractors. Indeed, where sub-contractors are instructed in some degree to apply the processes of the commissioning organization, that organization can now use ARIS as a tool in the development of specifications by modeling not only the conceivable collaboration scenarios, but also the interfaces that exist between the commissioning organization and its sub-contractors. This use for modeling thus also provides a simplified means of setting up audits to verify the activities of sub-contractors.
- Monitoring the effectiveness of the processes, and providing a working basis for internal audits and future audits of sub-contractors.

7. Outlook: ARIS Tomorrow...

In a subsequent phase, use of ARIS could be extended to fulfill the following functions:

An Aid to Simplifying Documentation

Based on certain observations made by the auditors, ARIS could be used to begin a new phase in the simplification of the documentation system.

In this case, it is most important to insist that the models be readable, not only directly on screen, but also in the printed form. In fact, it is very important that clear and comprehensible models are available to users in hardcopy format.

Then, it would be beneficial to reduce the number of procedures associated with the various models. Indeed, the standard ISO 9001 v 2000 provides for only six compulsory procedures, all the rest may take the form, for example, of intermediate level models. In these terms, the introduction of a "process record" type document, which would provide complete though synthetic coverage of the intermediate level, may represent an important contribution to the comprehensibility of the documentation system.

A Simulation Tool

The Simulation module in ARIS could be used to optimize management of workflows within Air France's Selection and Recruitment Department, and particularly workflows relating to processing applications, used in support of forecasts regarding the parameters of the department's activity.

ARIS in BT

Rob Davis
BTexact Technologies

Colin Paton
BTexact Technologies

Summary

"ARIS in BT" explains BT's reasons for choosing ARIS, their pilot plan, their implementation and roll out into different business units. It highlights the aspects involved in mapping business processes and the benefits of implementing ARIS. There are hints on how to make the most of ARIS, including creating guide sheets, developing process model standards and tips on how to use ARIS effectively. Additional ARIS features such as the application of web publisher and the use of balanced scorecard are also illustrated.

Key Words

BT, British Telecommunications, BTexact Technologies, Telecommunications, Design and management of processes, Common process architectures, Intranet for publishing process designs, Electronic publication of process designs, ARIS, ARIS Centre of Excellence, 'Bottom-up' approach, Pilot project, Model Generation, Simulation, EPC Methodology. Server migration, Web publisher, Intranet, Guide sheets, Balanced scorecard, Enterprise Modelling, Data modelling, Systems modelling, Workflow, Benefits, Business benefit

1. Company Background

British Telecommunications plc (BT) is a wholly owned subsidiary of BT Group plc, and is one of the world's leading providers of telecommunications services. Its principal activities include local, long distance and international telecommunications services, Internet services and IT solutions. In the UK, BT serves more than 28 million exchange lines as well as providing network services to other licensed operators.

With over 100,000 employees, the effective design and management of processes is essential to the success of the company. The telecommunications market is expanding and changing at a rapid rate, with new products being developed and deployed in increasingly fast time scales. Moreover, since 1999 BT has been going through a significant period of restructuring which has led to the creation of a number of semi-autonomous lines of business. The need for these lines of business to interact through well defined and measured interfaces puts extra urgency on the availability of effective processes.

The increasing complexity of the modern business environment means that companies that were once only customers, or only suppliers, can now be customers, suppliers and partners all at the same time. The supply chain relationships necessary to deliver a complex range of products and services to the market require that not only must companies' internal processes be effective, but also that intra-company processes must be world class.

2. The Need for Process Management Tools in BT

In such a large company it is inevitable that there will be a large number of people involved in the design and deployment of business processes. While some companies may have centralised process design teams, in BT the responsibility for process design is largely devolved to individual business units. However, processes do not operate in isolation, so it is essential for there to be a common format for process design that can ensure that processes work effectively together. This can be achieved using:

- Common process architectures
- Common process design methods and tools

Prior to 1997, BT had established a common high-level process and systems architecture based on the Telecommunications Managed Network (TMN) architecture (Furley 1997). This architecture had been made available to everyone in the company through an in-house developed Web-based interface known as TRIADS. While TRIADS was effective at promulgating process knowledge, it did not help process designers in their everyday task of undertaking process design, or help users to implement them. Process modelling tools were in use in some part of the business, but for the most part process design was done using Microsoft PowerPoint and Microsoft Word.

It was therefore proposed that an 'Invitation to Tender' (ITT) be instigated to find a process management tool that would:

- Replace TRIADS as the repository for the process architecture
- Provide users with a process design tool
- Provide a mechanism for publishing designs on the corporate Intranet
- Allow workflows to be enacted directly from process designs

The use of the corporate Intranet for publishing process designs was a key part of the strategy. Placing the BT procedural instructions on the Intranet had resulted in cost savings of millions of pounds from the reduction in paper usage. It was essential that similar saving should be achieved from the electronic publication of process designs. Furthermore, a key goal was to move process designs into becoming a major part of the lifeblood of the business rather than confining them to long forgotten dusty volumes that no one has ever read.

3. Choosing ARIS for Use in BT

A shortlist of ten process modelling tools was evaluated and the top three selected for further investigation. After scoring the results of the investigation, ARIS emerged as a clear winner. However, as is often the way, just as work was about to start new requirements intervened which lead to a different approach being taken for implementing the process and systems architecture repository. This removed the initial momentum for establishing ARIS as the preferred process design tool for BT. Fortuitously however, two new initiatives combined to pave the way for the implementation of ARIS in BT.

Firstly, the BT Corporate Strategy team (who had experience of ARIS) were keen to promote the use of a single process modelling tool in BT and wanted to set up a centre of excellence for the use of ARIS. Secondly, the Process Solutions Unit in BTexact Technologies wished to develop a more uniform approach to the way in which process design was undertaken.

BTexact Technologies, BT's advanced research and technology business, offers expertise and experience in communications technology and e-business, backed by a team of more than 3000 technologists and one of the world's largest communications research and development facilities. As the centre of technical expertise for the BT Group, BTexact established a record of world-first achievement and of successful delivery of projects, large and small. It has also created an intellectual property portfolio of some 14,000 patents based on almost 2000 inventions. BTexact *Process Solutions* undertakes the high-level (non-procedural) design of processes for all BT's major technology platforms.

The authors of this article are both members of the BTexact *Process Solutions* and were individually involved in these two initiatives. Rob Davis set up a small team to look at identifying process design tools and techniques for Process Solutions and Colin Paton was contracted by BT Strategy to set up the ARIS Centre of Excellence. These two initiatives were quickly combined and Rob Davis set up the BT ARIS Modelling Techniques Team (AMTT). Colin Paton subsequently took over management of the IP (Internet Protocol) High-level Process Design Team.

4. The Pilot Project

The ARIS Modelling Techniques Team (AMTT) decided early on its existence that it would not try to mandate the use of ARIS for process design in BT. Some companies have a management structure that facilitates the promulgation of centralised technical strategies. In BT, the devolved responsibilities and high-dègree of technical competence of management means that centralised decisions are not always well received unless championed by a senior board member. The AMTT decided that rather than lobby for senior management support, it would take a more practical approach by undertaking a pilot project to directly demonstrate the benefits of using ARIS. It was hoped that combining this 'bottom-up' practical approach with the 'top-down' mandate it had received from the BT Strategy team would lead to ready acceptance of the use of ARIS in the company. It was also hoped that by encouraging one part of the business to use ARIS, then other parts would also want to use it so as not to be seen to be missing out on the benefits.

When choosing a pilot project it is vital to ensure that the project is suitable:

- There should be strong support from the project managers
- It should be technically feasible
- It should effectively demonstrate the characteristics of the tool
- There should be sufficient time to implement the pilot
- There should be a need for the tool
- The pilot should not be on the project critical path
- There should be commitment to use the tool if successful

The chosen project, developing process models for one of BT's major network infrastructure platforms seemed to fulfil all these requirements. Rob Davis and Ordelia Sansford from the ARIS Modelling Techniques Team started work on the project. Both members of the team had been trained in ARIS 3 as part of the ITT, but the project was now using ARIS 4, so it was essential to update the training and enhance our knowledge to cover server administration and more advanced techniques.

We found much of our time in the early phases of the project concentrated on investigating the range of model and object types available in ARIS and deciding which ones to use. We were supported in this by Mike Pearce from IDS Scheer (UK) Ltd. We were fortunate in this early stage that (for once!) we were not under any great time pressure to achieve results and were able to concentrate our efforts on building our ARIS knowledge. Had we been under more pressure then we could have made more use of IDS consultants and perhaps achieved results more quickly. However, by spending our own time in exploring all the 'nooks and crannies' of ARIS we built considerable technical expertise that has reaped considerable benefits in future work.

We found that the project we had chosen was not as suitable as we first thought. It was technically very complex and was based on a number of systems, network and process releases that built on earlier versions. There were a number of variants of the product and the processes were delivered by a mixture of manual operations and the use of a legacy workflow system. The legacy system built workflows from a set of basic task components that it combined in different sequences for each purpose.

New releases of the product were issued at three monthly intervals and it had been our intention to model the information for the next release. However, the project documentation concentrated on describing the incremental changes since the last release. In order to 'base-line' the processes it was necessary to go back and read the documentation for all the previous releases. In practice it was not possible to go back and model all this past information in order to get to the point were we could describe the next release. Modelling just the incremental information for the next release was neither practical nor very useful.

With a lot of effort, the team managed a compromise that produced a set of models that described all the key aspects of the project. We used many of the advanced techniques of ARIS including Model Generation and Variants. The results were intellectually very interesting, but not very practical as the people who would have to use the techniques on a day-to-day basis could not understand them without a great deal of training and effort for which they did not have the time.

At first sight it seemed that the pilot project had not been a success. However, the reverse turned out to be the case. Firstly, in order to produce these models we had needed to learn almost everything there was to know about ARIS. Having both the opportunity and impetuous to do this was a luxury that most users do not get and it has been a great advantage to us establishing ARIS in BT. Secondly, word had spread about what we had been doing and many of our colleagues in BTexact Process Solutions and in the rest of BT had come to see ARIS and our work. As it turned out, it was this, rather than the pilot project, which started the road to implementing ARIS in BT.

5. IP High-Level Process Design

Managed by Colin Paton, the IP High-Level Process Design Team produces the initial process designs for all BT Ignite's Internet related products. These products range from high-bandwidth fixed internet access and virtual private networks (VPN) for large corporate customers, to complete access and networks provision for Internet Service Providers (ISPs), or for companies that require their employees to have network or dial-up access to a corporate internet.

The processes for these products include the ordering and provision of the service, the planning and provision of network infrastructure, billing, fault reporting, abuse monitoring, etc. BT has a vast array of complex processes which, while they are very similar for each product, vary due to the specific technical complexities of the product. To make things more complex, the rapid changes in the Internet market means that new products are being introduced at a frightening pace and existing products being combined and re-branded. Furthermore, the take-up of these products is so great that the network infrastructure to supply the necessary capacity to support them is continually being uplifted. As a result, processes must support the existence of several parallel network infrastructures as new networks are brought into service and old ones removed.

The increase in product volumes also means that processes that initially might have been done manually, now need to be rapidly automated. As a result the process designers have to work closely with the network designs and operational support system (OSS) designers to ensure a complete solution is delivered. In many cases, changes to systems or network specifications and delivery dates will require the process designers to produce a temporary 'work-around' to the process design. Once the high-level 'solution design' is complete, then process and procedural designers in the operational units will define the detail of how the process are to operate.

There are a wide range of customers for the output from the high-level process design team, including the systems and network solutions designs, product owners, operational design teams and those who write the detailed procedures for Operations. These designs must be produced rapidly and correctly and, where possible, reuse existing designs and infrastructure. The results must be published in a way that is quick and effective for people to assess and assimilate.

Before the implementation of ARIS in BT, the IP High-Level Process Design team used a mixture of Microsoft Word, Microsoft PowerPoint and a competing process design tool for their process design work. The process designs were always published in a Microsoft Word document that was primarily textual descriptions of processes and could often run to over 100 pages.

By chance the IP team share the same office as the ARIS Modelling Techniques Team. When the AMTT started the ARIS Pilot, the IP team had agreed that if the pilot was successful that they would implement a phased change over from their current methods to using ARIS. However, as a result of what they had seen of ARIS from the technical work on the pilot, the IP team were so impressed that they decided that they would change to ARIS without waiting for the pilot project to complete. Furthermore, because they were having difficulties with their existing process design tool, the IP team decided that they would not implement a phased change over, but change immediately. The IP team bought 8-10 ARIS licences and the AMTT brought in additional effort to support the IP team undertaking some of the initial modelling work to get them started.

6. ARIS in IP High-Level Process Design

The main goals in using ARIS for IP process design were to:

- Design and model more rigorously
- Produce designs more quickly
- Create a library of existing designs
- Reuse existing designs
- Eliminate as much written documentation as possible
- Publish more widely
- Speed up process review
- Validate designs using simulation

Initially, the team began by creating all its new process models in ARIS with the intention of gradually migrating existing designs across as they were updated. However, such is the pace of change in the IP environment, that within 6-9 months, all of its designs had been converted. The team started seeing the benefits of using ARIS almost immediately, as the discipline of updating and converting designs into ARIS exposed the shortcomings in existing process models, and the ability to re-use process modules across different process designs became apparent. The simulation module was used to analyse processes for bottlenecks, resulting in increased understanding of the problems facing some of the product lines. Customer feedback was largely positive from the start, as the long textual documents were replaced by easily navigable web-based designs. The only negative reactions received by the team were from some customers who were initially unfamiliar with the EPC methodology used by ARIS, but this largely disappeared as the team worked with its customers to review the designs and understanding was improved.

In these early days, the team members were all using ARIS with a standard set of method filters, on their local PCs. This lead to some customers noticing a lack of consistency in modelling style, exemplified by one comment that the customer could 'tell who produced the design just by looking at it!' This situation has been improved to a large extent by agreeing on a common set of standards documented in the Guide Sheets produced by the AMTT, but to make further progress in this direction, the team is now moving towards client-server working, using a common repository on the ARIS Server. This offers the following advantages:

- A centralised library of process models and re-usable objects
- Enforced use of method filters
- Managed access to models on an 'as-needed' basis
- Easier access to Change Management functionality
- Centralised security, backup and administration

It should perhaps be pointed out that this changeover to server working could not, and did not, happen overnight. Before existing process models could be migrated off local PC discs onto the server, there was a cleansing process to ensure that standards were followed, and to set up the libraries of functions, systems and organisational units. A small number of administrators were appointed and trained to manage the server and libraries. The team has now reached the stage where this process is virtually completed, all new modelling work is being done on the server, and the benefits are truly starting to flow.

7. The Benefits of Using ARIS in IP High-Level Process Design

In the thirty months that the team has been using ARIS, the IP revolution has taken the world by storm. As a result, BT's involvement in the IP industry has increased from being a virtual cottage industry, to a major part of the Group's global activities, and the amount of process design work required has increased exponentially. Without the use of ARIS, the team would still be writing long textual documents to accompany each new product release or change, and would be perhaps 2-3 times its present size. The benefits of server working listed above, coupled with the basic ARIS benefits of graphical designs and web publishing, have allowed the team to achieve its goals. Customers are now accustomed to seeing process designs in ARIS, and are increasingly looking to the tool for solutions to their own problems. Whereas the team started out using ARIS only for High-level design, a number of the low-level procedural writers are now using it, which brings additional benefits in the ease of integration of high and low-level designs.

An interesting measure of the benefit of using ARIS was highlighted when one of the IP designers was asked how long he had been using ARIS. At first he replied "two years". After reflecting for a moment he said: "I am mistaken, it is on fact only one year – it seems like two years because of the amount of work we have been able to do".

8. Implementing ARIS in BT

At the same time that ARIS was being used in the IP High-Level Process Design team, the word about ARIS was spreading. Many process people in the rest of the BT Group were requesting ARIS demonstrations from the ARIS Modelling Techniques Team. The team spent much of the later half of 1996, on the road demonstrating ARIS. ARIS was still not mandated as the only tool for process modelling in BT, but it was now on the portfolio of available tools and recommended by BT Strategy.

People outside of BTexact Process Solutions now started to purchase ARIS licences and it became clear that there was a need for:

- Formal support for ARIS in BT
- Standards for using ARIS
- A corporate licence

The ARIS Modelling Techniques Team started to provide ARIS support for the whole of BT and to develop standards that could be applied across the company. A first draft Method Filter had been created for the IP team, but now much more effort was put into defining company-wide Method Filter standards. While the task of creating Method Filters using the Configuration Wizard is relatively straightforward, identifying a coherent set of related model, object and relationships that will support all the modelling work required is a much more exacting piece of work. It was here that the detail technical work on the pilot project paid dividends, because the AMTT now understood in detail all the ARIS models, objects and relationships.

An internal Web site on the corporate Intranet was created and called "ARIS in BT" (see figure 1). Here people could get useful information, download copied of ARIS, the BT Method Filters and other ARIS resources. This, and an associated mailing list, became the focus for information on ARIS.

The first pilot project outside of BTexact set the need for detailed written ARIS standards. This project was to capture an existing process. It was to be done by three separate consultants, each working on part of the process and the results then combined into a complete set of integrated models. The consultants had received basic ARIS training, but it was essential for a detailed set of standards to be created to tell them what to capture and how to model so that the independently created models would fit together.

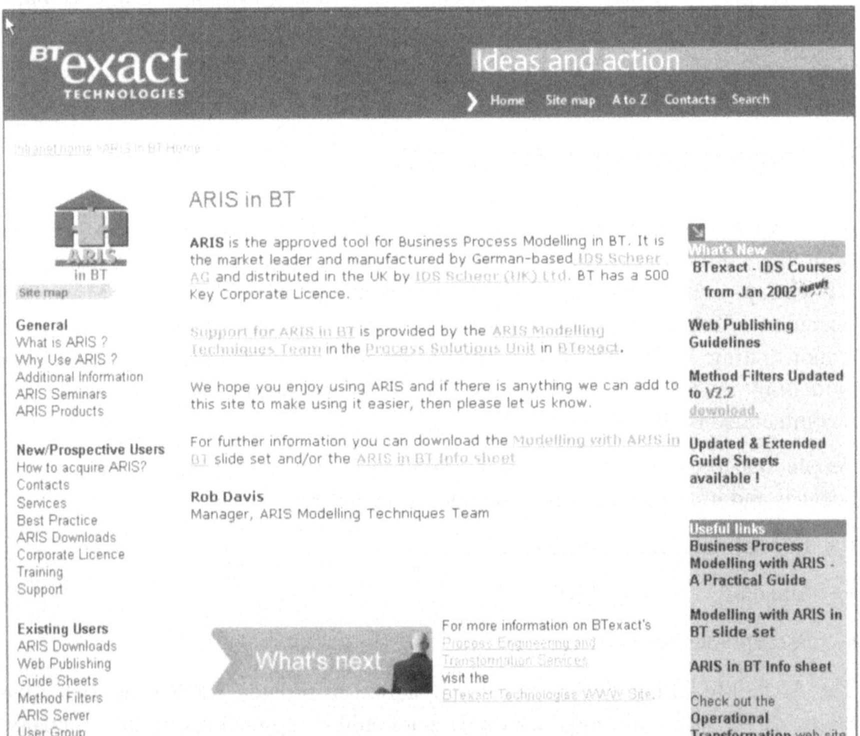

Figure 1: ARIS in BT intranet site

The AMTT's first attempt at writing a standards document was not a success. After writing the first thirty pages it was pretty clear that no one would ever bother to read it. A different approach was needed and this lead to the birth of the "ARIS in BT Guide Sheets" (see figure 2). It seemed pointless to describe in words how to use what is essentially a visual tool, so instead a series of A4 Guide Sheets was created. Each sheet comprised only one or two pages and contained mainly ARIS screen shots with numbered instructions and lists of hints and tips. The Guide Sheets were published on the ARIS in BT Intranet site.

The Guide Sheets were an instant success. Initially they covered basic modelling aspects such as how to model branches and decisions, but they quickly grew in number to cover more advanced techniques such as Model Generation, Variants, creating model hierarchies, linking models etc. Some other business units, in particular BT Wholesale, decided to set up their own ARIS competency teams and these teams collaborated with the AMTT in producing new Guide Sheets.

By now the number of ARIS users in BT had risen to about 70. Many people had switched from using other tools and it was clear that ARIS was now becoming the 'de facto' standard for process modelling in BT. The time was now ripe to consider making the use of ARIS in BT more formal and negotiate a corporate licence. The only disadvantage in the bottom-up approach to implementing ARIS that had been taken was that it was more difficult to get the corporate authorisation and funding for a corporate licence. However, with the support of a number of business units and in particular BT Wholesale, BT signed a £0.5M corporate licence contract with IDS Scheer (UK) Ltd in November 2000. The use of ARIS in BT is still not mandatory, but "why use anything else".

9. Using ARIS Throughout the Enterprise

Initially the main use of the ARIS in BT was for process modelling. Once the initial task of establishing ARIS in BT had been achieved, then the focus moved to using the wider facilities of ARIS. The main roll-out of ARIS in BT corresponded with the introduction of ARIS 5 that introduced many new facilities. BT now started to make use of ARIS facilities such as:

- Simulation
- Web Publishing
- Balanced Scorecard
- Enterprise Modelling
- Data Modelling
- Systems Modelling
- Workflow

BTexact has a well established simulation team that uses some of the market leading simulation software packages (Arena, Service Model, Witness). Not only has the team detailed knowledge of using the tools, but it also has considerable experience in gathering the data needed for simulation and in interpreting the results. It was important at the outset to understand where use of the ARIS simulation module fitted with the specialist tools. After a period of experi-

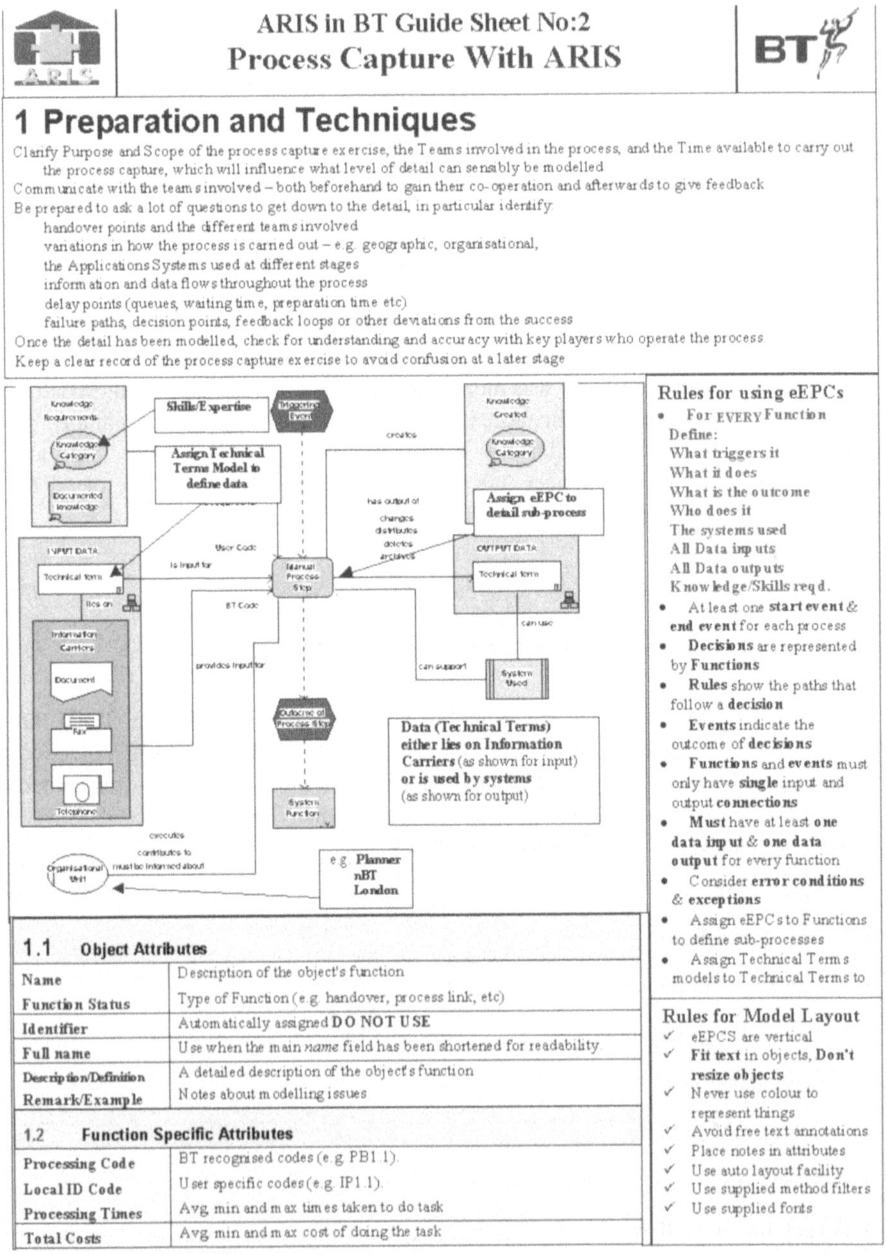

ARIS in BT Guide Sheet No:2

Process Capture With ARIS

1 Preparation and Techniques

Clarify Purpose and Scope of the process capture exercise, the Teams involved in the process, and the Time available to carry out the process capture, which will influence what level of detail can sensibly be modelled

Communicate with the teams involved – both beforehand to gain their co-operation and afterwards to give feedback

Be prepared to ask a lot of questions to get down to the detail, in particular identify

- handover points and the different teams involved
- variations in how the process is carried out – e.g. geographic, organisational,
- the Applications Systems used at different stages
- information and data flows throughout the process
- delay points (queues, waiting time, preparation time etc)
- failure paths, decision points, feedback loops or other deviations from the success

Once the detail has been modelled, check for understanding and accuracy with key players who operate the process

Keep a clear record of the process capture exercise to avoid confusion at a later stage

Rules for using eEPCs

- For EVERY Function Define:
  What triggers it
  What it does
  What is the outcome
  Who does it
  The systems used
  All Data inputs
  All Data outputs
  Knowledge/Skills req'd.
- At least one **start event & end event** for each process
- **Decisions** are represented by **Functions**
- **Rules** show the paths that follow a **decision**
- **Events** indicate the outcome of **decisions**
- **Functions** and **events** must only have **single** input and output **connections**
- **Must** have at least **one data input & one data output** for every function
- Consider **error conditions & exceptions**
- Assign eEPCs to Functions to define sub-processes
- Assign Technical Terms models to Technical Terms to

Rules for Model Layout

- ✓ eEPCS are vertical
- ✓ **Fit text** in objects, **Don't resize objects**
- ✓ Never use colour to represent things
- ✓ Avoid free text annotations
- ✓ Place notes in attributes
- ✓ Use auto layout facility
- ✓ Use supplied method filters
- ✓ Use supplied fonts

1.1 Object Attributes	
Name	Description of the object's function
Function Status	Type of Function (e.g. handover, process link, etc)
Identifier	Automatically assigned **DO NOT USE**
Full name	Use when the main *name* field has been shortened for readability
Description/Definition	A detailed description of the object's function
Remark/Example	Notes about modelling issues

1.2 Function Specific Attributes	
Processing Code	BT recognised codes (e.g. PB1.1)
Local ID Code	User specific codes (e.g. IP1.1)
Processing Times	Avg, min and max times taken to do task
Total Costs	Avg, min and max cost of doing the task

Figure 2: ARIS in BT guide sheet

mentation and discussion with IDS Scheer, it was concluded that ARIS Simulation was suitable for general purpose simulation of processes already modelled in ARIS. In particular, processes with relatively straightforward resources allocations and where it was needed to identify bottleneck problems and failures of process logic. The more specialist tools were better suited to complex problems were the simulation model was built especially to solve a specific problem.

The use of ARIS Web Publisher is a key element of BT's strategy in using ARIS and one of the main justifications for the purchase of the corporate licence. The key requirements are to make access to process designs more readily available and to reduce the amount of paper documentation. A big advantage with ARIS Web Publisher is that the browser-based interface provided by Web Publisher appears almost exactly like using an ARIS client. This means anyone familiar with ARIS can quickly navigate the same models on the Intranet. This has been used to great effect by the IP team who now publishes all of the models on the Intranet with only the minimum of paper documentation. Models published on the Intranet have also been extremely valuable for process reviews, reducing the amount of documentation that needs to be sent out in advance and enabling people to 'walk through' the processes in their own time. The team has also made extensive use of Microsoft NetMeeting to hold 'virtual process reviews' over the Intranet.

The ARIS-like appearance of Web Publisher is one of its strengths, but it is also a weakness. It is important that process designs are made available to a wide range of people who are not familiar with ARIS and hence the ARIS-like look and feel is a disadvantage. The new Web Publisher facilities released in ARIS 6 and through products like Hyperwave are starting to address these issues and BT expects to see significant developments in creating more user-focussed publishing in the coming months.

Once ARIS started to become a familiar tool in BT, then it was only natural that it should start to be used for more business related tasks. The Balanced Scorecard (BSC) Module is particularly useful. As well as being used specifically for BSC applications, the "Cause and Effect Model" is a valuable tool in modelling business objectives and benefits. BT has adapted the use of this model for several different purposes, even for modelling the personal objectives of the manager of the ARIS Modelling Techniques Team!

The most exciting development of the use of ARIS has been for modelling the structure of entire businesses. Since the restructuring of BT Group into separate lines of business (e.g. BT Wholesale, BT Ignite, BT Retail, etc), there has been a need to re-design these entities as businesses in their own right. Both BT Ignite and BT Wholesale have chosen to use ARIS to develop their Enterprise Models. In particular, BT Wholesale has adopted a formalised structured enterprise model and BTexact has developed an ARIS meta-model to describe how it should be modelled in ARIS. The meta-model is based on BTexact's Six Layer Enterprise

Architecture (see figure 3) and defines for each layer what business entities should be modelled and how they should be represented in ARIS.

Increasingly ARIS is now becoming of interest to the systems design community, particularly as the need to integrate system, process and data design is becoming accepted. It is likely that, in the near future, one of BT's lines of business will mandate the use of ARIS for both high-level systems and process design.

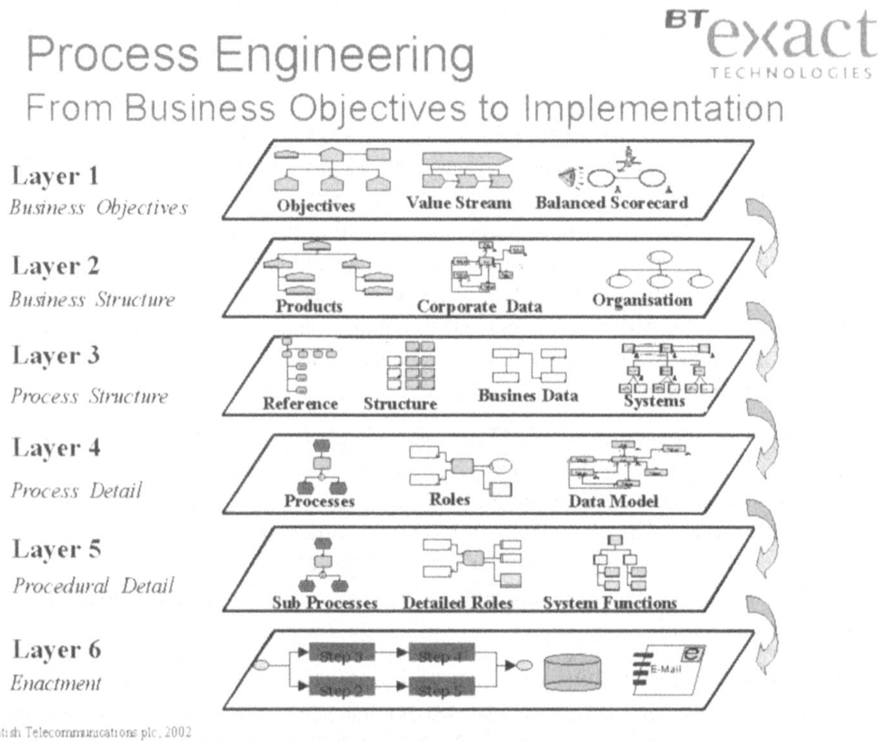

Figure 3: Btexact Six Layer Enterprise Model

A natural extension to the use of ARIS for process modelling is for those processes to be directly 'enacted' through the use of workflow tools and EAI (Enterprise Application Integration) system stacks. One of BT's strategic process automation tools is Oracle Workflow and during 2001 BT Wholesale commissioned IDS Scheer to develop an interface between ARIS and Oracle Workflow. This interface will be piloted in early 2002.

10. The Benefits of Using ARIS in BT

We are often asked about the benefits of using ARIS in BT. There are many:

- More rigorous and complete designs
- Increased process awareness
- Less opportunity for operational error
- Reduction in paper documentation
- Design reuse
- Faster time to market
- Demonstrable adherence to regulatory standards

Perhaps the greatest benefit to date has been the increase in rigour with which the designs have been produced. It is a common failing in process design to simply consider the ideal case. That is to create a success model that takes no account of alternative actions and what can go wrong. While it is important to model what happens in the majority of cases (hopefully success is the majority!) it is also essential to consider the failure modes. Often the majority of cost occurs in failure; both in terms of hard cash, but also, and perhaps more important, in terms of customer satisfaction. The use of ARIS and the Event-driven Process Chain method engenders a more rigorous approach to modelling and makes one ask all those difficult and embarrassing questions that are easy to skip over when modelling just using PowerPoint.

Another significant benefit is the ability to reuse existing designs. There is a great deal of commonality between the processes required to deliver different products, but there are always some differences of detail. The goal is to be able to reuse what is common while making clear the differences. This is almost impossible with processes of any complexity when using paper and pencil methods. However, the hierarchical nature of ARIS and facilities such as Variants and Model Generation allow process designs to be constructed that allow effective reuse.

For a large company such as BT, processes have to be managed in an effective and professional way. To do this in today's rapidly changing and complex environment it is not enough to use paper documents. ARIS is now playing a significant part in managing BT's business processes and we expect to see that increasing over the next two to three years.

11. ARIS in BT: Status and Challenges

ARIS is now firmly established as the business process modelling tool of choice for BT. It has found its way into all aspects of the business from process design to enterprise modelling to workflow enactment and we use nearly every ARIS facility and module. As new facilities and content (e.g. Quality Scout, Risk Scout, etc) are released it is almost certain that someone, somewhere in BT will use them. BTexact is currently evaluating IDS Scheer's new Process Performance Manager (PPM) product and it is likely that a pilot project will be installed during 2002.

There are over 400 users of ARIS in BT. The challenge is now to develop and enhance their use of ARIS to provide BT with a truly professional process engineering community and to make the results of their efforts available to the widest possible community. Many of the 400 users are spread thinly throughout the company, often working in isolation on small projects. Several of the lines of business are involved in programmes to put in ARIS servers to provide a more coordinated and integrated approach.

The biggest challenge is to ensure that the models produced in ARIS directly deliver business benefit. Increasingly models will be used to enact process directly through workflow, e-business and EAI, but for the moment models are mostly used by people looking at them. The challenge is for ARIS to be able to present process information to people in way that is tailored towards their specific needs. The information must be directly relevant to what they do. It must give them an overview of the entire process, but not clutter them with information that is not relevant. It must be easy to understand, easy to navigate and give them swift access to priority information. The information must be displayed concisely within the minimum number of models.

Most importantly, it should be possible to generate a variety of different viewpoints from the same underlying process definition. Those view points should be updated automatically when the underlying models change.

There is a parallel here with current developments in Web publishing. Up until recently web pages were presented in HTML. The information and the formatting were all defined in the HTML code. Moreover the two were intermixed, so changing either was difficult without affecting the other. The latest developments have separated format and content. Formatting is still done with HTML, but now a new language, XML, is used to define the content. Content described in XML can combined with different HTML files to present it in different ways.

We need to be able to do the same with processes. We need to be able to rigorously define our processes using a variety of ARIS models to give a complete and coherent description. However, our users may not want to see all of this information so we need to be able to have different formats for presenting content in different ways to different audiences. Many the facilities necessary to do this are becoming available with ARIS, Web Publisher and products such as Hyperwave. The challenge over the next two years is to bring all of this together to create a true enterprise-wide business process knowledge repository and portal.

12. BTexact in Partnership with IDS Scheer

The ARIS Modelling Techniques Team in BTexact provides technical support and consultancy to over 400 users of ARIS in the BT Group. BTexact Technologies also provides services to companies outside the BT Group. It is headquartered at Adastral Park, at one end of the Cambridge-2-Ipswich Hi Tech Corridor, and is a founder member of the Cambridge Network. BTexact has people based worldwide - including locations across the UK and in Asia, continental Europe, and North America.

BTexact's employees include many who are world leaders in their specialist fields, working at the forefront of standards development and new technologies in areas including multimedia, IP and data networks, mobile communications, network design and management, and business applications.

BTexact's use of ARIS is fundamental to this external services portfolio. To build on its strong relationship with IDS, BTexact has become an IDS partner to offer process engineering training, consultancy and PPM implementation skills to the UK and wider markets.

For more information about BTexact Technologies, please go to www.btexact.com

13. Conclusions

In some respects ARIS is like using a spreadsheet. It provides a rich range of models and functions that can model just about everything you may ever need, but exactly how do you go about modelling the company accounts and what do you do with them when you have done it?

To use ARIS effectively you must:

- Define clear business modelling objectives
- Identify your audience and their needs
- Define a process engineering method
- Establish modelling standards

- Use appropriately skilled people
- Provide training and support
- Encourage ARIS server-based working
- Publish results effectively
- Don't attempt to model the universe!

If you can achieve this there are many benefits:

- More rigorous and complete designs
- Increased process awareness
- Less opportunity for operational error
- Reduction in paper documentation
- Design reuse
- Faster time to market
- Enterprise-wide view
- Platform for process analysis and re-engineering
- Demonstrable adherence to regulatory standards

These are not just nice things to have, but an essential part of the due diligence required in operating a modern business.

Processes are not something your business does - they are your business.

14. Disclaimer

The views and opinions expressed in this article are solely those of the authors and do not represent the views of British Telecommunications plc.

15. References

Furley, N. "The BT Operational Support Systems Architecture". BT Technology Journal, Vol 15, No1, January 1997.

Appendix: The Authors

Abolhassan, Dr. Ferri

Co-Chairman and CEO

IDS Scheer AG

Altenkesseler Strasse 17

66115 Saarbrücken

Germany

Brady, Ed

IT Director

American Meter Company

300 Welsh Road

Building One

Horsham, PA 19044-2234

USA

Brown, George W.

Senior Staff Architect

Intel Corporation

CH3-61

5000 W. Chandler Boulevard

Chandler, AZ 85226-3699

USA

Browning, Steve

Business Improvement Manager

Television New Zealand

100 Victoria Street West

PO Box 3819

Auckland/ New Zealand

Castelbajac, Laurent de

Senior Consultant

IDS Scheer France

150, bureaux de la Colline

92213 Saint Cloud Cedex

France

Czarnecka, Roza

Controlling Manager

Zespló Elektrocieplowni Bydgoszcz S.A.

ul. Energetyczna 1

85-950 Bydgoszcz

Poland

Davis, Rob

Manager ARIS Modelling Techniques Team

BTexact Technologies

Postpoint B67/G10

BT Adastral Park

Martlesham Heath

Ipswich, IP5 3RE, UK

Dietrich-Nespěšný, Karel

Director Strategy and Company Development

Jihomoravská energetika, a.s.

Lidická 36

659 44 Brno

Czech Republic

Eschbach, Paul

Partner and Stakeholder

Manager Business Activities Czech Republic

BASE CONSULT GmbH

Steinsdorfstrasse 19

80538 München

Germany

Gruchman, Grzegorz B.

Vicepresident

IDS Scheer Polska

Plac Wiosny Ludów 2

61-831 Poznań

Poland

Gulledge, Thomas R.

Professor, Director

George Mason University

Enterprise Engineering Laboratory

MS 2E4

Fairfax, VA 22030-4444

USA

Hars, Alexander

Assistant Professor of Information Systems

Marshall School of Business

University of Southern California

Los Angeles, CA 90089-0809

USA

Heinzel, Herbert

Partner Consultant

Siemens Business Services

Carl Werystr. 18

81739 München

Germany

Horowski, Witold

Director

Strategy Advisory Department

IDS Scheer Polska

Pl. Wiosny Ludów 2

61-831 Poznań

Poland

Hrbek, Karel

Process Management Consultant

IDS Scheer CR, s.r.o.

Vídenská 55

63900 Brno

Czech Republic

Jost, Dr. Wolfram

Member of the Executive Board

IDS Scheer AG

Altenkesseler Strasse 17

66115 Saarbrücken

Germany

Kirchmer, Dr. Mathias F.W.

President and CEO

IDS Scheer, Inc.

CEO

IDS Scheer Japan

Member of the Extended Executive Board

IDS Scheer AG

1205 Westlakes Drive

Berwyn, PA 19312

USA

Mihaljevic, Antonela Divic

Analyst, BSc, Department of Business Processes

Slovenica Insurance Company

Celovska cesta 206

1000 Ljubljana

Republic of Slovenia

Miksch, Klaus

Manager Consulting

Utility Companies

IDS Scheer AG

Lindwurmstrasse 23

80337 München

Germany

Mitáček, Ing. Marek

Quality Management Specialist

ČESKÝ TELECOM

a.s. Olšanská 5

130 34 Praha 3

Czech Republic

Olsztyński, Paweł

Senior Consultant

Process Improvment Department

IDS Scheer Polska

Pl. Wiosny Ludów 2

61-831 Poznań

Poland

Paton, Colin

Manager IP Process Design Team

BTexact Technologies

Postpoint B67/G10

BT Adastral Park

Martlesham Heath

Ipswich, IP5 3RE

United Kingdom

Pluciński, Andrzej

Director of Quality Systems

ZE PAK

ul. Kazimierska 45

62-510 Konin

Poland

Rosemann, Dr. Michael

Associated Professor

Queensland University of Technology

Faculty of Information Technology

School of Information Systems

2 George Street

Brisbane QLD 4000

Australia

Scharsig, Marc

Director, Consulting Services

IDS Scheer, Inc.

1205 Westlakes Drive

Suite 270

Berwyn, PA 19312

USA

Scheer, Prof. Dr. Dr. hc. mult. August-Wilhelm

Founder and Chairman of the Supervisory Board

IDS Scheer AG

Altenkesseler Strasse 17

66115 Saarbrücken

Germany

Simon, Georg

Director

Product Consulting

IDS Scheer, Inc.

1205 Westlakes Drive, Suite 270

Berwyn, PA 19312

USA

Sommer, Rainer A.

Professor, Associate Director

George Mason University

Enterprise Engineering Laboratory

MS 2E4

Fairfax, VA 22030-4444

USA

Teysseyre, Laurent

Quality Manager of the Selection and Recruitment Department

Air France

45, rue de Paris

95747 Roissy Charles De Gaulle Cedex

France

Vannier, Benoît

Consultant

IDS Scheer France

150, bureaux de la Colline

92213 Saint Cloud Cedex

France

Wagner, Karl

Director ARIS

IDS Scheer AG

Altenkesseler Strasse 17

66115 Saarbrücken

Germany

Závodný, Ing. Zdeněk

Sales Representative

IDS Scheer ČR, s.r.o.

Vídeňská 55

639 00 Brno

Czech Republic

The manufacturer's authorised representative in the EU is Springer Nature Customer Service Centre GmbH, Europaplatz 3, 69115 Heidelberg, Germany. If you have any concerns regarding our products, please contact ProductSafety@springernature.com

Printed and bound by CPI Group (UK) Ltd, Croydon, CR0 4YY
25/09/2026
02222857-0010